Confronting Youth Unemployment in the 1980s

Pergamon Titles of Related Interest

Geismar/Geismar FAMILIES IN AN URBAN MOLD
Tropman/Dluhy/Lind/Vasey STRATEGIC PERSPECTIVES ON
SOCIAL POLICY
Tropman/Dluhy/Lind NEW STRATEGIC PERSPECTIVES ON
SOCIAL POLICY
Waxman THE STIGMA OF POVERTY

Related Journals*

CHILD ABUSE AND NEGLECT
CHILDREN AND YOUTH SERVICES REVIEW
JOURNAL OF CHILD PSYCHOLOGY AND PSYCHIATRY AND
  OTHER ALLIED DISCIPLINES
JOURNAL OF CRIMINAL JUSTICE
LEARNING AND SOCIETY
PERSONALITY AND INDIVIDUAL DIFFERENCES

*Free specimen copies available upon request.

PERGAMON
POLICY
STUDIES

ON SOCIAL ISSUES

Confronting Youth Unemployment in the 1980s

Rhetoric Versus Reality

Ray C. Rist
Guest Editor

A Special Issue of
Children and Youth Services Review

Duncan Lindsey
Editor

Pergamon Press
NEW YORK • OXFORD • TORONTO • SYDNEY • PARIS • FRANKFURT

Pergamon Press Offices:

U.S.A.   Pergamon Press Inc., Maxwell House, Fairview Park,
                    Elmsford, New York 10523, U.S.A.

U.K.   Pergamon Press Ltd., Headington Hill Hall,
                    Oxford OX3 0BW, England

CANADA   Pergamon of Canada, Ltd., Suite 104, 150 Consumers Road,
                    Willowdale, Ontario M2J 1P9, Canada

AUSTRALIA   Pergamon Press (Aust.) Pty. Ltd., P.O. Box 544,
                    Potts Point, NSW 2011, Australia

FRANCE   Pergamon Press SARL, 24 rue des Ecoles,
                    75240 Paris, Cedex 05, France
    cc,
FEDERAL REPUBLIC   Pergamon Press GmbH, Hammerweg 6, Postfach 1305,
OF GERMANY   6242 Kronberg/Taunus, Federal Republic of Germany

Published as Volume 2, Numbers 1 and 2 of
Children and Youth Services Review and
supplied to subscribers as part of their
subscriptions. Also available to non-subscribers.

Library of Congress Cataloging in Publication Data

Main entry under title:

Confronting youth unemployment in the 1980s.

   (Pergamon policy studies on social issues)
   "Children and youth services review, volume 2,
numbers 1 & 2, 1980."
   Bibliography: p.
   1. Youth—Employment—United States—Addresses,
essays, lectures. 2. Manpower policy—United States—
Addresses, essays, lectures. 3. Unemployed—United
States—Addresses, essays, lectures. I. Rist, Ray C.
II. Children and youth services review. III. Series.
HD6273.C66 1980   331.3'4137973   80-19730
ISBN 0-08-026077-2

Printed in the United States of America

CHILDREN and YOUTH SERVICES REVIEW

Volume 2, Numbers 1 & 2   1980

CONTENTS

11276

SPECIAL ISSUE:
CONFRONTING YOUTH UNEMPLOYMENT IN THE 1980s:
RHETORIC VERSUS REALITY

Ray C. Rist, Guest Editor

(Continued on next page)

Contents

ISBN 0-08-026077-2
ISSN 0190-7409
(556)

Children and Youth Services Review, Vol. 2, pp. 1–16, 1980
Printed in the USA. All rights reserved.

Confronting Youth Unemployment in the 1980s: Sorting Out the Issues and Trends

Ray C. Rist
Cornell University

The youth unemployment situation in the United States is a matter of the utmost national concern. With unemployment rates for all youth approximately 20% and for those of minority youth nearly double that figure, the country is in the midst of seeing literally hundreds of thousands of young people pass into adulthood without ever having been employed. The implications of this prolonged period of unemployment and schism between the young and the world of work are not encouraging. As has been documented in a growing number of studies, the relation between long term unemployment and the work experiences of persons while young is clear: Those who are marginal to or completely outside the labor force while they are young tend to be the same persons in the same predicament when they are adults. The process appears to be a cumulative one, and the cycle of unemployment persists.

It should also be stressed that the size of this population is not insignificant. On the average in 1977, 1.6 million young people between the ages of 16 and 19 were unable to find jobs, and their unemployment rate was almost three times that for persons 20 years and older. Stated differently, youth account for approximately one-tenth of the labor force, but almost one-quarter of all unemployed (cf. Westcott, 1979).

Ray C. Rist, Director, Youthwork National Policy Study, College of Human Ecology, Cornell University, Ithaca, New York 14853.

1

These proportions have held relatively constant since 1975 (Congressional Budget Office, 1980). In his address of January 10, 1980, where he announced his new initiatives in the area of youth unemployment, President Carter stated that there were:

Two million high school students in lower income school districts alone who are at least two years behind in their basic skills that are taken for granted in today's job market, and I need not tell you that the 2-year measurement is much better than many of these young peoples' educational level demonstrated. A large number of high school graduates in the United States of America are still functionally illiterate. They cannot read or write. They cannot add or subtract well enough to hold a simple job.

There is a second large group of disadvantaged young people also, coincidentally, about two million, who are already out of school but having severe problems getting a job, and if they ever get a job, of holding a job.

In sum, there is an "at risk" population in these two categories alone of nearly 4 million youth who are likely candidates for the unemployment rolls.

Youth Unemployment: The Federal Response

The response to this situation by the federal government has been through the initiatives contained in the Youth Employment and Demonstration Projects Act (YEDPA) of 1977. Created with a specific focus on the needs of youth, the effort was to signal a quantum leap in the support of youth employment and training projects. Indeed, in its first two years (1977–1979) YEDPA programs accounted for one-fourth of the measured employment growth for all teenagers and approximately three-fourths of all employment growth for black teenagers.

The Youth Employment and Demonstration Projects Act (YEDPA) became law on August 5, 1977. It amended the 1973 Comprehensive Employment and Training Act (CETA) so as to provide the initiative for an expanded effort to address the problems of youth unemployment. YEDPA added several new programs to improve employment and training opportunities for young people in their late teens and early twenties, particularly those from low-income families. It has sought to emphasize more experimentation and innovation on the part of the CETA local government sponsor system than has been the case with programs developed for unemployed adults.

The Act is particularly concerned with overcoming the barriers between school and work by more closely linking education, employment, and training institutions. It seeks to forge new relationships.

What provides a sense of urgency to this effort is that there is a desperate need both to improve the education of low-income minority youth and to find the means by which to create more employment for them. The evidence on this point is both conclusive and sobering: the situation for poor minority youth, as compared with white middle-class youth, has steadily deteriorated over the past 15 years. Whether one measures employment rates or labor force participation rates, the disparities have grown and continue to do so. This is in spite of all the education, employment, and training programs initiated since the mid-1960s and carried on to the present (cf. Adams & Mangum, 1978, pp. 19–34).

The spending level for YEDPA for both fiscal years 1979 and 1980 has been approximately $1.1 billion. The first priority for these funds has been to generate in the vicinity of 300,000 employment opportunities for youth. As such, they have become an integral component of efforts by the administration to reduce the present levels of unemployment. Nevertheless, and in recognition that present approaches to reduce youth unemployment are imperfect, both in design and implementation, the Act has authorized the Secretary of Labor to allocate up to one-fifth of YEDPA funds on demonstration projects to support knowledge development. The mandate from the Congress was clear:

Sec. 321. It is the purpose of this part to establish a variety of employment, training, and demonstration programs to explore methods of dealing with the structural unemployment problems of the nation's youth. The basic purpose of the demonstration programs shall be to test the relative efficacy of the different ways of dealing with these problems in different local contexts.

Sec. 328. To carry out innovative and experimental programs, to test new approaches for dealing with the unemployment problems of youth, and to enable eligible participants to prepare for, enhance their prospects for, or secure employment in occupations through which they may reasonably be expected to advance to productive working lives. Such programs shall include, where appropriate, co-operative arrangements with educational agencies to provide special programs and services.

The monies that were to be distributed according to formula among the local sponsors of programs for youth would alleviate some unemployment and "buy time." Yet there was little confidence that, in the end, these projects would either address the long-term needs of the youth or provide new insights into how programs might be more effectively organized and implemented so as to have a greater impact. New ideas, new approaches, and new actors would have to be on the scene if innovative and path-breaking approaches were to be found. And while it was not explicit in the legislation, it can be surmised that it was the hope of the authors that if successful projects could be located where jobs were created and the youth were prepared to assume them, then perhaps cities and states would be encouraged to redirect portions of the 80% formula funds towards projects of this kind. Thus, the discretionary funds projects could achieve a ripple effect throughout the entire infrastructure of youth employment and training programs.

But if YEDPA was to be more than simply ameliorative— desperately as such ameliorative efforts were needed—there had to be new approaches and new strategies for addressing the persistence of youth unemployment. The reason being, as Mangum and Walsh (1978) have cogently stated, that little or no systematic effort has been made over the past years to learn from previous efforts, both positive and negative. The decisions on what programs to instigate, what policies to pursue, and what objectives to seek have heretofore not been made. Their rather somber assessment includes much of what they understand to be in the YEDPA initiatives as well. They note:

It is ironic that after 17 years of experimentation with employment and training programs for youth, Congress found it necessary to legislate activities and programs aimed at discovering the causes of youth unemployment and its potential solutions. It seems fair to ask whether the assumptions upon which past youth programs were based were faulty, or whether the programs themselves were poorly designed or mismanaged. Yet, aside from the research provisions of the Youth Employment and Demonstration Projects Act (YEDPA), the programs authorized by the Act are the same as those which have been implemented over the past 17 years—work experience on community improvement and conservation projects, institutional and on-the-job training, counseling, placement and other kinds of supportive services . . . Congress undoubtedly hoped that programs initiated under YEDPA would be innovative and would unearth heretofore untried techniques, but one of the criticisms of past programs has been that they have been almost exclusively experimental. Experiment has been piled upon experiment, but a concerted, overall policy for treating youth unemployment and transitional problems has never emerged. (p. 11)

If Mangum and Walsh are correct in their assessment that "aside from the research provisions," little new or innovative could be anticipated from the YEDPA effort, then, of necessity, attention should focus on what the research sponsored by YEDPA might yield in the way of new insights or programmatic initiatives.

YEDPA and Knowledge Development

While the direct support for youth employment programs commands the bulk of YEDPA appropriations, improved knowledge development is of high priority. Indeed, the Congress authorized in the legislation that up to a full 20% of the YEDPA funding could be used for demonstration projects seeking innovative means by which to address the problem of youth employment. The first General Principle of the YEDPA Planning Charter of August 1977 stated:

Knowledge development is a primary aim of the new youth programs. At every decision-making level, an effort must be made to try out promising ideas, to support on-going innovation and to assess performance as rigorously as possible. Resources should be concentrated and structured so that the underlying ideas can be given a reasonable test. Hypotheses and questions should be determined at the outset, with an evaluation methodology built in. (p. 5)

With the first phase of YEDPA funding in FY 1978, an ambitious agenda of demonstration, research and assessment activities was implemented. The *Knowledge Development Plan* structured an array of discretionary efforts which would hopefully address a number of the most pressing questions facing national policy makers (U.S. Department of Labor, 1978). Within this 1978 plan were eight "first order" questions which needed to be answered to both design and implement the national priorities regarding youth unemployment. Among the questions were the following:

—Can the school-to-work transition process be improved?
—To what extent are short-run interventions and outcomes related to longer-term impacts on employability during adulthood?
—What is the universe of need for youth programs?
—What works best for whom?
—Does structured, disciplined work experience have as much or more impact on future employability than other human resources development services or a combination of services and employment?

It became apparent that as YEDPA moved into its second fiscal year (1979) that a number of "second order" questions also deserved attention. Seven such second-order questions were posed for the fiscal year 1979 effort. For the most part, these questions were refinements and further clarifications of the original eight. They focused more specifically, for example, on targeting for sub-populations of youth, on isolating the effects of specific service components, and on comparing among alternative delivery approaches.

Targeting on In-School Youth: Defining the Issues

Eli Ginzberg (1979) has written:

There are two contrasting views of what is wrong in the job market. The first holds that many applicants are not hired because they lack basic competencies required for effective performance or because they have acquired training for which there is little or no demand. If blame is to be apportioned, the educational system must be considered the major culprit. The opposing view holds that the educational system is a minor actor. The critical issue is the lack of strong and consistent demand for labor. A slack market means trouble no matter how well people have been educated and trained. I suggest that both positions are overstated: Both employers and employees, especially those with education and skill, possess considerable flexibility that should facilitate the absorption of new job seekers into the economy. (p. 45)

As suggested in the quote by Ginzberg, there are two contrasting views on the origins and persistence of youth unemployment. The first view posits that many applicants are not hired because they lack certain basic competencies or that the skills they do possess are outmoded or in little demand. The fault for this situation is laid on the doorstep of education, the sector of the society responsible for instructing the young in basic competencies and for orienting them towards appropriate adult roles. The alternative view holds that the issue is not one of the skills or competencies of the applicants, but rather that for some years now there has been a weak and inconsistent demand for labor—particularly the labor of the young. In this context, the point is raised that one can create a thousand and one different bridges for the transition from school to work, but if there is no work when the transition is completed, all is for naught.

Ginzberg writes that he believes both positions to be overstated. But overstatement is not the same as being incorrect. If both positions are fundamentally true, then each is tied in a reciprocal relation to the other. This, in turn, suggests that any effort that addresses only one of the two propositions will have a very low probability of success. No single strategy can be assumed to comprehensively address what is a multi-faceted and multi-dimensional phenomenon.

But having said that a single strategy will not suffice is simply to have stated the negative. Indeed, because it is not clear what will work, the emphasis within the YEDPA legislation is upon innovation and research. We must consider ourselves fortunate at this time if we later learn that we have been working with the correct questions, for it is obvious that we are some way off from providing the correct answers. Witness this summary of responses by program operators to the question of how to enhance the motivation and performance of the youth in their programs.

The majority of operators at the local sites agree that motivational and performance difficulties associated with youth are among the most severe operational problems. But there is disagreement on how best to resolve these issues. Some argue that programs dealing with youth should not contain other target groups, thereby allowing operators to concentrate totally on their special problems. Others assert the opposite, that the role models provided by older, more experienced workers are essential for the younger, less stable employees. Some operators contend that the problems of youth may not be particularly different from those of other hard to employ groups and that a well structured program with quality work sites providing meaningful work, training and opportunities for permanent transition is the key to success with all target populations. Other combinations of program treatment are being attempted with youth, such as the inclusion of remedial education and institutional job training in the basic work experience format. *What is clear is that definitive answers to these or other questions concerning the most effective methods for dealing with youth are not yet at hand.* (emphasis added) (Mangum & Walsh, 1978, pp. 68–69)

If definitive answers are not at hand, the first task then is one of sorting out which questions are likely to be answered and when. Secondly, it will be necessary to undertake systematic efforts to gain the answers in such a way that the impact is cumulative. In much the same way as the Department of Labor has prioritized a set of generic first and second order questions, the same has to be done on a more specific level for each of the areas in which we are woefully lacking in data and answers. We have to begin to chart our course, or we will end up once again as Mangum and Walsh described it earlier, without an overall policy for addressing the issues of youth unemployment and school-to-work transition.

We are at present in a stage of approximation—a stage where there are useful operating lessons to be learned from answering correctly posed questions. Our sophistication in sorting out what works best for whom is slowly accumulating, but again, we are learning more about the negatives, i.e., what not to do, and still uncertain on the prescription.

There are several additional insights to be gained from a closer examination of the duality and reciprocity of the casual relations posed by Ginzberg. These can be presented as complementary to his basic position.

First, the fact that effective strategies must include attention to both sides of the relation—training and employment—necessitates that those institutions which perform one or the other of these functions best must, of necessity, work collaboratively with other institutions to achieve the maximal impact. The issue is not one of "either-or," but rather that of what each is able most effectively to contribute to the success of the whole. It is no longer either education *or* employment, but an effective combination of the two. The task is to work out effective linkages between institutions so as to build on respective strengths. That such a view has been accepted by the Congress and the Department of Labor is also evident in the mandated 22% "set aside" in the YETP portion of the YEDPA legislation. These funds have been specifically targeted for those programs which are created as a result of collaborative efforts between the CETA and LEA in any local community. Literally hundreds of such awards have been made in the past two fiscal years, suggesting that collaboration is beginning and the exploration of mutual assistance is underway.

Second, the question of "What works best for whom" remains of the highest priority. If resources are to be used most effectively to assist those most in need, there must be an increased understanding of the education and employment needs of groups of youth and how it is that these can be fulfilled. The concern is for specificity, or as is used in the title of this section, with "targeting." The match between the needs of youth and the correct program response is a major concern of the current YEDPA demonstration efforts.

Finally, to remediate for the present lack of skills and competencies among millions of young people will necessitate a strategy different from that which must be employed to halt the continuing recurrence of this condition in the future. For teenagers and young adults who lack basic skills, the options are relatively limited, especially if they have already left the educational system. Remedial programs can be created, but current practices are not encouraging as to retaining youth in the programs, if in fact they can be persuaded to enter in the first place. The transmission of basic skills by non-traditional means is perhaps the preeminent educational challenge for this cohort of youth. On the employment side, the same can be said about the creation of stable employment opportunities.

For those youth who are still affiliated with a school, the clear implication is that programs on their behalf must be initiated much earlier in their schooling process. They also must be done with more systematic attention to the acquisition of skills and the demonstration of basic competencies. The creation of remedial programs for students in the last year or two of their formal education is simply too little and too late. The effort has to begin early and concentrate upon those in greatest need. (Here again there is a clear consistency between this position and the recently announced youth unemployment initiatives by the President on January 10, 1980.) The investment, early on and intensive, appears to be worth the cost. As Adams and Mangum (1978) have noted:

Investment in education and training during youth is closely correlated with subsequent investment over the life cycle. Those who invest early, continue to invest later. Thus, part of the economic returns to education and training during youth is realized through access to subsequent education and training opportunities. Not only is this important to early labor market success, but also to avoidance of later economic and social problems associated with declining investment and ensuing skill obsolescence with age. (p. 137)

Though the recent National Academy of Education report (Task Force on Education and Employment, 1979, p. 17) offered a more guarded assessment when it started, with respect to the long-term impact of work-education programs, "The average effects are modest at best," the point remains: participation in education and employment training programs does have an impact upon the life-chances of youth. The empirical question is not one of whether an impact, but to what degree.

Programs and Policies: Sorting out the Trends

While it is admittedly something of a reification, the following short list of six "knowns" highlights important dimensions of our current knowledge base with regard to creating programs to address the school-to-work transition for young people.

—More is known about the intentions of innovation programs than about program operations.
—More is known about measuring program outcomes than is known about the processes and program dynamics that created such outcomes.
—More is known about the conditions and factors that generate program failure than is known about generating program success.
—More is known about Federal initiatives than about local receptivity to these initiatives.
—More is known about the involvement of the public sector in school-to-work transition efforts than is known about the means to involve the private sector.
—More is known about serving youth as "clients" than is known about how to equip youth to be co-participants in decisions regarding their own future.

Taking this short list as a whole, there are several key implications that can be sorted out as suggestive of the trends in school-to-work transition programs for the 1980s. The first is that we will be moving rapidly away from the assumption of "actor proof" programs towards those that maximize the skills and expertise of the program participants. It is evident that the pursuit of actor proof programs in the area of youth education and employment/training programs is futile. Besides being a poor use of time and resources (when both are scarce), such an approach ignores the key strength of the current efforts in the field—a strength based on the inspired and competent efforts of staff. To look elsewhere than to the people who organize and implement the programs is to miss the central point. The projects only work when people involved successfully make them work. The contrary tendency, as Mangum and Walsh (1978) have noted, is:

to be searching for the "actor proof" program, or programs, that were so well conceived and constructed that their effectiveness does not depend upon the competence of the human beings who either operate them or participate in them . . . Evaluators may be correct when they blame the failures of programs or program components on the weaknesses of program personnel, but such criticism sheds very little light on the potential effectiveness of the programs or the components themselves. (pp. 14–15)

Several of the articles in this issue address specifically those areas of "potential effectiveness" so as to enhance the utility of the actors involved, not to render them irrelevant.

The second of our general conclusions with regard to the list of "knowns" is that while specific school-to-work transition efforts are necessary for youth, *we need to exhibit a certain degree of skepticism regarding their impact on either the economic structures of the society or the employment opportunities for the youth themselves.* Data from our own national assessment (Rist et al., 1979a, 1979b, 1980) suggest that there exists a persistent discomfort at program sites and in the offices of their sponsors that "not all is being done that ought to be done." This is a misdirected concern, especially in light of those expectations for projects to accomplish more than what is possible. Given the multiple constraints of funding, of scheduling, of existing on "soft money," often as short term demonstration projects, of some numbers of youth being reluctant to commit themselves to yet another federal project, and the lack of prior collaboration between the CETA system and other agencies or institutions, the current projects have performed remarkably well. But they cannot be expected to ensure employment opportunities with promotion possibilities, nor can they be expected to retain all youth in their programs.

Third, *that we have learned so little from our efforts over the past two decades ought not to pressure us into seeking instantaneous results.* Current efforts will need careful scrutiny, not to provide premature "outcome" data, but to learn what we can about implementation, of the trials of program start-up, and of how slowly but confidently to build the inter-institutional linkages necessary for effective program operation. Had we been more concerned in these past years with the questions of implementation, and less with the pursuit of the "quick fix," we would not be in the dismal condition that we currently find. *We have been seeking outcome measures before we even understood the process.* Thus we continue to grope about seeking to learn "what works when and why?" With this cart-before-the-horse mentality, it is sobering to read from Pressman and Wildavsky (1979):

Our normal expectations should be that new programs will fail to get off the ground and that, at best, they will take considerable time to get started. The cards in this world are stacked against things happening, so much effort is required to make them move. The remarkable thing is that new programs work at all. (p. 109)

Not taking the time to learn when programs did work and why they did has brought us once more to the making of a beginning. We are in the midst of trying again.

The fourth of our general conclusions is that the transition from school to work is a complex endeavor for young people, involving not only occupational choices, but choices about living arrangements, education, spending larger sums of money (or buying on credit), assuming adult roles, and any number of other such changes. *The task is one of learning how to weave together the social net to be placed below youth as they make their way into adulthood and the world of work.* This view is consistent, for example, with that of the National Commission for Manpower Policy (1978) which has recommended that the focus of study on CETA programs be that of the strengths of the various approaches. As was noted:

In view of the rapid and continuing growth of federal manpower programs, together with the deliberate shifts in programmatic emphasis, it would seem reasonable to assume that the efficacy of manpower programs, in their various forms, was well established. This is not the case, however. Not only is the efficacy of any single program more an article of faith than documented evidence, but also there are very few clues regarding the relative efficacy of alternative programmatic approaches. (pp. 107–108)

Youth need to get started somewhere in building their experience with work. It is inappropriate to measure program performance and outcomes when the youth have barely left the starting blocks. To assist youth in making choices as a result of exposure and experience in an in-school project ought to be acknowledged for what it is.

The fifth of the general findings is one that has been extensively documented previously (Mangum & Walsh, 1978; Rist et al., 1979a, 1979b, 1980). The one *"treatment" which has consistently appeared as important to the youth and to the overall success of current projects has been "individualized attention."* The student populations being served by YEDPA projects tend, as a generalization, to be students who have not experienced success in conventional schools and in conventional classrooms. They are students whose constant accumulation of unmet academic and interpersonal needs are not well redressed by large-scale, mass programs. The students appear to have best responded in those settings where there has been quiet and consistent interaction with adults, where the individualized assessment of their basic skill needs has led to an individually tailored and closely monitored course of study, and where the adults in the programs have taken the time to assist the youth in sorting out their options and choices for the future (the very opposite of an "actor proof program!") This finding appears to hold across various program strategies and across various age ranges of students. Students have flourished when they have been treated as "whole persons."

The sixth and final conclusion to be drawn from this discussion is that if our continuing efforts are not to be a repetition of our past mistakes, we are going to have to actively seek mechanisms of offering technical assistance to new efforts and sharing successful practices among currently operating programs. The current isolation of projects and their perpetual "rediscovery of the wheel" is a luxury and use of resources that simply cannot continue. Much as has been done in other areas of education (e.g., the 26 General Assistance Centers located across the nation and working to facilitate school desegregation), a means of providing comprehensive technical assistance will soon be past due for those involved in the school-to-work transition. So long as there is no single blueprint for the creation of school-to-work transition programs, then those who are, as it were, in a constant state of improvisation need all the assistance they can muster. We are likely to find, if no mechanisms of assistance are created and put in place, that history does indeed repeat itself.

On this Special Issue

The original rationale for this issue grew out of a concern for providing within the professional literature a discussion of a number of pressing issues related to youth unemployment. Heretofore, the vast majority of material in this area has not been in the formal literature, but has existed as conference proceedings, interim and final reports to various sponsoring agencies, drafts of papers being circulated for comment, and program specific evaluations. Little of the discussion and analysis of what has come rapidly to the front as one of the key domestic issues of the 1980s has seen the light of the easily accessible literature.

The nucleus of papers in this issue comes from the College of Human Ecology at Cornell University. In addition to faculty and administration interest in the youth unemployment issue, the College is the home of the Youthwork National Policy Study (YNPS). The YNPS is a multi-year study of nearly 60 exemplary school-to-work transition programs currently being conducted in 31 states. The projects have been funded by the Department of Labor and are served on a day-to-day liaison basis by Youthwork, Inc., a non-profit intermediary corporation established specifically for this purpose.

The YNPS has sought through the application of on-site intensive qualitative data collection and analysis to provide a different yet critical vantage point for the study of transition programs. By foregoing a concern with "outcome" measures and focusing, instead, on the processes and dynamics of program implementation, the study seeks to provide information to program personnel and policy makers alike on what program options are available and how these options can be implemented. Four of the papers in this issue are based on data gathered in relation to the national study.

The other papers and the book review essays have been solicited to strengthen and expand the range of issues to be covered. The materials, in total, reflect the spectrum of concerns with the transition unemployment nexus, including policy agenda, current programmatic analysis, research findings and implications, and assessments of what we have learned to date. We would stress, as a means of furthering communication among people interested in youth unemployment, that the readers of this issue are welcome to contact any of the authors for further information regarding material, data, or discussion of points raised here.

References

Adams, A., & Mangum, G.L. *The lingering crisis of youth unemployment*. Kalamazoo, Michigan: W.E. Upjohn Institute for Employment Research, 1978.

Congressional Budget Office. *Causes of youth employment problems— a preliminary analysis*. Washington, D.C.: Government Printing Office, 1980.

Ginzberg, E. *Good jobs, bad jobs, no jobs*. Cambridge, Mass.: Harvard University Press, 1979.

Mangum, G., & Walsh, J. *Employment and training programs for youth: What works best for whom?* Washington, D.C.: Office of Youth Programs, Employment and Training Administration, Government Printing Office, 1978.

National Commission for Manpower Policy. *CETA: An analysis of the issues*. Washington, D.C.: Government Printing Office, 1978.

Pressman, J.L., & Wildavsky, A. *Implementation*, (2nd ed.). Berkeley: University of California Press, 1979.

Rist, R.C., et al. *Forging new relationships: The CETA/school nexus*. Ithaca, N.Y.: Youthwork National Policy Study, Cornell University, 1979. (a)

Rist, R.C., et al. *Strategies for coordinating education and employment services: A preliminary analysis of four in-school alternatives*, Occasional Paper #1. Ithaca, N.Y.: Youthwork National Policy Study, Cornell University, 1979. (b)

Rist, R.C., et al. *Targeting on in-school youth: Four strategies for coordinating education and employment training*. Ithaca, N.Y.: Youthwork National Policy Study, Cornell University, 1980.

Task Force on Education and Employment. *Education for employment: Knowledge for action*. Washington, D.C.: Acropolis Books, 1979.

U.S. Department of Labor. *A knowledge development plan for the Youth Employment and Demonstration Projects Act of 1977*. Washington, D.C.: Office of Youth Programs, Employment and Training Administration, Government Printing Office, 1978.

U.S. Department of Labor. *A knowledge development plan for youth initiatives, fiscal 1979*. Washington, D.C.: Office of Youth Programs, Employment and Training Administration, Government Printing Office, 1979.

Westcott, D. The nation's youth: An employment perspective. *Children and Youth Services Review*, 1979, *1*, 87–100.

Children and Youth Services Review, Vol. 2, pp. 17–39, 1980
Printed in the USA. All rights reserved.

Youth Employment and Education: Federal Programs from the New Deal Through the 1970s

Michael W. Sherraden
Washington University

Education, in a variety of forms and for a variety of purposes, has played a role in federally sponsored youth employment efforts since the 1930s. The purpose of this historical review is to describe educational components of major youth employment programs from the New Deal through the Youth Employment and Demonstration Projects Act (YEDPA) of 1977. Attention is given to historical continuities as well as major shifts in policy and administrative strategy. Particular attention is given to the transition from school to work and the role education has played in this transition.

The New Deal

The federal government became actively involved in youth employment efforts for the first time during the Depression of the 1930s. When Franklin Roosevelt assumed the Presidency in 1933, unemployment was high among all age groups. "Youthful tramps" were a recognized social problem. The Congress and the public were ready for change and Roosevelt responded quickly. Among the first "alphabet soup" agencies of the New Deal was the Civilian Conservation Corps (CCC), a program which employed young men in conserva-

Michael W. Sherraden, The George Warren Brown School of Social Work, Washington University, St. Louis, Missouri 63130.

17

tion work camps in rural areas.[1] The CCC existed from April,
1933 to June, 1942. Enrollment averaged approximately
300,000 at any given time, although the peak enrollment was
over half a million. Average individual stay in the CCC was
ten months. The total number of enrollees during the nine
year program period was more than three million. Income
redistribution and conservation work were the two principal
goals of the CCC. Education and job training were, at best,
ancillary goals. Overall, the CCC was popular and generally
has been evaluated as highly effective in terms of its major
objectives (Salmond, 1967, p. 121; Sherraden, 1979, pp. 5–7).

The second major youth employment program of the
New Deal was the National Youth Administration (NYA). The
NYA was established in June of 1935 as an agency within the
Works Progress Administration (WPA). The primary goal of
the NYA was economic relief in two forms—student aid and
out-of-school work projects. Unlike the CCC, the emphasis of
the NYA was clearly economic support rather than work,[2] and
education played a more prominent role. In terms of the total
enrollment, the NYA was even larger than the CCC; nearly
five million young men and women were served altogether.
Both the CCC and NYA have served as influential precedents
in youth employment efforts in the 1960s and 1970s. For this
reason, it is useful to briefly examine their characteristics. We
turn now to a closer look at the role of education in these two
prominent New Deal programs.

Education in the Civilian Conservation Corps. The educational program of the CCC was not emphasized (Rawick,
1957, chap. 5; Salmond, 1967, pp. 149–150). Although it was
a topic of much debate and study, education never became a
major CCC goal.[3] The primary reason was that President Roo-

[1]The CCC was originally called the Emergency Conservation Work. In 1937
the popular name, Civilian Conservation Corps, was officially adopted.
[2] The strong influence of Harry Hopkins, who was WPA Director from
1935 to 1938, is apparent in the goals and structure of the NYA. A social
worker by training, Hopkins was more interested in feeding and clothing
the needy than in productivity. One of the best sources on Hopkins is
Sherwood (1948).
[3] Educators were interested in the CCC because of the innovative educational possibilities it presented. It is informative, for example, that the majority of Ph.D. and Master's theses produced on the CCC during the 1930s
were by graduate students in education.

sevelt and CCC Director Robert Fechner did not view the CCC as an educational program. At one point Fechner stated: "The prime purpose of the CCC is to furnish work and to conserve natural resources . . . These cannot be work camps and educational camps at the same time" (U.S. Congress, Committee on Labor, 1937, pp. 98–99). President Roosevelt was frequently dissatisfied with educational initiatives, suggesting that education was likely to interfere with the more important goals of the CCC. Although there was much pressure from some members of Congress, Roosevelt never permitted working hours to be shortened to allow more teaching (Salmond, 1967, pp. 77–78). Classroom vocational training was even less popular with CCC policy-makers because organized labor was opposed to it (Rowland, 1937).

In spite of these responses, a voluntary educational program was created for Civilian Conservation Corps enrollees. The educational program consisted of basic academic and craft classes held in the evening. In addition, a few CCC enrollees obtained a formal high school or college education by attending classes in towns near the camps. The U.S. Army, which was in charge of CCC camp operations, resisted hiring civilian personnel for educational purposes. The Army lost this battle, but succeeded in maintaining control over the educational program. The Office of Education was justifiably frustrated by this arrangement. By and large, the Army served as a repressive influence in educational matters. In fairness to the military, however, this seemed to be Roosevelt's and Fechner's intent.

Despite the constraints which limited the CCC educational program, some benefits resulted. At least half of all CCC enrollees took some kind of classes. CCC enrollees most in need of education, however, were not always those who received the education. One study reported a positive correlation of .40 between measured I.Q. and participation in the educational program (U.S. Office of Education, 1939); in other words, enrollees with higher I.Q. scores tended to take classes more than enrollees with lower I.Q. scores. Nevertheless, thousands of formerly illiterate enrollees left the Corps with reading and writing skills (Oxley, Note 1, p. 5). There is some evidence that black youths, who made up 10% of the regular CCC population and 25% of the illiterate CCC population, took better advantage of the educational program than white youths. Literacy gains for black youths were significant ("Reducing Illiteracy in the CCC," 1940).

Regarding transitions from the CCC to other employment, CCC education had minimal effect. In one of the most thorough studies of post-CCC outcomes for enrollees, Walker (1938, p. 42) found no relationship between camp educational experiences and later jobs, and she concluded that poor transitions were due in part to poor performance of camp Educational Advisers in job placement activities. Lorwin (1941, p. 18) concluded that the CCC as a whole was not very successful in terms of future jobs for enrollees. All things considered, however, economic conditions were so bad throughout most of the CCC's existence that quality of education was not the major problem. Skillful job placement was more important (Salmond, 1967, p. 134), and Headington (1938, p. 134), studying enrollees from 21 camps, found that "home contacts" was the most often cited reason for obtaining a job upon leaving the CCC.

Some observers have noted that CCC graduates were "well received" by employers (Kesselman, 1978, p. 183, citing Salmond, 1967, p. 111), but such observations are misleading. CCC graduates may have been looked upon favorably, but there were few jobs available and the CCC job placement program was never very good. In the only large-scale surveys of former CCC enrollees, it was found that the unemployment rate was 60–77% a few months after leaving the CCC. Unemployment rates were even higher in populous industrial states such as New York, Ohio, and Illinois, indicating that business employers' favorable outlook on CCC graduates was overshadowed by the severity of the Depression (U.S. Federal Emergency Relief Adminsitration, Note 2). The Civilian Conservation Corps, although its accomplishments were impressive, did little to help enrollees overcome unemployment after leaving the program.

Education in the National Youth Administration. The National Youth Administration had two major components—the in-school program and the out-of-school program. The in-school or student aid program was the larger of the two and operated in elementary and high schools, colleges, and to some extent in graduate schools. It was the first major "work-study" effort sponsored by the federal government. Educational institutions were provided funds to hire students to undertake "practical and useful projects." Although there was a peripheral intention of job training in such projects, the major emphasis was economic support. Aid was distributed proportionately with population in rural and urban areas, which meant that about 55% of NYA student aid went to towns and cities with populations under 25,000 (Johnson & Harvey, 1938, pp. 32–33). As of December 1937, the program served 47% males and 53% females; at the college and graduate level, however, the proportion was 60% males and 40% females. Eleven percent of NYA in-school enrollees were non-whites (Johnson & Harvey, 1938, pp. 34–35).

The role of education in the NYA student aid program was clear—education was the principal objective. Employment was provided for the purpose of keeping young people in school. In this regard, the NYA in-school program was unquestionably a success. Hundreds of thousands of young people were able to continue their education with NYA support. At a minimum this program insulated these youths from a very inhospitable labor market. Although an adequate formal evaluation is unavailable, there is little doubt that students able to continue their educations were, on the whole, better prepared to compete for jobs after leaving school.

The NYA out-of-school or work projects program was established in January of 1936 as a work relief effort similar to its parent program, the WPA. Females made up 45% of the enrollment (U.S. National Youth Administration, 1944, p. 109). Most NYA out-of-school projects were non-residential. Much of the work was semi-skilled or unskilled. Projects included construction, conservation, education, clerical work, research and production of simple goods. Basic academic education of enrollees, although given lip service, was not part of the program and there was little formal job training. NYA administrators were unequivocal regarding the basic program purpose, which was simply to provide employment (U.S. National Youth Administration, 1944, p. 24). Nevertheless, many enrollees gained valuable work experience in the NYA and this work experience facilitated transitions to unsubsidized employment (Johnson & Harvey, 1938, pp. 55–58). The NYA also put more emphasis on post-program job placement than did the CCC and the NYA was more successful in this effort.

There were some cooperative educational efforts between the CCC and NYA, especially in later years (Woods, 1964, p. 326). And young men would occasionally leave one program and sign up for the other. In the final analysis, the demise of these two major New Deal youth employment programs was due to their temporary image. They were viewed by the public and Congress as short-lived responses to an economic emergency. When employment opportunities expanded as a result of U.S involvement in World War II, the Civilian Conservation Corps and National Youth Administration were terminated.

Between the New Deal and the War on Poverty

There were no youth employment programs at the federal level between Franklin Roosevelt's New Deal and Lyndon Johnson's Great Society. For the most part, the nation's attention was focused on foreign rather than domestic issues during this period. However, proposals did surface from time to time and they were usually modeled after the Civilian Conservation Corps. The first revival of the CCC idea occurred in the Congress in 1949 and 1950. Resource management agencies favored this legislation but educators and labor analysts were skeptical. Roll Grisgby, Deputy Commissioner of Education for the Federal Security Agency summarized the opposing viewpoint:

In short, assuming no rapid worsening of the unemployment situation, we believe the re-establishment of the Civilian Conservation Corps should await accumulation of experience with measures for improving the education and training of youth in the presently established educational institutions. (cited in Weeks, 1967, pp. 24–25)

The Korean War and cold war politics, accompanied by general economic prosperity, delayed further consideration of a federal youth employment program until 1958. During the early and middle 1950s however, a number of private, county, and state programs were initiated in California, Idaho, Michigan, and other states. These programs all bore a resemblance to the earlier CCC. At the federal level, it was Senator Hubert Humphrey who led the effort for renewal of a youth employment program. Humphrey proposed legislation in 1958 to create a Youth Conservation Corps (YCC), again patterned largely after the CCC of the 1930s (U.S. Congress, Senate, 1958; and U.S.Congress, Senate, 1959). As in the CCC, emphasis on education in Humphrey's YCC proposal was limited. Senator Humphrey also took his idea to the American people in a widely distributed *Harper's* magazine article entitled, "Plan to Save Trees, Land, and Boys" (Humphrey, 1959). Although there was great public support, the White House opposed Humphrey's initiative. The bill barely passed in the Senate, and a companion bill in the House received no action.

There was a specific promise of a Youth Conservation Corps in the Democratic platform of 1960. However, as legislation was introduced in 1961, it became clear that President Kennedy was weakly committed to the idea, offering a very limited "pilot" formula designed to hold down expenditures. Over White House opposition the Senate Labor Committee approved a somewhat watered-down Humphrey plan rather than Kennedy's proposal. The House Committee on Education and Labor, on the other hand, more nearly supported the President's requests. Neither bill reached a vote on the floor.

During 1962 and 1963, discussion of various versions of the YCC continued. Debate was intensified by James Conant's report, *Social Dynamite* (National Committee for Children and Youth, 1961), which identified an explosive unemployed and out-of-school urban youth population. The Conant report recommended a variety of roles for education in enhancing youth employment programs. Among 142 example programs cited in *Social Dynamite*, at least half described cooperative arrangements between public schools and local businesses or government for career awareness, pre-employment preparation, work experience, summer job programs, job placement or other employment oriented projects. The emphasis on various education-employment links in Conant's report was clear. This emphasis, however, was not translated into proposals in the Congress. The prominent bills before the House and Senate continued to focus on public service job creation.

Support expressed for a Youth Conservation Corps before congressional committees was remarkable—almost no one was opposed. A Gallup poll in 1961 reported that 80% of the American people thought it was a good idea to revive the CCC; 59% thought it should be required for young men unemployed and not in school (reported in the *Washington Post*, August 23, 1961). In 1963 President Kennedy also proposed a National Service Corps, but this proposal was soon lost in a muddle of appropriation and task force funding limitations (Weeks, 1967, p. 44). None of these initiatives resulted in new programs during the Kennedy administration.

Regarding the role of education, Representative Carl Perkins introduced a bill in the 1961 debate which included many of the educational aspects of the old NYA, but even this effort did not serve as a rallying point (Woods, 1964, pp. 360–363). The Manpower Development and Training Act (MDTA) of 1962 emphasized education and training to keep up with rapidly changing technologies. The central MDTA programs were not targeted specifically toward youth; however, MDTA did create experimental and demonstration projects, many of which were designed to test various educational roles in solving youth unemployment problems (U.S. Department of Labor, 1969). There was a near success for vocational education of unemployed youth in the Vocational Educational Act of 1963, which contained a section authorizing funding of five experimental vocational schools giving "special consideration to the needs of large urban areas having substantial numbers of youths who have dropped out of school or are unemployed." Unfortunately, Congress failed to appropriate funds for this section, due in part to disagreement over location of the schools (Weeks, 1967, p. 45).

The War on Poverty

It was not until Lyndon Johnson became president that congressional bottlenecks to social legislation began to dissolve. The 1964 Economic Opportunity Act (the legislative foundation for the "War on Poverty") created the Neighborhood Youth Corps and Job Corps, descendents of Hubert Humphrey's proposals for a "Youth Conservation Corps."

The Neighborhood Youth Corps (NYC) began in 1965 as a paid work experience program for low-income 14- to 21-year-olds. NYC had two major objectives: (1) to increase the employability of youths, and (2) to reduce school dropout rates. NYC had separate in-school, out-of-school, and summer programs. In some ways, NYC was similar to the programs of the National Youth Administration of the New Deal. A second incarnation of the out-of-school program, called NYC-2, began in 1970 and concentrated on employment preparation via job skills training, supportive services, and remedial education. The size of NYC was substantial. Nearly 138,000 enrollees participated during the first year; the program reached a peak of 556,000 first time enrollments in 1967, and fluctuated around 500,000 over the next three years (Clague & Kramer, 1976, p. 19). These numbers almost rivaled the size of the old NYA.

Job Corps began in 1965 as a residential program offering vocational training and basic education to disadvantaged youths. It was designed to improve employment prospects among 16- to 21-year-old male and female youths. Originally, the conservation lobby had pushed through a provision that 40% of Job Corps enrollees would be located in Civilian Conservation Centers doing conservation work (Levitan & Johnston, 1975, p. 14). Today, after an inauspicious early performance, Civilian Conservation Centers play a less significant role in the Job Corps and emphasis has shifted even more toward job training and education. In its early years Job Corps had numerous problems and withstood a barrage of negative publicity. Early evaluations were not complimentary. Program objectives appeared to be unclear and enrollee dropout rates were high. In recent years, however, Job Corps has been viewed as a "social experiment that works" (Levitan & Johnston, 1975) and data indicate that Job Corps has indeed become an effective program in terms of successful transition of enrollees to unsubsidized employment (U.S. Department of Labor, Note 3).

Education in the Neighborhood Youth Corps. The in-school NYC program was designed to prevent youths from dropping out of school by offering financial support through

part-time employment. Other program emphases included
self-image development, vocational skills training, workman-
ship training, and career exploration (Systems Research Incorporated, 1973). A 1970 review of research on the NYC
in-school program concluded that youngsters may have
stayed in school longer and, at a minimum, the financial
burden of staying in school was reduced (U.S. Department of
Labor, 1970, pp. 9–10).

The NYC out-of-school program has been described as a
"work experience" program, but the goals were in reality
more complex, including return to school, skill training in
some cases, and job placement. The NYC out-of-school program consisted primarily of small supervised work teams
engaged in a wide variety of jobs. Remedial education was
supposed to be part of the program, but was generally unsuc-
cessful due to insufficient effort among program personnel
and insufficient interest among enrollees (U.S. Department of
Labor, 1970, p. 15). There is little evidence that the remedial
education component of the out-of-school NYC affected transitions to future jobs. Nevertheless, transitions were good
among some groups, especially urban black female enrollees
and enrollees in rural areas and small towns. On the other
hand, the program was little help to urban black males, and
even less help to urban white youth, male or female (U.S.
Department of Labor, 1970, p. 11).

Education in Job Corps. Education has always played a central role in the Job Corps program. At the outset, educational
goals were vague and the entire Job Corps program faltered
(see Weeks, 1967; Lewack, 1973). The urgent need for remedial education was not effectively met (Clague & Kramer,
1976, p. 20). Today, educational goals are more specific and,
largely as a result, Job Corps is more successful.

One of the important lessons learned from Job Corps experience—
one that may be particularly relevant to future institutional training
programs—is that Job Corps performance improved rather than deteriorated when many of the frills were slashed. Training and education were narrowed to specific job requirements. The key seemed to
be the ability to gain access to jobs rather than efforts to alter attitudes
and values of enrollees. (Magnum & Walsh, 1978, p. 84)

Mangum and Walsh (1978, pp. 84–85) have also concluded that it is helpful to establish specific links to employers and unions and it is essential to provide adequate placement services. Cooperative arrangements between Job Corps and some labor unions have been one of the most effective approaches to youth employment in the past forty years. Under these arrangements, Job Corps education is shaped to fit union jobs; and enrollees enter the union as apprentices with a foot in the door toward a promising career.

With the above-mentioned changes in Job Corps, combined with more careful screening of applicants, retention of enrollees has improved. And improvement in enrollee placement upon leaving the program has been dramatic. According to government statistics, the Job Corps national placement rate for fiscal year 1977, including enrollee dropouts, was close to 93%. This included all enrollees who entered the military (6%), returned to school (23%), or were placed in jobs (64%) (U.S. Department of Labor, Note 3 pp. 9–10). The placement rate for fiscal 1978 remained at 93% (*Employment and Training Report of the President*, 1979, p. 45). Following Congressional recognition of the program's effectiveness, appropriations were approved in 1978 to double the size of Job Corps from 44,000 to 88,000 enrollees per year.

Youth Conservation Corps

One major youth employment program was created between the War on Poverty and the Comprehensive Employment and Training Act (CETA) of 1973. The Youth Conservation Corps (YCC) was initiated in 1970 as a summer residential conservation-oriented work and education program. YCC has been targeted more broadly than other youth employment efforts, i.e., enrollees are not necessarily disadvantaged. In fact, YCC has been criticized for not enrolling a fair proportion of urban, black, and economically disadvantaged young people (Mangum & Walsh, 1978, p. 60). The program, however, has been popular with enrollees and generally viewed as successful in terms of work accomplished and enrollee satisfaction (Marans, Driver, & Scott, 1972; Mowitt, Note 4).

From an educational standpoint, YCC is unique. The

program "bears only a tenuous relationship to traditional employment and training programs" (Mangum & Walsh, 1978, p. 60). Environmental education is a major goal of YCC. Time is set aside on a regular basis for educational purposes and the program is evaluated partly on the basis of increased environmental knowledge among enrollees. For the most part, this emphasis is taken in the YCC as a value in itself. Little attempt is made to tie YCC education to future jobs. Although there may be a hope that some YCC enrollees are inspired to a conservation career, job training and future employability are not goals of the YCC educational program. No other major youth employment program has used education in quite this way.

The general popularity of YCC, however, should not escape us. It is the only existing youth employment program that does not suffer from a "welfare" image. A universally applied program, i.e., a program open to applicants regardless of economic means—has the advantage of being accepted without stigma by the Congress and the public. This is an old lesson in social welfare policy which the YCC is again demonstrating.

The Comprehensive Employment and Training Act of 1973 (CETA)

The Comprehensive Employment and Training Act of 1973 (CETA) was part of President Nixon's larger strategy to decentralize federal government services to state and local government control. The emphasis was to be on block grants rather than categorical programs. And as a result of the block grant approach, a large proportion of federal support for employment programs has been transferred to local "prime sponsors." However, some existing categorical youth employment efforts were incorporated within the original CETA legislation, including the Neighborhood Youth Corps, Job Corps, and Youth Conservation Corps. In addition, other categorical programs have been initiated under CETA which focus on youth as a special group. The largest and most well-known has been the Summer Program for Economically Disadvantaged

Youth (SPEDY), a direct descendent of the Neighborhood Youth Corps. SPEDY has become larger than NYC. In calendar year 1975, for example, 888,000 young people aged 14 to 21 were provided short-term jobs in SPEDY (*Employment and Training Report of the President*, 1976, p. 108). In the summer of 1978, 1,009,300 persons were served (*Employment and Training Report of the President*, 1979, p. 44). SPEDY is the largest youth employment program in the nation's history in terms of number of youth served per year. The nature of these jobs has been very similar to jobs in the National Youth Administration and the Neighborhood Youth Corps. Beginning in 1978, however, there has been an effort to upgrade the quality of work experience and to increase opportunities for vocational exploration (*Employment and Training Report of the President*, 1979, p. 44). These recent emphases in SPEDY represent a shift from simply providing employment to a greater concern for future employability of enrollees.

Another CETA program of direct interest in the present discussion is the School to Work Transition Program (SWTP). This program has included a number of pilot projects designed to develop new ways to prepare youth to move smoothly from educational institutions to places of work.

Objectives of the program include integration of classroom instruction with work experience; design and development of curriculum materials that will better prepare students for occupational entrance requirements; and preparation of youth for new occupational fields. Other aims are to develop career information and knowledge of local training, employment, education, and service opportunities and to provide better counseling, guidance, and placement assistance, using employment related resources of the community. (*Employment and Training Report of the President*, 1977, p. 53)

Expenditures for all SWTP projects totaled $9.5 million in fiscal year 1977. These projects have been a productive series of experiments, comparable to the experimental and demonstration youth projects under MDTA (see U.S. Department of Labor, 1969). With the accumulation of this experience, Congress passed new legislation in 1977 to further explore possible solutions to rising levels of youth unemployment.

The Youth Employment and
Demonstration Projects Act of 1977 (YEDPA)

CETA was expanded in 1977 by the Youth Employment and Demonstration Projects Act (YEDPA). YEDPA legislation created four new programs: Young Adult Conservation Corps (YACC); Youth Incentive Entitlement Pilot Projects (YIEPP); Youth Community Conservation and Improvement Projects (YCCIP); and Youth Employment and Training Programs (YETP). The Department of Labor interpreted the legislation for these four programs and identified ten principles to guide program administration. These principles included knowledge development; improving the quality of work experience; involvement of youth in program designed delivery; targeting resources to those most in need; and involvement of community and neighborhood-based groups. One additional principle focused directly on the transition from school to work: "to promote institutional change, particularly program linkages between education and work activities" (U.S. Department of Labor, 1978a, p. 3). Educational provisions serve different functions in each of the YEDPA programs.

Young Adult Conservation Corps. YACC is another descendent of the Civilian Conservation Corps. Disadvantaged young people ages 16 through 23 years are employed in conservation work and other projects with the U.S. Forest Service, The U.S. National Park Service, and the State Park Departments. YACC is a straightforward work program. The major goals are carbon copies of CCC goals—jobs and conservation work. Education, as in the old CCC, is not emphasized. Indeed, an early evaluation of YACC implementation reported that "enrichments" were generally not incorporated into the program (U.S. Department of Labor, Note 5, p. viii). Total expenditures for YACC reached $233 million in fiscal 1978 and, as of September 30, 1978, 27,000 youths were enrolled in the program (*Employment and Training Report of the President*, 1979, p. 42).

Youth Incentive Entitlement Pilot Projects. YIEPP is a series of pilot projects designed to test the entitlement approach, which is the guarantee of a year-round job for in-school youths.

The basic purpose of YIEPP is to test the notion of whether school-year (part-time) and summer (full-time) jobs can be feasibly guaranteed for 16–19-year-old economically disadvantaged youths who are in secondary school, or who are willing to return to such a school or enroll in a course leading to a certificate of high school equivalency. It will test whether such jobs will be an "incentive" to increase their high school retention, return, and completion. (U.S. Department of Labor, Note 6, p. 1)

Entitlement is a concept similar to the old NYA and NYC in-school programs. However, the YIEPP experiments are unique in two respects: (1) they are comprehensive within a given area, i.e., the program is a "saturation" test wherein the entire service population is entitled to a job; and (2) there is a goal beyond merely keeping young people in school—career development, employment, and training efforts are emphasized in the selected experimental areas (U.S. Department of Labor, 1977, pp. 13–14). This latter emphasis indicates a greater awareness of the role schools might play in the transition from school to work. During an 18 month period in 1978 and 1979, about 30,000 jobs were being provided in 17 CETA prime sponsor locations, with a total federal expenditure of $115 million (*Employment and Training Report of the President,* 1979, p. 41).

Youth and Community Conservation and Improvement Projects. YCCIP seeks "to employ youth in well-supervised work with tangible output which will be of benefit to the community. The work itself will be the source of training, with academic credit arranged where appropriate" (U.S. Department of Labor, 1977, p. 15). In short, YCCIP is designed as an experiment to test whether the "work approach" can lead to successful transitions to unsubsidized employment (U.S. Department of Labor, 1978a). YCCIP is designed to serve 16- to 19-year-olds with the greatest difficulty finding employment. In fiscal year 1978, approximately 20,000 jobs were created at a cost of $115 million (*Employment and Training Report of the President,* 1979, p. 41).

Youth Employment and Training Programs. YETP is designed for both in-school and out-of-school youths ages 16 through 21 who have the most severe problems entering the labor force. A major goal of YETP is to create linkages between CETA prime sponsors and local educational agencies. According to the initial 1977 YEDPA legislation, at least 22% of YETP grant funds were to be set aside to encourage collaboration between CETA prime sponsors and local educational agencies in planning and providing services to in-school youths. This significant allocation of resources ($88.5 million) specifically to establish linkages between education and employment and training institutions is unprecedented in the history of youth employment programs in the U.S. Never before has the transition from school to work received such direct attention. There is great flexibility for experimentation in these projects at the local level. An early report of five case studies of the YETP in-school projects tentatively found that communication between CETA prime sponsors and the public schools had improved. A noticeable positive impact on education and job training program quality had occurred in several cases. It was found that the YETP in-school projects were reaching students who would not otherwise have been served (U.S. Department of Labor, 1978b, pp. 3–4).

Knowledge development efforts under YEDPA include many projects related to the transition from school-to-work. Some of these are the Career Intern Program; establishment of work-education councils in selected communities; a grant to the National Occupational Information Coordinating Committee to improve delivery of occupational information to youth; establishment of a National Longitudinal Survey focusing on the school-to-work transition of a large sample of economically disadvantaged youth (U.S. Department of Labor, 1978a, pp. 17–18). Three intermediary nonprofit corporations have been established to assist the Department of Labor in YEDPA knowledge development projects. These organizations are the Manpower Demonstration Research Council, the Corporation for Public/Private Ventures, and Youthwork, Inc. These intermediary non-profit corporations represent another important cooperative emphasis within YEDPA programs—cooperation among federal and local governments and non-governmental research organizations to learn as much as possible from the YEDPA experiments.

The diversity of projects and knowledge development efforts under YEDPA has begun to yield valuable experience and information. Already it is clear that the increased emphasis on education-employment linkages will continue. President Carter has proposed a one billion dollar program within the new Department of Education which would concentrate on basic academic skills—reading, writing, and simple math—at the 3000 most impoverished junior and senior high schools in the nation. In addition, this money would finance job counselors, local labor market information systems, teacher training and vocational education. Simultaneously, the Department of Labor would initiate a one billion dollar program to provide job training and work experience for high school dropouts. This cooperative two billion dollar effort would also provide incentive grants to school systems and local employment programs which demonstrate effectiveness in basic literacy training and establishing links to private sector jobs. Increasingly, the federal government is adopting youth employment policies which recognize that disadvantaged young people stand a better chance of succeeding in the labor market when they have a basic education and when some effort is made to connect, coordinate and facilitate the transition from school to work.

Conclusions

Over the years many approaches to youth unemployment problems have developed. Emphasis on education within these programs has varied greatly and the roles which education has played have been diverse. It is difficult to summarize this vast range of experience in a few words, but taking a long-range perspective, the following conclusions emerge:

1. *Educational objectives have played a role in youth employment programs consistently since the New Deal.* Even though the Civilian Conservation Corps and the National Youth Administration of the 1930s were principally job creation programs, education of enrollees was not ignored. The NYA in-school program sought especially to keep young people in school. Even the CCC, a classical public employment effort, had a well-organized educational program. During the 1960s and 1970s the educational components of

Neighborhood Youth Corps, Job Corps, Youth Conservation Corps, and the Youth Employment and Training Projects have been pronounced. Overall, educational components have played more prominent roles in youth employment programs than in adult employment programs. This long-term policy emphasis implies a general recognition that education, in some form, is an important element in preparing young people to enter the labor force.

2. *Educational roles within major youth employment programs have taken one of four general forms.* Historical experience with each of these educational approaches leads to separate conclusions:

   (a) *Supplemental education within a job creation program.* Supplemental education consists of classroom work or tutoring, usually in basic skills, within a program designed essentially to create jobs. The Civilian Conservation Corps is the best example. Other examples are the out-of-school National Youth Administration and out-of-school Neighborhood Youth Corps. Overall, the supplemental approach has not been successful. The primary reason has been the low priority accorded to educational goals within these programs. Educational components of the CCC and out-of-school NYA and NYC were "tacked on," almost as afterthoughts. Education has conflicted with work objectives within these programs and education has been consistently overshadowed.

   (b) *Work Study.* In this category are all those programs which have combined paid work and regular public or private education. The first federally-sponsored work-study effort was the in-school NYA. More recently we have seen the in-school NYC and the Youth Incentive Entitlement Pilot Projects. The summer programs of the NYA, NYC and SPEDY also fall into this category because they have primarily served in-school youths. At the college level, federal support for work-study has been extensive. The chief objective of work-study efforts has been to provide economic support to keep young people in school. In this regard, these programs have generally been successful. The benefits of keeping youths in school are at least two-fold: (1) these young people are, for the time being, kept out of an inhospitable labor market; and (2) the additional education and credentialization enhances future employability of program participants. In addition, the jobs provide some work experience and may establish connections for future full-time employment.

   (c) *Classroom or institutional efforts designed to prepare young people for jobs.* This broad category consists of programs in basic or remedial education, career awareness, pre-vocational training, skills training, and/or counseling which are aimed directly toward future employment of enrollees. Such programs may be either for in-school youths or for out-of-school youths. The number of experiments during the 1960s and 1970s in this area has been vast (for the most complete summary, see Mangum & Walsh, 1978, pp. 76–111, 129–145). However, the only major federal program for institutional remedial education and skill training has been Job Corps. Job Corps has achieved a remarkable turnabout since it was implemented in 1965. Post-program outcomes have been good in recent years and one major reason has been an increased specificity in basic education and skill training. A lesson to be learned from Job Corps' experience is that institutional or classroom educational components should focus on a clearly defined employment opportunity. The remedial education program currently proposed by President Carter is unlikely to succeed if preparation is not connected directly to a job.

(d) *Programs which facilitate the transition to work.* Programs which emphasize successful transition to unsubsidized employment may or may not be combined with any of the three approaches described above. Youth employment efforts have developed this emphasis relatively recently and, in general, it is an area which holds promise. Connections to jobs is probably the most critical element in any youth employment program. Again, the striking example is Job Corps. Simultaneously with specific job-related training, Job Corps has developed relationships with potential employers and organizations of community volunteers. Largely because of these relationships, job placement rates are high. The education-employment linkages being developed within the Youth Employment and Training Program experiments also show promise. It seems very likely that new federal initiatives will expand these efforts. It is almost twenty years since James Conant wrote *Social Dynamite;* and his message regarding education-employment connections, at last, seems to be heard.

The historical view suggests that educational institutions can continue to play important roles in combating youth unemployment problems. Most promising are: (1) work-study arrangements which enable young people to continue their educations and simultaneously provide work experience; (2) specific job-related remedial education and training programs; and (3) programs which facilitate the transition from school to work by interorganizational connections, job information systems, job matching, and/or job development.

Education, however, has not and cannot solve youth un-

employment problems by itself. Historical perspective brings
to mind a fundamental observation by Eli Ginzberg (1979).
Ginzberg describes two contrasting views of what is wrong
with the job market. The first view is that individual job
seekers need better preparation, training, and placement. The
second view is that individual characteristics are of minor importance; the real issue is lack of a strong and consistent demand for labor. Ginzberg wisely observes that there is truth in
both positions (1979, p. 45). Educational institutions alone
cannot compensate for an economy which does not generate
enough jobs. On the other hand, many jobs and potential jobs
currently stand vacant because no one is trained, ready and
asking to fill them. The challenge to educational components
within youth employment programs is to focus directly and
concretely on these employment opportunities. Simultaneously more jobs must be created. Educational institutions have
important roles to play in job development—as promoters,
advocates, organizers, and employers. But the scope of the
problem is massive and employing large numbers of disadvantaged young people in productive jobs will require concerted efforts among government at all levels, business, the
military, and labor unions as well.

Reference Notes

1. Oxley, H. *Education in Civilian Conservation Corps camps.* Washington,
   D.C.: U.S. Emergency Conservation Work (mimeograph), 1936.
2. U.S. Federal Emergency Relief Administration. *Report of the findings in a
   survey of former members of the Civilian Conservation Corps, winter, 1933–34
   term.* Washington, D.C.: U.S. Federal Emergency Relief Administration
   (mimeograph), 1934. U.S. Federal Emergency Relief Administration. *Report of the findings in a survey of former members of the Civilian Conservation
   Corps, summer term 1934.* Washington, D.C.: U.S. Federal Emergency Relief Administration(mimeograph), 1935.
3. U.S. Department of Labor. *Job Corps in brief: Fiscal year 1977.* Washington, D.C.: U.S. Department of Labor (mimeograph), 1978.
4. Mowitt, P. Deputy Director, Office of Manpower Training and Youth
   Activities, National Park Service, U.S. Department of the Interior. (Interview) Washington, D.C., February 8, 1978.
5. U.S. Department of Labor. *Implementation of the Young Adult Conservation
   Corps.* Office of Program Evaluation Report #48. Washington, D.C.: U.S.
   Department of Labor (mimeograph), 1978.

6. U.S. Department of Labor. *Youth Incentive Entitlement Pilot Projects, Application guidelines for CETA prime sponsors.* Washington, D.C.: U.S. Department of Labor (mimeograph), 1977.

References

Clague, E., & Kramer, L. *Manpower policies and programs: A review, 1935–75.* Kalamazoo, Michigan: W.E. Upjohn Institute for Employment Research, 1976.

Employment and training report of the President. Washington, D.C.: U.S. Government Printing Office, 1976.

Employment and training report of the President. Washington, D.C.: U.S. Government Printing Office, 1977.

Employment and training report of the President. Washington, D.C.: U.S. Government Printing Office, 1978.

Employment and training report of the President. Washington, D.C.: U.S. Government Printing Office, 1979.

Ginzberg, E. *Good jobs, bad jobs, no jobs.* Cambridge: Harvard University Press, 1979.

Headington, L. *A study of the duties of company commanders, educational advisors, and project superintendents in the Civilian Conservation Corps of West Virginia.* Master's thesis, Ohio State University, 1938.

Humphrey, H. Plan to save trees, land, and boys. *Harper's Magazine,* January 1959, *218*, 53–57.

Johnson, P., & Harvey, O. *The National Youth Administration,* prepared for The Advisory Committee on Education. Washington, D.C.: U.S. Government Printing Office, 1938.

Kesselman, J. Work relief programs in the great depression. In J. Palmer (Ed.), *Creating jobs: public employment programs and wage subsidies.* Washington, D.C.: The Brookings Institution, 1978.

Levitan, S., & Johnston, B. *The Job Corps: A social experiment that works.* Policy Studies in Employment and Welfare, No. 22. Baltimore: The Johns Hopkins University Press, 1975.

Lewack, H. I. Requiem for a dream: The job corps on trial. In I. Goldenberg (Ed.), *The helping professions in the world of action.* Lexington, Massachusetts: Lexington Books, 1973.

Lorwin, L. *Youth work programs: problems and policies.* Washington, D.C.: American Council on Education, 1941.

Magnum, G., & Walsh, J. *Employment and training programs for youth: What works best for whom?* A Report from the National Council on Employment Policy to the U.S. Department of Labor. Washington, D.C.: U.S. Government Printing Office, 1978.

Marans, R., Driver, B., & Scott, J. *Youth and the environment: An evaluation of the 1971 Youth Conservation Corps.* Ann Arbor, Michigan: Institute for Social Research, 1972.

National Committee for Children and Youth. *Social dynamite.* Report of the

Conference on Unemployed, Out-of-School Youth in Urban Areas. Washington, D.C.: National Committee for Children and Youth, 1961.

Rawick, G. *The New Deal and youth: The Civilian Conservation Corps, the National Youth Administration, and the American Youth Congress.* Doctoral dissertation, University of Wisconsin, 1957.

Reducing illiteracy in the CCC. *School and Society,* 1940, *51,* 472–473.

Rowland, H. Can the CCC blaze a new trail? *Survey Graphic,* 1937, *26,* 321–325.

Salmond, J. *The Civilian Conservation Corps, 1933–1942: A New Deal case study.* Durham, North Carolina: Duke University Press, 1967.

Sherraden, M. *The Civilian Conservation Corps: Effectiveness of the camps.* Doctoral dissertation, University of Michigan, 1979.

Sherwood, R. *Roosevelt and Hopkins.* New York: Harper and Brothers, 1948.

Systems Research Incorporated. *In-school youth manpower.* Final Report on the Survey and Analysis of Innovative In-School Youth Corps Program Models to U.S. Department of Labor. Lansing, Michigan: Systems Research Incorporated, 1973.

U.S. Congress, House, Committee on Labor. *Hearings on H.R. 6180, a bill to make the Civilian Conservation Corps a permanent agency.* 75th Congress, 1st Session, April 14–15, 1937. Washington, D.C.: U.S. Government Printing Office, 1937.

U.S. Congress, Senate. *A bill to establish a Youth Conservation Corps, S. 3582.* 85th Congress, 2nd Session, 1958.

U.S. Congress, Senate. *Hearings before the Subcommittee on the Youth Conservation Corps of the Committee on Labor and Public Welfare.* 86th Congress, 1st Session, Regarding S. 812, A Bill to Establish a Youth Conservation Corps, May 11, 12, 19, 22, and 25, 1959. Washington, D.C.: U.S. Government Printing Office, 1959.

U.S. Department of Labor. *Breakthrough for disadvantaged youth.* Washington, D.C.: U.S. Government Printing Office, 1969.

U.S. Department of Labor. *The Neighborhood Youth Corps: A review of research.* Washington, D.C.: U.S. Department of Labor, 1970.

U.S. Department of Labor. *A planning charter for the Youth Employment and Demonstration Projects Act of 1977.* Washington, D.C.: U.S. Government Printing Office, August, 1977.

U.S. Department of Labor. *Youth initiatives.* Washington, D.C.: U.S. Government Printing Office, 1978. (a)

U.S. Department of Labor. *Impacts of YEDPA on education/CETA relationships at the local level: Five case studies.* Office of Youth Programs Special Report Number 1. Washington, D.C.: U.S. Government Printing Office, 1978. (b)

U.S. National Youth Administration. *Final report of the National Youth Administration, fiscal years 1936–1943.* Washington, D.C.: U.S. Government Printing Office, 1944.

U.S. Office of Education. *Individual guidance in a CCC camp: It's effect upon participation and quality of work in a voluntary educational program.* Bulletin No. 7, Washington, D.C.: U.S. Government Printing Office, 1939.

Walker, H. *The CCC through the eyes of 272 boys: A summary of a group study of the reactions of 272 Cleveland boys to their experience in the Civilian Conservation Corps.* Cleveland: Western Reserve University Press, 1938.

Weeks, C. *Job Corps: Dollars and dropouts.* Boston: Little, Brown and Company, 1967.

Woods, J. *The legend and the legacy of Franklin D. Roosevelt and the Civilian Conservation Corps (CCC).* D.S.S. Dissertation, Syracuse University, 1964.

Children and Youth Services Review, Vol. 2, pp. 41–61, 1980
Printed in the USA.

0190-7409/80/010041-21$02.00/0
Pergamon Press Ltd

Youth Employment: A Challenge for the 1980s

Robert Taggart and Evelyn Ganzglass
Office of Youth Programs
Department of Labor

Patterns of Youth Employment

The employment problems of young Americans are widely recognized. The alarming statistics have become so familiar that they are almost accepted with equanimity. During 1979, an average 16% of sixteen to nineteen-year-olds were unemployed including 36% of non-white youth. This was during a period of rapid employment growth. Youth are the most vulnerable in periods of unemployment decline when the near term prospects are dismal.

What is not as widely known is the importance of education, schools and school attendance patterns in these measured problems. During the 15-year period ending in 1977, school enrollment increased substantially and the number of employed youth 14–24 doubled. The employment to population ratio for in-school 16- and 17-year-old youth rose significantly as compared to a very modest increase for all out of school youth. In September, 1979, official statistics reported that more than half of all employed and unemployed 16–19 year-olds were students. But this may underestimate the number. A new labor market survey interviewing youth directly, rather than parents, found that the labor force participation rate of students was two-fifths, above that reported by the

Robert Taggart, Administrator, Office of Youth Programs, Department of Labor, Washington, D.C., 20210

Bureau of Labor Statistics, and the number of unemployed
was more than double (Borus, 1980).

The severe job shortage for non-white youth is also sur-
prisingly an in-school problem and not just a dropout problem. The gap in employment to population ratios between
white and non-white youth is one-third larger for in-school
youth than for out-of-school youth. The new data indicates
that the labor force participation rate of non-white students is
double that previously reported, and that most of those youth
are unable to find jobs (Borus, 1980).

As has always been the case, those youth with limited
education are more severely affected than those who complete
school. The high school dropout pattern by age, race and sex
has shown an equalizing trend, again with the most significant
improvement among non-whites. Nevertheless in 1976, dropouts represented 20% of the non-white youth population age
18 and 19 compared to 16% for whites. Among out-of-school
youth, the unemployment rate is twice as high for dropouts as
for high school completors. The chances of being unemployed
within the first 2 years of dropping out of school are one in
three for all youth and one in two for non-white youth.

Furthermore, the employment experience of dropouts is
quite unstable, with more frequent job turnover, shorter job
tenure, and longer spells between jobs. Many youth experience initial job instability associated with the transition from
school to work, but dropout youth continue this pattern
longer and have difficulty in securing desirable employment
into adulthood.

Finally, there is increasing evidence that employment experiences during the school years are an important factor in
future labor market success (U.S. Department of Labor,
1979).

Long-Term Implications. The long-term impacts of experiences along the path of development and transition are difficult to measure and are probably understated by most available
assessment techniques. There are so many factors affecting
youth during these critical years, and these factors are so inter-
related over time, that statistical sorting techniques can provide
only a sense of direction of causality and a crude approxima-

tion of the degree. Descriptors of youth are limited so that it is difficult to control for the differences. Such controls are a necessary precondition for sorting. For instance, to measure the long-run impact of high school part-time employment, the future employment and earnings of a group of youth who work more must be compared to those of a group who work less, all else being equal. But all else is seldom equal. Regression analysis may control for age, socioeconomic status, race and other variables, but motivation might be involved in the choice of work, or perhaps disenchantment with schooling, and this would certainly be reflected in future outcomes although not controlled by the demographics. Statistical techniques also have problems in dealing with cumulative and longitudinal phenomena. The simple fact is that the explanative power of *any* youth status or change on future status is limited by the inadequacies of measurement and statistical techniques. There is, nevertheless, an increasing body of evidence documenting the long-term importance of positive youth career development and transition experiences. It is to a brief review of this evidence that we now turn.

To assess the impacts of work and nonwork on future employability and income for teenage males, Meyer and Wise (1979) studied the 1972 National Longitudinal Survey of high school seniors. They concluded that an additional 10 hours of work per week during the senior year produced an 11% increase in weeks worked following graduation and a 3% increase in weekly earnings. However, after controlling for individual differences, there was no evidence of a lasting effect 5 years subsequently.

A study by Ellwood (1979) used the data from another National Longitudinal Survey to determine impacts of work on the future employment and earnings of out-of-school males. The study found that an extra 10 weeks of employment one year was related to between two and three more weeks of employment the next. Ten weeks out of work in the first year after school reduced wages 5% eight years subsequently.

The National Longitudinal Survey data were used by Corcoran (1979) to assess impact of youth employment for females. The study found that, controlling for all variables, the odds a woman would work in a given year were eight times higher if she had worked the previous year than if she had not. Ten years after completing school, a woman who spent 2 years out of the labor force immediately after school earned between 3 and 5% less per hour than women who worked continuously.

A study of differentials for blacks and whites by Osterman (1978) found that whites who had no unemployment in 1968 had 26% less than average unemployment in 1966 and 22% less in 1970. For blacks, those with zero unemployment in 1968 had 12% less in 1966 and 34% less in 1970. Becker and Hills (1979) found that for the "average" unemployed youth, short joblessness did not have negative consequences. For black teenagers with 15 weeks or more unemployment, however, the future impacts were significant.

Studies have also looked at the long-range impacts of occupational information and training. Parnes and Kohen (1975) studied 18–26 year-old employed men not enrolled in school. Controlling for years of school completed and mental ability, an increase in occupational knowledge equivalent to a five-point rise in occupational test score (out of a possible 56) was related to an annual earnings increment of about $140 for a steadily employed white youth and $290 for a black. A study by Stevenson (1978b) corroborated these findings.

Meyer and Wise (1979) studied the effects of high school vocational or industrial training on employment and wage rates after graduation. They found that no measure of high school vocational or industrial training was significantly related to subsequent employment or wage rates. However, on-the-job training subsequent to school leaving was related to higher future wages.

A study by Stevenson (1978a) found that training, if applied on a job, had a high payoff, ranging from $1500 higher annual earnings for white males to $2300 per year for black females. The effects were lasting.

Grasso (1975) studied the relative merits of various high school curricula on earnings. He found that while youth in high school vocational training programs did not receive higher starting rates of pay, white youth benefited from post-school training although blacks did not.

Again, these studies are far from definitive concerning

the magnitudes of long-term impacts. Different assumptions and analytical techniques will produce different findings. However, as a generalization, the evidence seems to be mounting that youth labor market experiences are cumulative and that short-term problems have long-term consequences.

Policy Direction. Recognizing these realities of the youth unemployment situation, it is clear that we need to:

1. begin addressing the problems that impact on youth employment earlier in order to keep youth in school and better prepare them for making the transition from school to employment;
2. enlarge employment opportunities for in-school youth during the school year; particularly for non-white and disadvantaged youth who lack part-time employment opportunities;
3. increase targeted efforts for disadvantaged students in gaining the educational competencies and credentials they will need in order to successfully compete in the adult labor market;
4. eliminate the employment and education barriers that often prevent youth from more efficiently combining education and work;
5. concentrate much more attention on remedial education and training assistance for youth who have dropped out of, or completed, high school without attaining needed competencies but who are mature and committed enough to benefit from more intensive career investments.

Programs aimed at facilitating the access of minority students to jobs have the potential for equalizing the employment experiences of students across race and sex lines and thereby helping reduce post-school differences in employment.

Bold steps along these lines have been taken in recent youth initiatives under the Youth Employment Demonstration Projects Act (YEDPA). Under its authority we have, within the last 3 years, been able to accomplish an historically unprecedented expansion of employment and training efforts for youth supported by strong linkages between education and work.

In the 1960s the War on Poverty gave heavy emphasis to youth. The Neighborhood Youth Corps Program tried to create more in-school and summer jobs as well as jobs for out-of-school youth. The Job Corps was initiated to provide an alternative education and vocational training system for the most disadvantaged hard to reach out-of-school youth. Area Skills Centers were established under MDTA to link education and training activities for out-of-school youth.

In 1973 the Comprehensive Employment and Training Act was enacted and in 1976 the Vocational Education Act was amended providing increased emphasis to work and education linkages. Yet, during the 1970s year-round employment and training opportunities for youth actually declined even as the need increased as a result of the massive growth of the youth population. By 1977, the situation had deteriorated to the point where dramatic action was required. YEDPA was enacted signalling a dramatic expansion of youth employment and training efforts. In its first two years, YEDPA programs accounted for one-fourth of the measured employment growth for all teenagers and approximately three-fourths of the growth for black teenagers.

YEDPA was not just "more of the same." It sought to change ways of doing business particularly in the relationship between education and employment and training activities, and between local education agencies and prime sponsors.

The provision most directly aimed at bringing about this change was the requirement that at least 22% of the Youth Employment and Training Program (YETP) funds provided to State and local prime sponsors be spent on in-school programs under agreement between the prime sponsors and local education agencies. The Act required that all in-school work experience must combine work with career counseling, occupational information, placement assistance and special efforts to overcome sex stereotyping. For both in-school and out-of-school jobs, it mandated efforts to arrange academic credit for work experience. YEDPA also broadened the role of the National Occupational Information Coordinating Committee (NOICC), originally created under the 1976 Amendments to the Vocational Education Act, by including a mandate stating that in the development of an occupational information system particular attention should be directed to the needs of economically disadvantaged youth. These mandates were reinforced by the Career Education Incentive Act of 1978 which provided formula money to States for expanded occupational information and career-related instruction, and the Elementary and Secondary Education Act Amendments of 1978 which provided for in-school youth employment programs linked to education. In reauthorizing CETA in 1978, coordination was required with activities under the Career Education Incentive Act. The CETA setaside for supplemental vocational education programs was increased from 5% to 6% of Title II resources. A new setaside of 1% of Title II funds was provided to States specifically for facilitating CETA-education coordination.

Coordinated Federal Efforts

The Departments of Labor (DOL) and Education (formally Health, Education and Welfare (HEW)) have used all available mechanisms to lead the education and employment and training systems in a coordinated assault on the problems of youth employment and youths' preparation for employment. The goals have been given priority in the design and implementation of new programs as well as the reorientation of existing ones. A range of joint technical assistance activities have been undertaken. Discretionary resources have been used to provide incentives for cooperation at the State and local levels between the education and employment and training systems. Finally, a vast array of research, evaluation and demonstration activities have been initiated to learn more about education and work problems and programs.

Program Design and Implementation. From the initial planning stage of YEDPA implementation, the Department of Labor worked closely with the Department of Education and national educational associations in formulating policy for the various education-related provisions of the Act. Correspondingly, there has been extensive interagency consultation in developing regulations for the Career Education Incentive Act and the youth employment provisions of the Elementary and Secondary Education Act.

The regulations governing the Youth Employment and Training Programs under YEDPA were designed to allow for maximum local flexibility while ensuring that the mandates for integration of work and education objectives were achieved. The regulations regarding CETA/LEA Agreements outlined broad parameters for these agreements but left the form and substance to the process of negotiation at the local level in order to allow for the wide variance in local conditions. To carry out the intent of the 22% setaside to promote linkages primarily with public secondary schools, the definition of a LEA for purposes of YETP was narrowed to focus on public schools, with the expectation that colleges and junior colleges could be funded with resources above the 22% level. In an attempt to improve the quality of programs for in-school youth under the Youth Employment and Training Programs, the regulations required that in-school programs provide career employment experiences which were defined as a combination of well supervised employment, counseling, guidance and placement assistance. Requirements for the provision of academic credit were stressed with a clear delineation of the roles and responsibilities of the educational system in awarding credit for specified programs.

The regulations for the Summer Youth Employment Program (SYEP) published in 1978 attempted to move the in-school summer youth program toward a year-round focus stressing educational enrichments and career counseling. Likewise, there was an encouragement to arrange academic credit for work experience.

Policies regarding Job Corps operations also placed greater emphasis on educational aspects of Job Corps programming. A new Advanced Career Training program at the post-secondary level was added to Job Corps. Currently, 1200 of the 33,000 Job Corps enrollees are being trained in residence at colleges or junior colleges. Job Corps reading and mathematics curricula were revamped and greater attention was focused on innovative educational approaches. In addition, Job Corps began using vocational education facilities as part of its expansion efforts, and brought on vocational education personnel to aid in curricula improvement.

Finally, the Departments cooperated extensively in the staffing and development of the National Occupational Information Coordinating Committee, expanding its mission as rapidly as possible in order to assure meaningful coordination.

Technical Assistance and Support. Both Departments have sought and enlisted the active support and involvement of public and private agencies and organizations representing the many diverse interests concerned with the CETA-education linkage. The goal of this joint effort has been to promote better working relationships and to help clarify and propose solutions to the issues confronted in bringing the systems closer together. These actions have been aimed at influencing key decision makers within each of the systems at the national, state and, most importantly, local levels. As part of this networking activity, the Departments have individually and jointly supported and participated in conferences, workshops and policy forums sponsored by a wide variety of groups throughout the nation.

The Department of Labor, with substantial input from the Department of Education, has published a series of technical assistance guides for prime sponsors on education-related issues. These include guides on: the awarding of academic credit in YEDPA programs; considerations regarding the development of CETA/LEA agreements under YETP; career information delivery systems; and the possibilities of work-education councils.

Through educational associations, public interest groups and national organizations representing community based organizations, the Department of Labor has helped facilitate CETA-education collaboration by identifying model programs including those demonstrating effective CETA-education collaboration. Summary descriptions of these model programs have been distributed to CETA prime sponsors on a regular basis with the intent of fostering replication of exemplary models. The U.S. Office of Education has similarly funded a project to identify and document exemplary CETA/vocational education programs currently operating in the field.

Collaboration Incentives. In areas where legislative mandates already overlap or are complementary, the Departments of Labor and Education have mounted a series of discretionary incentive programs. The major purpose of these programs is to draw the CETA and educational systems together through the creative coupling of federally-funded and other programs. An important secondary aim is to gain a better understanding of the dynamics of these coupled programs and to document identified collaborative models which maximize the utilization of available resources at the State and local levels.

The largest and most broad ranging effort is the Exemplary In-School Youth Program demonstration project. This has been administered with the assistance of Youthwork, Inc. Youthwork is a new intermediary organization created by the joint efforts of five private foundations to marshall the combined education and labor expertise and perspectives necessary to mount a collaborative effort. Under the Exemplary In-School Program, projects have been developed in the areas of counseling, guidance and job-seeking skills; the awarding of academic credit, improved private sector involvement, youth operated projects, and projects focused on high risk and handicapped youth.

Another major incentive project is the CETA and Vocational Education Incentive Program which is aimed at demonstrating models of linkage between vocational education and CETA youth programs at both the State and local levels. The three year project jointly funded by the Departments of Labor and Education will include replication of successful models through incentive grants, expansion and extension of existing projects and the dissemination of notable project findings.

The Departments have also been working together to try to improve coordination between CETA and programs in post-secondary educational institutions through a number of incentive and demonstration projects managed and evaluated by the Fund for the Improvement of Post-Secondary Education (FIPSE). These program models which provide a broad spectrum of educational and training services at the post-secondary level for CETA qualified youth. During the summer of 1979, HEW and DOL conducted a Vocational Education/CETA Summer Youth Employment Program (SYEP) which tested the efficacy of granting SYEP monies to post-secondary institutions to involve primarily minority economically disadvantaged youth in an integrated program of career development, basic skills development and vocational training.

Finally, the two departments cooperated on the Upward Bound-CETA demonstration project which is supporting programs in ten sites providing a combined career-oriented education program and career-related summer work program for economically disadvantaged high school students. The program is intended to channel students away from lower level occupations and into expanding occupational areas particularly those in which minorities and others from disadvantaged backgrounds are severely underrepresented.

The Department of Labor has sought to promote linkage between the private sector, education and employment and training activities at the local level through the Work-Education Consortium Project, which is being assessed by the National Institute of Education. The project involves more than 30 communities throughout the Nation in which local Work-Education Councils have been formed to help facilitate youth's transition from school to work within their communities. The Department has also provided matching grants to five States to enable them to undertake statewide initiatives which build on existing work-education councils and the experience gained during an exploratory State level initiative in four States funded by the Department of Education.

Lastly, under the auspices of the National Occupational Information Coordinating Committee (NOICC), the Department of Labor has supported a $2 million incentive program funding statewide career information systems in fourteen States. Using a matching strategy, NOICC has successfully elicited program and financial support from CETA, Vocational Education, Educational Information Center Career Education, and other programs with resources available at the State and local levels. Furthermore, NOICC's leadership has heightened interest among other States to undertake similar coordinated delivery systems on their own.

These many incentive programs should encourage cooperation on a number of fronts. The activities also become a laboratory for learning about program design, implementation and replication. Each has a built-in research component to determine how well linkages are working and why. The aim, then, is not to foster coordination in the near term, but to provide the foundation for more effective linkages in the future.

Knowledge Development. The Youth Employment and
Demonstration Projects Act (YEDPA) of 1977 provided extensive authority to the Secretary of Labor to experiment with
and evaluate alternative employment and employability development approaches for economically disadvantaged youth.
Under a carefully designed "knowledge development" plan, a
structured array of multi-site demonstration projects, large-
scale evaluations and complementary research efforts were initiated on a scale and scope of unprecedented dimensions.
Education and work issues were a major focus of these
knowledge development activities.

The cornerstone is the Youth Incentive Entitlement Pilot
Projects (YIEPP), a legislatively mandated demonstration program which ranks as the largest social experiment in history.
Within 17 demonstration sites, the program guarantees a job
and/or training (part-time during the school year and full-time
in the summer) for all economically disadvantaged 16 to
19-year-olds who are in school or willing to return to school
and who subsequently perform adequately in school. One of
the major aims of the demonstration is to assess the impact of
a job guarantee on school retention, return and completion. It
is intended to demonstrate whether youth who have dropped
out of school can be attracted back into school through curriculum adaptations and alternative education approaches,
and whether improved school capacity in combining education
and work activities will improve the future employability of
students. A structured test of different modes of enriching
educational services within schools was undertaken in January
1979. There is an extensive research effort to capture the
effects of the program not only on school return, retention
and completion as well as future employment, but also on
performance in school and time devoted to studies. The background surveys are beginning to provide a wealth of information about the educational experience of the disadvantaged,
including comparable youth outside Entitlement areas
("Schooling and Work," 1979).

Another knowledge development activity with significant
policy implications is the Education Entitlement Voucher
demonstration project which is testing the feasibility and value
of applying the GI Bill approach to youth employment pro-

grams by providing an "Education Entitlement Voucher" to youth participants in selected programs. It will determine whether increased training and education at the post-secondary level is appropriate for CETA youth.

The Education Improvement Effort (EIE) under Job Corps is testing alternate instructional methodologies developed and screened by HEW. In the controlled setting of Job Corps, it will carefully test their effectiveness on disadvantaged youth through a large scale random assignment experiment including pre/post and follow-up testing.

The School to Work Transition demonstration project is another structured experiment in which community based and other groups are providing transition services to high school juniors and seniors. Data collected from this project and others with similar objectives, will be assessed to determine the comparative effectiveness of different deliverers of services and the impact of such services on economically disadvantaged youth. As one variant, there are also a group of projects which are bringing the apprenticeship system into the school, making arrangements for juniors and seniors with the anticipation that they will move smoothly into full-time apprenticeships upon graduation.

A number of YEDPA funded research activities related to the delivery of career information for youth are being carried out by HEW and DOL under the coordination of NOICC. These are (1) a national survey of career information delivery at the secondary school level; (2) a structured test of the effectiveness of different types of information and delivery on the measured career awareness of youth; and (3) a test of the impacts of intensive exposure of career information on disadvantaged youth.

DOL is experimenting with the replication of the Career Intern Program, a tested alternative education program originally developed by the Opportunities Industrialization Centers (OIC's) under contract to the National Institute of Education (NIE). The Institute is operating this program under the terms of an interagency agreement.

Finally, there are a range of complementary research activities on education work issues, utilizing data gathered under the Survey of Income and Education, and the National Longi-

tudinal Surveys. A major new longitudinal survey has been
undertaken with interagency input; this will provide a wealth
of information about work-education relationships.

Status of Coordination. Under Youth Employment and
Training Programs, three-fifths of all participants were in-
school youth and half of all funds went for in-school activities,
more than double the 22% required by law. A total of a
quarter of a million in-school youth were provided jobs or
pre-employment services under YEDPA in Fiscal 1978. However, these are only the quantitative dimensions. In the two
years since YEDPA was enacted, substantial progress has been
made in forging workable and productive linkages between
the CETA and educational systems.

In April 1978, eight months after the signing of YEDPA,
an HEW-DOL team made onsite reviews in five locations.
Based on this very limited sample, the review team observed:

YEDPA has contributed to improved CETA communications with
the public schools. In some cases, YEDPA has provided the impetus
for communication . . . YETP is reaching students who would not
otherwise be served . . . The ability to hire additional school counselors and staff has contributed to the ability of schools to offer services for students who are noncollege-bound. (U.S. Department of
Labor, 1978, p. 3)

An interim report on YEDPA implementation prepared
early in 1979 by the National Council on Employment Policy
reflected the pace of institutional change that has in fact resulted from the coordinative provisions in YEDPA. The reported stated:

The Council's first report on YEDPA implementation told a story
about optimistic prime sponsor plans for CETA/LEA agreements.
The plans reflected more aspirations of the sponsors than was realistic. The second report documented problems encountered in implementing the first hasty plans; a breakneck implementation pace that
left little time for considerations about quality; incompatibility between prime sponsor and LEA calendar years; disagreements over
whether academic credit was appropriate for employment aspects of
work experience. There were positive results to report, but expectations in the first LEA cycle ending in June 1978 outran what was

feasible. Expectations for the start of the second academic year may have been lowered, but, at the margin, sponsors and LEA's seem to be moving in the directions of more progress. (Wurzberg, 1979, p. 5)

Referring to the early strains of implementation of the Exemplary in School Demonstration Project, a recent report prepared by Cornell University documented positive impacts of incentive activities:

There is considerable evidence that the outcome has been a valuable one for both organizations (CETA and education) —the staff have had experience at working together and have shared responsibilities in the completion of joint tasks. Successful negotiation of this level of collaboration apears to have resulted in more intense collaboration in other areas, e.g., discussions on further coordination, recruitment of youth for programs, and the crossover of staff from one program to serve as advisors to another. (Rist et al., 1979, p. xi)

A study of CETA/LEA impacts in large cities by the Council of Great Cities Schools reported that:

Aside from the improvements in institutional communication which the legislation promoted, it spurred several immediate changes in the delivery of school-based employment services. The requirement that schools design their services to meet prime sponsor specifications resulted in heightened attention on the part of educators to a traditionally manpower-oriented set of concerns. Incorporation of occupational interest and aptitude testing into program intake services was one result. Increased efforts to coordinate program training and job sites with local manpower needs was another. More attention was devoted to work site development than had formally been the case under NYC and the summer jobs programs. ("Youth and Training," 1979, p. 3)

All these studies point out the false steps as well as progress, the frictions which are part of change, and the obstacles to further collaboration at the local level. However, the following positive themes run through all these analyses.

—There is a willingness, even an eagerness in many localities to cooperate and work things out.
—State agencies have increasingly assumed a supportive and facilitative role.
—The level of collaboration between the Departments of Education and Labor has never been so high.

—A certain momentum has developed at all levels as individuals are beginning to work together.
—Specific barriers have been identified that now can be addressed in a positive, knowledgeable way.

Many of the efforts undertaken to date will have their payoff in future years. The incentive projects are now having an immediate impact in encouraging collaborative application for incentive funds, but as new linkages are forged and more is learned about the process, coordination will improve. The technical assistance activities represent a continuing commitment; it takes time for messages to circulate to local decision makers, and for cooperation at the Federal and State levels to filter down. New institutional mechanisms such as the State Occupational Information Coordinating Committees are just getting in operation, and their impact will be in the future. Knowledge development activities will yield critical information about how to improve our education and work policies in future years.

Policy Reformulation

One of the most important results of recent collaboration has been to establish a foundation for the rethinking of youth work and education policies for the 1980s. At the end of FY 1980, the current authorization for YEDPA expires. As both the Administration and Congress consider major legislative changes, the knowledge gained during the past two years of operational program experience and detailed research and demonstration activities will be utilized as the basis for decision making.

The cooperative spirit that has been engendered through these activities should permit the education and employment and training communities to tackle the difficult issues and barriers to collaboration that have been brought to the foreground as a result of increased communication between the two systems.

During this last year a task force under the leadership of the Vice President with input from nineteen federal agencies and hundreds of national, state and local organizations carried out a careful review of program activities, surfacing new concepts and serving as a forum for broad policy discussion. The task force recommendations were presented to the President late in 1979 and have served as the basis for the Administration's recently announced legislative initiative on youth employment. The proposals attempt to address the fundamental issues that are of concern to both the education and employment and training systems.

Alternative Education Approaches. Alternative education approaches have been supported by YETP formula and discretionary funds. In some cases, usually when funded under CETA-LEA agreements utilizing the 22% setaside, close linkages have been developed with the regular school system. In other cases, little, if any, communication exists between CETA educational programs and local and State education agencies. The Job Corps, a major CETA youth program is itself an alternative education system of significant magnitude. With staggeringly high dropout rates, reduced enrollments resulting from declining birth rates, and shrinking availability of State and local funds for education, school systems by necessity are considering alternative approaches to the education of many youth who would, otherwise, not be served by the traditional school system. With this convergence of interests and operational concerns such as staff development and credentialing, facilities utilization, budgetary and other administrative issues, there is a need for agreement on common approaches and consistent standards that can be used in alternative education and related programs. There is also a need to sort out roles and responsibilities in order to utilize the comparative advantages of both the education and employment systems.

Employability Development Plans. The major rationale for facilitating institutional linkages and improving program planning is to enlarge opportunities for individuals whether they are in- or out-of-school youth. The concept of employability development plans brings program linkage down to the individual client level and suggests a commitment to provide assistance in the form of a structured sequence of interventions in response to the assessed long-term developmental needs of each person.

Individualized educational plans for the handicapped are already in use throughout the nation. Various educators are suggesting the need for Employability Development Plans (EDP's) for all youth. On the CETA side, the concept was written into law in the 1978 CETA reauthorization. The Consolidated Youth Employment Program demonstration project consolidates local youth programs and seeks to test out ideas which are being considered for future implementation. It also incorporates EDP's as a central concept and is seeking local interagency cooperation in the development and utilization of this approach.

Competency Certification and Academic Credit. Ideally, youth employment and training and education programs which seek developmental goals should evaluate program success by measuring progress of individuals toward attainment of specified competencies. For this to occur, program objectives must be clearly stated in terms of measurable outcomes or competencies. An important step forward in creating a common basis for service delivery would be the development of certification criteria for competencies gained through educational and employment and training programs. These standards would be in four basic areas: (1) pre-employment competencies indicating a basic awareness of the world of work; (2) work maturity; (3) basic educational achievement; and (4) job skills acquisition. Acceptance of these standards by private employers, educational institutions and other community institutions would hopefully make it easier to develop positive next steps for program participants and would serve as the basis for maintaining or improving the quality of program services. The education system is increasingly adopting systems of certification, and it is clear that employment and training programs would help youth if they could document their progress. Here is an area where cooperative action is needed at the local level with guidance from the national level.

Basic Skills. The education system's primary role in employment programs is to improve the basic educational competencies of youth who are not adequately prepared for labor market entry. In order to accomplish this objective, emphasis will have to be placed on the teaching of reading, writing, communication and computation at the secondary school level including increased linkage of these resources with basic skills components of vocational education programs. Alternative approaches to teaching basic skills within existing secondary school programs as well as alternative programs for school dropouts will have to be strengthened. In addition, greater access to such programs by special needs populations will have to be developed through improved coordination with employment programs and greater sensitivity within schools regarding the needs of youth who are deficient in basic skills.

Quality Occupational Preparation and Skill Training. Both the CETA and Vocational Education systems have been criticized for poor quality or inappropriateness of skill training provided. Often the overlapping objectives of developing vocational skills and other competencies compete with each other and the real objective of specific programs is lost. The development of criteria for the certification of competencies should provide the basis for a reassessment of program objectives and approaches to meet these objectives. A more individualized approach should permit exposure to multiple occupations during the career preparation phase, followed by more intensive, occupation-specific training for young adults who are mature and have a good sense of career objectives. Currently, because of lack of financial resources in inner cities and isolated rural areas, opportunities for vocational training are inadequate. One of the major issues that must be addressed is how the availability and access to facilities, equipment, instructional programs and supporting services in these areas can be increased, and how access to these facilities can be assured for mature, career-oriented young adults.

School-to-Work Transition Services. A wide range of services such as counseling, guidance, the provision of career information, as well as services to overcome sex role stereotyping and teach job seeking skills, are designed to assist youth in more successfully making the transition from school to work. Little is known about the comparative benefits of various approaches to providing such services nor has it been possible thus far to pinpoint the benefits to different age groups and different types of youth. Research undertaken during the past two years should provide policymakers with new insight in this area. Under YETP formula funded activities, and even more under discretionary projects, outside groups such as community-based organizations, labor unions, and private sector employers have provided such services within the school setting as a supplement to and enrichment of such school provided programs as cooperative and career education. A critical assessment of the experiences of these projects is needed in the process of developing mechanisms for the effective involvement of outside institutions in the school setting.

Postscript: Looking to the Future

Any comprehensive youth strategy for the 1980s will require effective linkages between employment, education, economic development and other efforts as well as a broadened base for involvement among all institutions connected to such efforts. A determined drive is needed to improve the understanding and capabilities of the employment and training and education systems so that they can build on and improve the cooperative model that has served us well thus far.

No matter what legislation is implemented, every deliverer of services to youth, whether CETA prime sponsor, local school administrator or director of one of the many youth serving agencies, will need to know more about how to organize and administer employment, training and education services for youth.

The broad scale investment in knowledge development activities under YEDPA can be expected to begin feeding back to the system information about what works and why. Although the full payoff from these activities will not be felt for a number of years as projects reach their conclusion and follow-up data on participants is collected and analyzed, the knowledge gained thus far has helped us better identify the demanding tasks that lie ahead. Likewise, the linkages which have been established must continue to be institutionalized. At present, we have a rare opportunity to achieve needed changes in both the education and employment systems.

References

Becker, B.E., & Hills, S.M. *Teenage unemployment: Some evidence of the long-run effects on wages.* Columbus, Ohio: Center for Human Resource Research, Ohio State University, 1979.

Borus, M. *Pathways to the future: A longitudinal study of young Americans—preliminary report: Youth and the labor market-1979.* Columbus: Center for Human Resource Research, Ohio State University, January 1980.

Corcoran, M. *The employment, wage and fertility consequences of teenage women's nonemployment.* Ann Arbor: University of Michigan Survey Research Center, May 1979.

Ellwood, D. *Teenage unemployment: Permanent scars or temporary blemishes.* Washington, D.C.: National Bureau of Economic Research, 1979.

Grasso, J.T. *The contributions of vocational education, training, and work experience to the early career achievements of young men.* Columbus, Ohio: Center for Human Resource Research, 1975.

Meyer, R.H., & Wise, P.A. *High school preparation and early labor force experience.* Washington, D.C.: Nat. Bureau of Economic Research, April 1979.

Osterman, P. Youth, work, and unemployment. *Challenge,* 1978.

Parnes, H.S., & Kohen, S. Occupational information and labor market status: The case of young men. *Journal of Human Resources,* 1975.

Rist, R.C., et al. *Forging new relationships: The CETA/school nexus.* Ithaca, N.Y.: Youthwork Inc., 1979.

Schooling and work among youths from low-income households. A baseline report from the entitlement demonstration. Manpower Demonstration Research Corporation and ABT Associates, Inc., 1979.

Stevenson, W. The relationship between early work experience and future employability. In A. Adams & G.L. Mangum (Eds.), *The lingering crisis of youth unemployment.* Kalamazoo, Michigan: W.E. Upjohn Institute for Employment Research, 1978.(a)

Stevenson, W. The transition from school to work. In A. Adams & G. L. Mangum (Eds.), *The lingering crisis of youth unemployment.* W.E. Upjohn Institute for Employment Research, 1978. (b)

U.S. Department of Labor. *Impacts of YEDPA on education/CETA relationships at the local level: Five case studies.* Washington, D.C.: Office of Youth Programs, Department of Labor, Government Printing Office, 1978.

U.S. Department of Labor. *Youth employment policies and programs for the 1980s: Analysis and proposals of the Department of Labor.* Washington, D.C.: Office of Youth Programs, Department of Labor, Government Printing Office, 1979.

Wurzberg, G. *Overview to the local focus on youth: A review of prime sponsor experience implementing the Youth Employment and Demonstration Projects Act.* National Council on Youth and training programs and the urban school: Profiles and Youth Programs Report, 1979.

Youth training programs and the urban school: Profiles and commentary. Council of the Great City Schools, Office of Youth Programs Report, 1979.

Children and Youth Services Review, Vol. 2, pp. 63–80, 1980
Printed in the USA. All rights reserved.

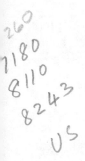

Barriers to Full Employment of Rural Youth

Jerome M. Ziegler
Cornell University

The concern of this inquiry is the question of the full employment of rural youth, including rural minority youth, the barriers to full employment and the policy initiatives required at all levels in order to attain full employment.[1] Since the official acceptable rate of unemployment is now defined by the Humphrey-Hawkins legislation as four percent, full employment means 96% employment. This may or may not be "realistic" given the economic conditions in the country at the start of the 1980s as the unemployment-inflation policies trade-offs remain a critical issue in the FY81 and ensuing Federal Budgets, but as long as H-H is the national goal and standard for policy, it should apply equally to rural as to urban areas. National policies in the employment field, therefore, are now being developed to attain 96% employment and four percent unemployment.[2]

The term "institutional barriers" has been used in connection with a discussion of the employment problems of youth—all youth whether rural or urban—meaning, I take it,

Jerome M. Ziegler, New York State College of Human Ecology, Cornell University, Ithaca, New York 14853.

[1]This paper was originally prepared for presentation at the Institute for Economic Development's Conference on Youth Unemployment, Pan American University, Edinburgh, Texas, March 4–5, 1980.

[2]Since an analysis of the numbers of rural youth, including the breakdown of various minorities, male-female, age cohorts and geographical distribution is dealt with in another paper; it will not be addressed here.

those barriers which are caused by poor schooling, lack of industrial/commercial enterprise, inadequate government programs and the like. To this, I should add the term "structural barriers" in order to indicate those personal and individual factors and family conditions as well as the lack of social policies which affect and impede the full employment of rural youth. I shall use both terms but they are not precisely interchangeable.

The problem of unemployment among all youth, rural and urban, has been persistent over decades, geographically widespread—few if any sections of the nation have not experienced unacceptably high unemployment—and proof against past efforts to resolve it. Two generations ago, the Civilian Conservation Corps and the National Youth Administration were designed in part to meet this problem. In the middle 1960s, a number of initiatives were developed under the War on Poverty. The Job Corps was national in scope and enrolled youth from rural as well as urban sectors; the Neighborhood Youth Corps was more urban in its operation. The first program in President Kennedy's administration which began to deal with the problems of unemployment and economic development was the Area Redevelopment Act of 1962; it included a job training component but that effort was directed mainly at adult unemployment.

Federal policy in the 1960s and 1970s was deeply concerned with the problems of the cities, including unemployment, and manpower program followed manpower program together with other initiatives in an effort to reduce unemployment. Youth unemployment received a share of the national attention during this period but never, in my view, sufficient for the depth and dimension of the problem. Now, at the start of the 1980s, after almost twenty years of policy and program, the nation and the federal government realize afresh that youth unemployment is more difficult to solve than previously imagined, and that particularly for minority youth or for pockets of rural youth, the issue is more intractable and requires new and different approaches and a different level of resource. That is all to the good; one can be grateful to policy-makers and analysts in Washington and elsewhere who have impressed Mr. Carter with the urgency of solving this question. The new money contemplated for this purpose in the President's FY81 budget, two billion dollars, will also be welcome; but it must be tied to new approaches in order to achieve results more significant than what has been reached by the expenditure of previous billions.

Not every rural (or urban) unemployed youth exhibits the full spectrum of problems or social pathology or is subject to all the conditions affecting youth unemployment. But most youth are beset by multiple factors operating simultaneously in their local environment upon them. The structural and institutional barriers intersect in such a way that policies and programs dealing with only one factor and not all of them are bound to fail. The best example of this is the separation of vocational or job training from job creation. The two must go hand-in-hand and in the same locality; investment in one must be duplicated by investment in the other. It does no good to train youth in school vocational programs or in manpower programs for jobs that do not exist in the area or city or for jobs in an industry which is declining.

Another example: neither training nor employment opportunity is worth much if rural youth cannot reach the workplace for lack of transportation. Even with adequate transportation, public or private, youth in poor health or prone to drug or alcohol abuse or who are members of famiies in distress are unlikely to find and hold steady employment. Youth with no access to vocational guidance in poorly financed rural high schools and junior high schools have no opportunity to understand the job market and their own possibilities. Youth enrolled in inadequate schools fail to develop the basic personal and intellectual skills suitable for employment in any but the most transitory jobs. Minority youth are subject to the additional indignity of racial discrimination.

In short, it is the thesis of this paper that the barriers to full employment for rural youth must be addressed together at one and the same time.

A favorite word in the Washington lexicon as new federal programs are created is "comprehensive." But truly comprehensive program development seldom occurs for reasons well known to analysts of the federal bureaucracy. Yet the term is applicable here: a comprehensive or holistic approach to the problems and conditions of youth unemployment, rural or urban, is clearly required if the nation is serious about solving this issue in our time. All of the factors must be addressed concurrently; public investments must be applied concurrently; the questions of human resource development and area, regional (or urban) economic development must be regarded as closely interconnected aspects of the same basic issue.

Differences and Similarities Between Rural and Urban Youth Unemployment

It may be useful to say a word about the differences and similarities between rural and urban youth unemployment problems as they appear to this writer as prelude to a consideration of new policy and program development initiatives. Youth employment opportunities are based mainly on the state of local economies; therefore some comparison of rural and non-rural sections of the country needs to be drawn. First, the differences.

There are fewer job opportunities for rural than for urban youth: geographic dispersal in rural areas versus compactness in urban areas. Second, there is less variety of economic activity in rural than in urban areas, industrial and commercial. Third, the lack of adequate public transportation, while a problem in many major and middle-size cities is a condition endemic to rural areas. Rural bus companies have been disappearing for decades; railway transportation connecting rural areas to each other and to larger towns and cities hardly exists although it once did even thirty years ago; and 100 years ago we had an extensive trolley car system that connected center cities with many of their outlying suburbs which were really rural communities.[3] Fourth, again because of the nature of rural communities, the variety and number of social, health and educational services and agencies typically found in cities are not found in rural areas. Small towns and villages in coun-

[3]Before World War I, one could go from New London, Connecticut, by trolley in either direction, to Boston or to New York City with changes along the way; these street railway lines provided easy access for the rural and suburban areas to the large cities.

try areas cannot support the network of services associated with cities; the population is too sparse, the economics are impossible. Fifth, although there may be some dispute about this in certain sections of the country, rural school systems are apt to have less comprehensive programs, vocational training shops, and vocational guidance programs than urban/suburban. Whether rural schools are, in general, educationally less effective than their urban counterparts for those students who graduate is a matter about which serious analysts disagree. But for the purposes of policy formulation, we know that the rural school is less well financed by local property taxes than urban/suburban systems and that state tax equalization formulas do not, in fact, equalize. Rural schools need greater per capita investment than they receive in order to equip them to educate and train youth for the economy of the next twenty years and beyond.

Rural areas differ from urban in numerous ways that have been the subject of much imaginative literature, social analysis, and government policy since the founding of the country. Cultural differences undoubtedly play an important part in attitudes toward work, the kinds of work considered acceptable, and in attitudes toward the roles of men and women, in the home or in employment. Differences in cultural values and expectations probably have considerable influence on the differences between rural and non-rural school programs, for example, and what local tax money should pay for, or the level of responsibility which local government should assume for individuals or families needing some form of assistance. Rural values may still be associated in many sections with the tradition of frontier independence, "doing for oneself", suspicion of "outsiders" including social agency personnel, government folk, and programs.

But beyond or beneath the differences between urban and rural culture, and the obvious differences between rural dispersion and urban congestion of population, housing patterns, commerce and industry, there are important similarities. Perhaps the most important is the fact or phenomenon of *modernization*. Modernization is first and foremost the application of scientific discovery and technological invention to the common problems of society. It is the application of the most recent knowledge to customary ways of doing things, thereby transforming practice and culture—small, individual machine shop into sequenced, repetitive mass production factory, family farm into agri-business, private physician into health maintenance organization, to take just three examples. Modernization is also defined by changes in communication and transportation, bringing homogeneity to the entire country. Modernization creates a national culture which overrides and overcomes regional and sectional differences. Moreover, modernization affects human aspiration and expectation so that, for example, people want the same gains from life. With respect to youth, and the problem of youth unemployment, it may be that modernization is also a short-hand term for the impulse to move from rural to urban. While some rural sections of the country are experiencing migration from the cities and towns, many rural counties are still being depopulated. This is a point which bears close analysis on a regional/sectional basis as new policy and programs for youth unemployment are being considered. The effect of modernization on the rural areas and the similarities and differences between rural and urban areas must be carefully analyzed in order to estimate how certain policies will affect youth employment. Again, what is occurring now in rural America with regard to development, employment, education, migration, family formation, and the like? What is expected in the 1980s and beyond? We need better data and better forecasting.

Similarities: rural youth who experience employment problems are probably not so different from urban youth who are in the same case. Distressed families, ill health or disablement on the part of one or both parents, adult unemployment, inadequate housing, conditions of severe poverty—all produce similar effects within the family and upon children and youth no matter where they may live. The sense of emotional or mental isolation that attends the rural poor is alike to the sense of isolation produced in the heart of an urban ghetto. Despite the very real strengths and workings of informal family-and-friend networks among the poor (which are often disregarded or underestimated by government programs), both in rural areas and inner-city ghettos, there are insufficient social networks and service agencies to help the family or the children overcome their isolation. Housing patterns contribute to greater physical isolation in rural than in urban sectors, however. The lack of appropriate role models in parents and other adults is more a result of poverty and of discrimination, I suggest, than it is of the geographic location of the family. Lack of motivation in youth for achievement in school leading to steady employment is no less an effect of poverty and other conditions in the family in rural than it is in urban areas. These negative personal and familial factors operate in much the same way upon rural as upon urban youth, preventing both from maturing and from acquiring the basic personal and intellectual skills necessary to cope with the world and to achieve steady employment. Lack of role models in the family, lack of parental education and experience contribute to the stunting of motivation and sense of possibility for youth everywhere.

For minority rural youth, the fact of racial antagonism leading to discrimination in employment is no less, I surmise, than for urban minority youth. It may be more. Hispanics, blacks, and Indians who live in rural areas are perhaps seen as culturally different in greater degree in certain rural sections than in the cities. (I do not know the research data on this point.) But whether racial discrimination is greater or lesser in the one than the other is not important. The fact of discrimination bears on minority youth and their families no matter where they live; it is personally destructive and socially nefarious and must be eliminated as a barrier to employment insofar as government policy can do so. State Fair Employment Practices Commissions or Equal Employment Opportunity Commissions have the same responsibility to deal with discriminatory employment patterns wherever they occur. The problem is that it is easier to monitor compliance with federal and state law in urban than rural areas, again because of the difference between concentration and dispersion. Thus it may well be that racial discrimination in rural sectors of the country has a more malign effect on youth employment.

Barriers

1. The Economy. The fact is the rural economy of the country is poorer than the urban. Median family income in rural areas in 1973 was $10,327 compared to $11,343 in central city and $14,007 in suburban (U.S. Department of Commerce, Bureau of Census, 1975, 15, Table P). The rural sections of the country have 30% of the nation's population but 40.1% of the poor (U.S. Department of Commerce, Bureau of Census, 1975, 16, Table R). In 1974, of persons over twenty-five years of age, 53.9% had completed high school, compared to 59.8% in central cities and 68.5% in the suburbs.

The rural economy is more likely to be a single-industry economy, with far less occupational diversity than is found in cities and therefore possessing fewer employment opportunities. Once the local work force need is met, there is not much chance for employment among successive cohorts of youth. A local industry can absorb just so many employees. But in an area with greater occupational variety and density, all persons, youth or adult, seeking work have a better chance.

The chief economic enterprise of America's rural areas has always been agriculture with timber and mining following. In terms of employing people, agriculture is a declining industry and will doubtless continue to be so overall. The decrease in family farm population may not be made up by an increase in farm laborers employed by large-scale commercial agriculture. The pattern of economic growth, since the end of World War II, has followed the movement of population into the suburbs of the north central and northeastern cities and out of the northeast toward the south, southwest and west coast. The central facts about population movements and economic developments in the last thirty-five years are: (1) there are not enough jobs in the rural areas to meet the needs of the rural population, (2) while technology has changed the face of agriculture in the rural areas and of manufacturing in the urban areas, diversification of industrial development has not occurred in sufficient depth to equalize the loss of agriculture, and (3) the change from agriculture, mining and lumbering has made necessary a different kind of vocational preparation for the younger generations of students leaving school to enter the labor force in rural areas.

2. Schools. Despite school district consolidation, there are still a very large number of small rural schools in the country.

In New York State, 85% of the districts are rural. Rural schools are smaller, have less faculty and staff, less equipment, fewer resources all around, and therefore provide fewer opportunities for their students to prepare themselves for a sophisticated, rapidly changing national economy. Vocational guidance, counseling and training, for example, in small rural high schools with large numbers of migrant, or native American or black youth would not normally equal that of urban/suburban schools. Resources are fewer, and community expectations about the school's responsibility in this realm are different.

For decades, the traditional rural occupations, agriculture, mining and lumbering, did not need specially trained youth to take those jobs. They learned by apprenticeship, leaving school early to work alongside family members. Vocational training and vocational services in rural schools were nonexistent until recently and were never as important as in city schools. But with the post-World War II decline in the traditional rural occupations, a new educational and social need comes to light, for which the schools like the parent communities are ill-prepared. What are the new kinds of jobs for which rural youth are to be prepared? What kind of industry locates itself in rural areas? What rural areas? These are questions that must be carefully analysed as prelude to new policy.

Answers must be found to these questions for any given area or section before the schools can create a vocational training program for their youth which has a fair chance of succeeding. If a training program is not connected to a tangible job at the end, if students do not see a realistic opportunity to go to work in their community, why should they stay? School systems, therefore, must work very closely with those local officials and private business persons who are planning rural economic development. *Rural Economic Development Commissions* and local *School-to-Work Councils* should be organized to address this issue. One result for the schools would be the creation of vocational training programs with a strong distributive or cooperative education component, that is a work experience built into the curriculum, which would enable students to learn work skills and habits while in school and in many cases provide direct access to a post-graduation job in the same firm or industry.

3. Transportation. If there is a lack of jobs in rural areas, then unemployed youth must travel to where the jobs are—in the cities and the suburbs. They must have a method of getting there. Private transportation is limited by personal income which in the case of unemployed, teen-age rural youth is bound to be low. For migrant worker families with out-of-work and out-of-school children, for rural black and Hispanic and Indian youth, what is the likelihood of their being able to afford dependable automobiles to get them from home to worksite? The question answers itself.

With respect to public transportation, bus service has been decreasing in rural areas for years, at just the same time that railroad service has also been diminishing to the point of eradication in many parts of the country. Moreover, rural commuter train service has not been present in most parts of the country for over half a century. (From about 1880 until the First World War, one could take a train from outlying farm areas into Ithaca, New York.) Present-day, commuter rail transportation has a difficult enough time breaking even in the heavily populated suburban areas of metropolitan Chicago, Philadelphia and New York. There seems no likelihood that local train service will be restored in the near future. So if youth are to be helped in finding employment where most of the jobs are, it seems clear that rural bus service will need to be resuscitated, supported by new public investment in overall rural transportation networks. Again, planning for such a network will need to be coordinated with economic and industrial development efforts in order to select the most promising and useful routes.

4. Social and Institutional Networks and Individual and Family Factors. That rural youth are isolated, social planners, government officials and agency personnel are undoubtedly well aware. But with the problems of the cities taking precedence in recent years, and with resources already spread too thin to cope with conditions of urban poverty, congestion and lack of services, the depth of isolation for the rural poor is probably not fully appreciated. What level of social services can be expected in communities of 1,000 population and under, of which there are 9,515, or even in communities of 10,000 and

under, of which there are 18,467? Young people with health
conditions, for example, that militate against their searching
for jobs, or keeping them once found, cannot expect to secure
the help they need in the areas where they live. The full
spectrum of social service agencies which urban communities
have created to meet the variety of individual and family
needs found in the cities is not likely to be duplicated in the
rural areas. Individual and family problems are therefore
more likely to be unnoticed, unmet and unresolved by social
structures which could assist unemployed youth (and adults)
to surmount their difficulties. Again, distances among rural
communities and dispersion of population work against timely
social intervention and assistance.

It is precisely because social network and institutional
help is less available and less specialized in small rural communities that the problems experienced by youth take added
point. Fewer or narrower role models of adult employment,
lack of social and job-fitting skills, lack of personal self-confi-
dence, a narrow or non-existent school vocational training
program taken together with individual or family health or
mental health problems, disablement, adult unemployment,
family breakdown and poverty constitute a set of conditions
almost insuperable.

5. *Racial and Sex Discrimination.* To all the above conditions, now add racial discrimination acting upon minority
youth and sex discrimination against young women, minority
or not, and one can estimate the weight of the barriers to rural
youth employment. Successive Employment and Training Reports of the President have demonstrated all too clearly the
disparities between white and non-white youth employment,
figures with which we are all familiar. These disparities are
national, although the crisis in black youth unemployment has
been seen as primarily urban because of the greater concentration of black youth in the ghettos of the large and middle-
size cities. Racial discrimination, as the Kerner Report pointed
out and as successive reports by the Urban League on "The
State of Black America" have described, exists and persists in
our society. In rural areas with mixed white and black or white
and Hispanic populations and with less well-developed econo-

mies to begin with, who is likely to get the available jobs? In rural areas which are predominantly minority, youth would have to make their way to the cities anyway in order to find work. Racial discrimination operates in subtle as well as blatant ways, and can be difficult to pin down. In the face of federal and state laws against it, employers in general are officially color-blind. Nevertheless, the power of state agencies could and should be invoked to consider the *employment patterns* of hiring, training and retention of minority youth by firms and industries located in areas which would normally draw upon this population for their labor force.

The case is similar for sex discrimination, although with respect to rural areas, there may well be cultural traditions and family customs operating against women working outside the home. Despite modernization, spoken of earlier, as a movement affecting all parts of the country, its effects on traditional attitudes toward women as wage-earners may be less pronounced among certain rural groups. Also, young women may be required in the home to care for younger children when the adults are working. Or again if there is ill health or disablement among adult family members, it would be the young woman's role, rather than the young man's, to stay home and give care. Again, sex discrimination in employment could be determined by examining hiring patterns.

Probably in very few individual cases is there but a single barrier to employment for rural youth. Most youth would face several if not all of these barriers. Therefore, policy and program initiatives to increase rural youth employment must take all factors into account and treat them at one and the same time.

Policy Initiatives

The following policy initiatives are necessary if rural youth unemployment is to be resolved in a timely fashion—which means to me within the next four or five years. Indeed, the basic problem of youth unemployment wherever it exists should be an absolute national priority until it is solved, and concentrated efforts ought to be made at all levels of government to finish with this problem for the rest of this century.

We must not allow successive generations of young people to be set apart or to set themselves apart from the economic and social order.

1. Job Creation. The central issue is more jobs in the rural areas; despite the importance of treating and solving other problems, there must be new public investment in the rural economies and better coordinated use of current programs which are targeted to rural sections.

There is no hope for better coordination at the federal level. Sub-cabinet coordinating committees with a directive from the President or the respective Secretaries simply do not work. Coordination, planning and distribution must be accomplished at a sub-regional, state or local level. *Rural Economic Development Commissions* should be established for precisely this purpose either at a state, sub-regional or regional level and federal funds should go from the Departments directly to these Commissions without passing through departmental regional offices or state agencies. The Governor's office, at the state level, should have sign-off authority and be represented on the Commission but the funding must go directly to the Economic Development Commissions.

The machinery established under the Regional Commission Act can be used for this purpose except that thought must be given to the optimum size of particular rural areas which may have rather distinct local or sub-regional economies. As the President's Small Community and Rural Development Policy notes, federal funds are available from many agencies in most of the Departments of the Federal Government for a wide array of rural development purposes. Taken together, they comprise a large resource, but their use must be the result of concerted coordinated planning.

2. Job Creation and Job Training. Job creation and job training must go hand-in-hand. The nation can no longer afford the waste, confusion and downright stupidity of policies which separate employment training from local economies. First, school systems must be represented in local, sub-regional and regional planning departments or commissions for economic development. Second, rural school systems must receive financial assistance in order to modernize their vocational training programs which means new equipment, retraining for vocational education teachers and vocational counselors and a commitment by the school board and school personnel to raise the whole level and status of vocational training. Elementary and junior high school curricula should be modified to include new emphasis and new materials on the world of work, and the development of basic literacy and intellectual skills should be regarded as preparation for work. Fortunately, there are plenty of curriculum materials available which focus on this goal. The importance of the role of elementary and junior high schools in preparing young children for further vocational training and eventually for employment must be given fresh emphasis by appropriate state and federal agencies and teacher training programs must be made more sensitive to this entire issue. Vocational training must expand from shoemaking, cosmetology, print shop and auto repair and school systems must find new faculty or retrain old faculty to teach new job skills.

3. School-to-Work Councils. To bring about close collaboration between school and employment opportunities, rural communities must be encouraged by appropriate federal and state agencies to create School-to-Work Councils. These Councils can bridge what has been for far too long a large gap between school and work. Very modest financial assistance might be necessary or useful to their formation and staffing but the cost should be small. These Councils could have a profound and positive effect upon connecting school program and personnel and local regional labor markets, commerce and industry. Business and industry representatives on these Councils would bring to the school people a sense of current and developing needs for personnel, and knowledge of how workers need to be prepared and trained vocationally before employment. School-to-Work Councils would be a new link between rural communities and industry. They would be under local control, a very important point, and they would meet a clear need. The formation of such Councils ought to receive immediate attention.

4. Enhancement of Rural Infrastructure. In this category of policy initiative and program development, must be included:

•new and improved transportation
•new and rehab housing
•improved social and health services
•new and improved roads, water and sewer facilities and utilities

All of these are necessary to overcome barriers to youth employment, and to retain youthful workers and their families in rural areas. It should be obvious that without investment in this kind of infrastructure, economic development can proceed only so far. The first essential must be jobs; but there must be a sound and healthy labor force, too, with all that that means. They must be able to live decently, to have services and to get from home to work conveniently.

5. Use of the Volunteer Sector. Neither national nor local government, nor school systems nor local commerce and industry can by themselves or even together reach the rural youth and their families who must be served. The volunteer sector of our society must be involved: 4-H, Future Farmers of America, Scouts, church groups, the Grange and community and adult organizations of all kinds. Investment in these organizations and associations of adults who work with children and youth will produce a sure response. For example, in 1978, 4-H alone reached 1,665,219 children and youth living in towns under 10,000 and open country. That was the largest group of 4-H members, larger than the number reached in towns and cities of 10,000 to 50,000 population (680,660) or in suburbs and cities over 50,000 (401,586) or in central cities (561,993). To reach almost 4,200,000 members, 4-H involved just under 580,000 volunteer leaders. That is an immense piece of machinery which exists in every part of the country.

Volunteer agencies with their adult leadership understand the informal network. Indeed, they are often part of the network. If the efforts of 4-H and other organizations akin to it were harnessed to the task of overcoming barriers to youth employment, if these groups were invited to become part of the local School-to-Work Councils, if they were tied into other

service-providing organizations and if they were everywhere
recognized by local school systems and by local government as
vital parts of community development, the prospects for progress and change would be wonderfully enhanced.

6. *The Problem of Program Development and Coordination.* The
intergovernmental system has grown too complex to enable
program coordination to occur at the federal level. A reading
of the President's "Small Community and Rural Development
Policy" or the catalogue of Federal Assistance Programs or the
FY81 Federal Budget reveals the truth of the generality. But
program coordination must take place, and the correct level is
at the local, sub-regional or regional level. Congress and federal administrators must come to recognize this point if the
array of resources in direct grants, employment training programs, loans and the like are to have their intended and proper
effect. Interdepartmental collaboration can be encouraged by
set-asides targeted to areas or communities with defined characteristics but it won't suffice to bring about the kind of sustained coordinated approach necessary to solve rural youth and
rural minority unemployment. Local, sub-regional or regional
management and control is required.

7. *Natural Resource Development and Economic Diversification.* Both natural resource development and economic diversification are challenging opportunities for rural revitalization
in the decades ahead. The one clearly interacts with the other,
and both kinds of development need sustained effort from all
governmental levels. Because environmental protection is so
much a part of national and state policy, and because large-
scale capitalization is necessary to natural resource development, it cannot be left to local control alone. But it is worth
saying, once again, that economic planning and development
programs with job training and job creation as integral parts
must involve local officials from the outset. Planning and coordination from the top down won't work. There are very strong
employment opportunities in rural areas for youth and adults
if natural resource development, coupled with industrial diversification, can be generated by federal, state and private
sector investment.

8. Knowledge Development. It seems that the country may finally be ready to embark upon a concerted effort to solve youth unemployment, rural, urban, wherever it exists. As resources become available and programs are devised, we need to observe and analyze what we are doing. In short, we need sustained action research in order to evaluate progress, results, failures, make mid-course corrections and improve performance. We can learn from our mistakes as well as from successes, but independent evaluation and research will be necessary, for program managers are too busy and too committed (or ought to be) to render impartial judgments about what works and what doesn't. Therefore, policy and program initiatives need an evaluation-research component built in from the outset.

9. Rural Community Development. Rural community development means at one and the same time human development, infrastructure development, use of natural resources and economic development. They must all proceed together in a balanced plan. The rural community must have both jobs and services to attract and keep youth and their families, and to give them the kind of life which fits their aspirations and expectations. Otherwise, they will continue to leave rural areas for towns, cities and suburbs, and the rural sections of the country will continue to be depopulated.

If one of the nation's goals in the 1980s and for the rest of this century is to maintain vitality in the rural areas of the country or to revitalize those areas which have lost population and economic purpose, then the kind of holistic approach advocated here is required. For there is a seamless web between individual and family health and the health and strength of the community. Education and training must suit the local economy. Individual aspirations must have a chance to be fulfilled. Services must be available in a timely and convenient fashion to meet human needs. The economy must provide decent jobs. Racial discrimination must be eliminated. There must be a *reason* for people to want to stay in a community and build it. In short, there must be a kind of human and social reconstruction in the rural areas. The rest of the nation must contribute from its resources to effect this reconstruction in just the same way that one hundred years ago, the rural areas began to contribute to the industrialization and urbanization of America. Most of us realize that as we turn into the next century, we cannot fashion a decent and just society with one part of the country strong and prosperous, another weak and poor. That is the central point of the domestic agenda for the next twenty-five years.

NOTE. I am most grateful for comments and suggestions for this paper from my colleagues in the New York State College of Human Ecology, Cornell University: Professor Ray Rist, Professor Jeanne Mueller, Professor Stephen Hamilton, and Extension Associates Florence Cherry and Herbert Engman.

References

Adams, A., & Magnum, G.L. *The lingering crisis of youth unemployment.* Kalamazoo, Michigan: W.E. Upjohn Institute for Employment Research, 1978.

A charter for improved rural youth transition. Washington, D.C.: Center for Education and Work, National Manpower Institute, 1978.

Magnum, G., & Walsh, J. *Employment and training programs for youth: What works best for whom?* Washington, D.C.: Office of Youth Programs, Employment and Training Administration, U.S. Department of Labor, 1978.

Rist, R.C., et al. *Forging new relationships: The CETA/school nexus,* Interim report #1. Ithaca, N.Y.: Youthwork National Policy Study, Cornell University, 1979. (a)

Rist, R.C., et al. *Education and employment training: The views of youth,* Interim report #2. Ithaca, N.Y.: Youthwork National Policy Study, Cornell University, 1979. (b)

Rist, R.C., et al. *Targeting on in-school youth: Four strategies for coordinating education and employment,* Interim report #3. Ithaca,, N.Y.: Youthwork National Policy Study, Cornell University, 1980.

Sher, J.P. (Ed.). *Education in rural America.* Boulder, Colorado: Westview Press, 1977.

Small community and rural development policy, Washington, D.C.: The White House, 1979.

Children and Youth Services Review, Vol. 2, pp. 81–96, 1980
Printed in the USA. All rights reserved.

0190-7409/80/010081-16$02.00/0

Federal Intervention and Youth Programs:

An Essay on the Viability of the In-School Work Experience/Education Model

Wilfred B. Holloway
Cornell University

Introduction

Schools have been viewed as the place to solve many of the nation's ills.* They have taken on responsibilities which were previously discharged by other primary institutions such as the family, church, and community. With the decline of these other institutions, schools have been seen more and more as the place to rehabilitate society. By changing the young, it was thought, the problems of America would also be solved.

Such is the background from which America approaches the problem of youth unemployment. There are as many as "4 million" at risk young people in the country today according to government statistics. These youth cannot find jobs and generally do not have the basic competencies to successfully compete in the modern labor market. In-school youth are described as illiterate and out of school youth are seen as unable to acquire a job, and if they do get a job, are unable to hold it.

Wilfred B. Holloway, Youthwork National Policy Study, College of Human Ecology, Cornell University, Ithaca, New York 14853.
*The author would like to thank Steven Johnson and Ray C. Rist for their helpful comments on an earlier draft.

To deal with this problem, President Carter recently proposed a two billion dollar increase in spending for programs
to curb youth unemployment. This will bring the total spent
on such efforts to six billion dollars. The emphasis of the new
initiative is to be on teaching disadvantaged youth the basic
skills which are necessary for participation in the modern labor market.

While it is obvious from the President's initiative that
many youth are not receiving an adequate education, the merits of his solution to the problem are not so obvious. There is
much honest disagreement as well as cynical skepticism about
the administration's proposal. For example, Greeley (1980)
brands the President's proposal "a campaign ploy" with little
chance of passage in the Congress. Greeley goes on to suggest
that:

Not even the most enthusiastic admirer of the War on Poverty
(Johnson era) would suggest, however, that we know how to incul-
cate literacy and job skills in the chronically disadvantaged. Mr.
Carter's version of the War on Poverty would mean more jobs for
Labor and Education Department bureaucrats and few, if any, jobs
for the poor.
    Neither (the new Secretary of Education) nor the President
seems to grasp the devastating irony of admitting that professional
educators have not produced literacy in 40 percent of their black
students . . . while proposing to pour yet more money into the hands
of such educators.
    If they cannot teach young people to read and write in school,
what possible grounds can there be for expecting them to teach such
basic skills once the young people have dropped out of schools?
(Greeley, 1980)

There have been more congenial evaluations of the President's proposal but the consensus seems to be that the initiative represents not much more than what has been tried
before.

Some authors, most notably McGowan and Cohen (1977),
have trumpeted a change in the way schools are viewed by
society. McGowan and Cohen note:

But rather than picturing schools as a refuge, the current wisdom
portrays them as pathologically isolated products of the failure of

primary institutions to socialize the young and of economic pres-
sures to keep youth out of the work force. School children are said
to be walled off from healthy social realities by irrelevant compulsory attendance and school-leaving laws, and by an unwise professional devotion to book learning. According to these reports, schools
prevent students from learning; the answer to the barrenness of
formal schools is real experience.

For generations schools have been regarded as the indispens-
able preparation for work: They would provide the skills and connections that once were handed down informally on the job or in the
family. This idea underlay the earliest manual training programs,
the later movements for vocational education, and the turn-of-the-
century torrent of high-school and trade-school specializations in
everything from accounting to veterinary medicine. It is also the
inspiration for the more recent flood of post-secondary white and
blue collar training programs.

But if schooling once seemed a prerequisite for the vicissitudes
of work, it is now pictured as a barrier to learning about it. Schools,
it is argued, teach things that are useless for jobs or careers. (p. 30)

Far from being disillusioned with schooling as a setting for
learning the skills necessary for work, the President has shown
the utmost respect for and confidence in the institution of
schooling as an instrument of social change.

The Carter administration is intent upon increasing the
amount of time poor in-school youth spend working as a part
of the institution of schooling. What are the benefits to such
an experience for this target group? To what extent can we
expect work experience programs to impact on the development of disadvantaged in-school youth? Policy makers suggest
that the experience will increase the youths' job holding skills,
improve their academic skills, and raise their level of self-
esteem by providing successful experiences.

Let us examine briefly the rationale for the creation of
work experience programs for youth.

Why the need for youth programs?

With a plethora of statistics to back them up, both proponents and critics of the system have pointed to the inordinately high levels of youth unemployment as a serious problem in America today. The call for integration of youth into

the society (President's Science Advisory Committee Panel on Youth, 1974) and the development and implementation of youth employment programs come as a direct result of a disillusionment with schooling, student unrest, and the civil rights movement. Each of these crises has been addressed in one form or another by employment/training programs for in-school youth. Mangum and Walsh (1978) suggest that:

The mission of employment and training programs for this target population (in-school youth) is extremely complicated. Obviously, one of their purposes is to help prepare in-school youth for eventual participation in the labor force. Others are to reduce school dropouts, provide income to needy students, and to increase student motivation to master academic and vocational curricula. (p. 168)

What Mangum and Walsh do not mention as a goal of employment/training programs (but what is implied by the designation of the target population) is the need for increased opportunities for those who have been denied access to the labor market in the past through discriminatory practices. The need for the development of greater opportunities is apparent from the disproportionate numbers of minority group members who are represented among the nation's poor.

The Work-Education Consortium of the National Manpower Institute (1978, pp. 3–4) cites eight benefits of work or service experience for youth: sustained exposure to a particular career, adult work attitudes and habits, interaction with adults, responsible behavior, mastery of nonclassroom skills and problem-solving techniques, citizenship skills and attitudes, increased academic motivation, and lifelong learning skills. In a recent review of literature these variables, Hamilton and Crouter (1980) conclude that the evidence from work and service program evaluations are mostly unimpressive (see also Barton & Fraser, 1978).

The often cited Panel on Youth study (President's Science Advisory Committee, 1974) asserts that work experience has developmentally beneficial impacts on young people. The study suggests:

Although the data are limited and relevant variables often confounded, on balance the weight of the evidence suggests that work experience outside the home is more likely to have positive than deleterious effects . . . Work seems to have psychological significance for youth as a step toward maturity via personal-social characteristics whether or not it promotes vocational development per se. Even rather humdrum gainful employment may yield these benefits. (1974, p. 108)

As Hamilton and Crouter (1980) note, "this conclusion is not heavily documented and reflects the Panel's hopes and assumptions more than actual empirical knowledge" (p. 3).

From the implementation of the Neighborhood Youth Corps under the Equal Opportunity Act of 1964 to the current developments of the YEDPA Act, there has been increasing interest by government agencies in the funding of employment/training activities for in-school youth. Much of this activity has been encouraged by theorists who have argued that we should look to the work-place as a complement, or even as an alternative to the high school (e.g., Illich, 1971; President's Science Advisory Committee Panel on Youth, 1974). They and other commentators have suggested that early experience in the work-place would enhance the integration of youth into the larger society, promote social responsibility and independence, and provide an alternative to the school in which cognitive skills could be acquired (Adams & Mangum, 1978; Greenberger & Steinberg, 1979).

The Problem

Given the tremendous increase in employment (both private and public) in-school youth are experiencing and the number of suggestions by champions of work experience programs about the evils such opportunities will cure, it is surprising how little actual research can be found which has examined the impacts of work on in-school youth. In a report prepared for the federal government's Interagency Panel for Research and Development on Adolescence ("Work experience," 1973), the authors conclude an exhaustive review of federally sponsored research on work experience programs with the following observation:

Perhaps the most significant question . . . is whether actual experience in a real working situation promotes social and cognitive development beyond that which classroom learning can provide. This question has not yet been answered and few of the studies reviewed are attempting to answer it. (p. 206)

In their own recent review of the literature on adolescent employment, Greenberger and Steinberg (1979) corroborate the Interagency Panel's findings: "Although there is a vast amount of research on adolescents, including many studies of their future occupational plans, there has been relatively little in-depth research on the actual job experiences of adolescents and the effects of working on adolescents' social and cognitive development" (p. 10).

Since 1973 and the implementation of the Comprehensive Employment and Training Act, the government has spent billions of dollars to fund work experience programs to improve job holding skills, academic achievement, and self-esteem for disadvantaged young people. What evidence has accrued in this time to either support or refute the idea that work experience programs do have favorable impacts on the development of in-school youth? Since the Interagency Panel's report in 1973, there have been at least five studies which have addressed the issue, "does a work experience promote development beyond that which can be acquired through classroom learning?" The purpose of this paper is to review the findings from those studies to examine what implications work has for in-school youth. The primary focus of the paper will be on changes in self-esteem and academic achievement.

Employment Programs and Developmental Impacts: Some empirical evidence

For the period 1974–1979, five empirical research articles examined the relationship between work experience and such variables as self-concept, self-esteem, academic achievement, attitudes toward school, work values, and intelligence. The first of these, Bernardo (1973), examined the effects of a pilot work-study program on the school adjustment of delinquent male youth returning from institutions. The study was interested in ascertaining changes in self-concept as the result of participation in a work experience program. The treatment program consisted of paid work-experience, academic class-work, technical-vocational training, individual and group counseling, and individual tutoring. Subjects, both treatment and control, were selected from a group of boys, 16 through 19 years of age, who had been released from institutions within the last six months, and who were due to return to one of four Cleveland inner-city high schools. All subjects were black and were economically disadvantaged by Neighborhood Youth Corps standards. The Tennessee Self-Concept Scale was administered in the Fall/Winter, 1971 and again in June, 1972. Using linear multiple regression models, a comparison was made to determine if there was a significant difference between groups on posttest scores on the Total Positive Score (overall measure of self-esteem) and 11 other variables of the Tennessee Self-Concept Scale. Pretest scores were compared to assure that the groups were equivalent. The findings indicated that participation in the work experience program did not result in a significant change in self perceptions. It was also found that experimental group gains on the Total Positive Score did not correlate positively with any program variable. There was a consistent negative correlation between gain scores and all program variables.

Mayer (1974) looked at self-concept and the drop-out prone high school student. The study was designed to examine the effect of a work-study program on the self-concept of tenth grade potential drop-outs. Academic achievement was also examined. Three groups were used; two experimental and one control. All groups were administered the Bills' High School Index of Adjustment and Values in September and again in June. No significant treatment effects were found in comparison with the control group for either self-concept or academic achievement.

LaPointe (1977) used Neighborhood Youth Corps participants to compare the effects of a program of paid summer and school year work and a motivation group program on the achievement, self-concept, attitudes toward school, school attendance, and school discipline of disadvantaged youth. Positive changes were hypothesized for all of the dependent variables for participants in both the work experience and motivation group treatments. There were 120 low-income,

primarily minority group students, randomly assigned to one
of the four experimental groups: (1) work experience; (2)
motivation group; (3) combination work experience and motivation group; and (4) control group. Teacher grades and the
Comprehensive Test of Basic Skills were used to measure
achievement. The Piers-Harris Children's Self-Concept Scale
was employed to determine self-concept. Attitudes toward
school were measured by the Attitudes Toward School questionnaire. School attendance was measured by official school
attendance records and school discipline by the number of
school discipline referrals filed on a student. Pre- and posttests
were gathered on all variables. The major findings of the
study were:

(1) Significant positive changes in achievement, as measured by
    grades but not by a standardized test, were found as a result of
    the work experience and the combined group treatments.
(2) Significant positive changes in student attitudes toward school
    and school attendance were found as a result of the combined
    work and motivational group.
(3) No significant change was found for self-concept or school dis-
    cipline referrals as a result of the experimental treatments.

Katyal (1977) sought to determine the effect of work experience on the self-concept, work values, and school interest
of high school students. The subjects of the study were 53
students who had elected to take the work experience program in first semester of the 1974–75 school year in Alberta,
Canada. The Tennessee Self-Concept Scale, Super's Work
Value Inventory, and Cottle's School Interest Inventory, respectively, were used to measure the three variables studied.
An experimental-control group design was used for this study
and the student's "t" scores were computed to study the differences in the group scores.[2] The results of the study indicated
that:

(1) On the self-concept variables examined, the work experience
    students showed significant gains in all except physical self. No
    finding for total self-esteem was given.

[2] The major limitation with this study is that it lacks random assignment of
subjects to treatment and control groups and no pretest was given to assure
the equivalency of the two groups. There was also no evidence that the
groups were matched on any set of criteria.

(2) Of the 15 work values studied, significant gains for the experimental group were indicated for 10 values: achievement, surroundings, supervisory relations, way of life, security, esthetics, prestige, variety, economic return, and altruism.

Greenberger and Steinberg (1979) explore the costs and benefits of early work experience in the part-time labor force in relation to such variables as school attendance, attitudes toward school, academic performance, and attitudes toward working. Data was collected from a sample of 531 tenth and eleventh graders in Orange County, California. This sample was drawn from a pool of 3,100 young respondents who participated in a survey regarding their employment histories and family background characteristics. The findings were based on a cross-sectional comparison of workers and non-workers at one time only. In this type of design, it is not possible to clearly separate differences due to selection into the work force and those which are due to the experiences of working. In other words, the analysis is done post hoc and differences in the makeup of the groups which are not controlled may be influencing the findings (same as Katyal study).[3] Groups were not randomly selected or matched. The findings of this study are presented in the following:

(1) Workers are significantly more likely than non-workers to be absent from school.
(2) Workers are more likely than non-workers to report that they do not enjoy school.
(3) Workers obtain significantly lower grade-point averages than non-workers. Intensity of employment is also negatively related to academic success. The more one works the worse are one's grades. Workers spend less time on academic work.
(4) Delinquent behavior is higher among workers than non-workers.

Discussion

Of the five studies reviewed, four looked at some measure of self-concept/esteem. One study, Katyal, found a sig-

[3] The lack of an ability to clearly separate findings due to selection into the work force and differences due to the experiences of working limits the usefulness of this study. The authors compensate for this design flaw somewhat by comparing youth who are seeking work with those who are not seeking work.

nificant relationship between work experience and self-concept. Three others, Bernardo, Mayer, and LaPointe, found no
significant relationship between the two variables. Bernardo,
LaPointe, and Katyal all used the Tennessee Self-Concept
Scale. Mayer used the Billings High School Index of Adjustment and Values.

Three studies examined the relationship between work
experience and academic achievement. Two, Mayer, and
Greenberger and Steinberg, found either no relationship between the two variables or a negative relationship (working
leads to worse academic achievement). LaPointe, on the other
hand, found that work experience was related to improvements in achievement measured by changes in grade performance. There was no significant increase as measured by a
standardized test employed by LaPointe.

It has been over a decade since the early critics of schooling began calling for the inclusion of work experiences as a
vital option in secondary education for disadvantaged youth.
More recently, there have been calls for making this experience available to all regardless of financial need. What evidence is there to support the theoretical suppositions made by
the critics concerning the effects of work experience on self-
concept/esteem and academic achievement?

*The literature reviewed in this paper suggests that work experi-
ence programs do not positively affect either self-concept or academic
achievement. By a margin of three to one, studies since 1974 have
concluded that work experience does not improve self-esteem. By a
lesser margin, two to one, the same review concludes that work experience does not correlate with improved academic achievement.*

The question of whether work experience improves social
and cognitive development is an important one because if it is
found that there is no difference between what classroom
training offers and what a combined classroom and work experience offers, then that will be valuable information which
should influence how policy makers utilize their resources in
trying to improve the lot of disadvantaged youth. While it is
clear that more research is needed to clarify the relationships
between these variables (only five published studies on programs that have spent billions), this review concludes that the
weight of the evidence to this point suggests that work experi-

ence does not promote social and cognitive development beyond that which already occurs in the classroom setting.

Why is this? It appears to me that two arguments can be made at this point. First, the critic of schools can now become a critic of government programs and suggest that employment programs as presently recognized and constituted do not provide the kinds of experiences which would lead to improvements in adolescent development. The critic is then left with the task of defining what kinds of work experience programs would improve adolescent development. The second approach would be to acknowledge that work experience has not been the panacea which the experts had expected. As Levitan, Mangum, and Marshall (1976) have suggested:

NYC was ostensibly justified as a route to employability, [it] is primarily income maintenance accompanied by a minimum of useful activity. This does not mean that it is not desirable, only that it should be approached more honestly. Poor people need income and something at which to keep busy as a bridge between school enrollment and work or to help them at a vulnerable age when opportunities may be scarce . . . The tendency over the years has been for the quality of the work experience to improve and the accompaniment of basic education to grow. There is evidence that the Neighborhood Youth Corps makes a positive contribution to employment. (p. 57)

In paraphrasing these authors, Mangum and Walsh (1978) suggest:

What the authors seem to be saying is that we should lower our expectations: that the cultural, environmental, and personal reasons why some youth drop out of school may be beyond the healing powers of simple work experience. If policy makers and program operators are at last ready to face this fact, the time may have arrived when the more profound reasons for school dropouts and youth labor market failure can be the subject of research. If this ever happens, it is almost certain that the results will indicate that solutions to many of these problems are beyond the scope of ordinary employment and training programs. (p. 57)

Indeed, at a time when achievement scores in secondary education for math and reading are decreasing, it seems that adolescents may need more time in an academic setting instead of less. Greenberger and Steinberg (1979) provide evidence that those in-school youth who work are significantly more likely to be absent from school, more likely than non-workers to report that they do not enjoy school, and to obtain significantly lower grade-point averages than non-workers. While their research design does not allow for the sorting out of differences due to selection into the work force and differences which are due to the experience of working, the findings suggest that poor academic achievement and working are correlated for secondary students. The direction of that relationship is less than clear. Whether poor achievement leads to working or whether working contributes to poor achievement is still a question for further research to answer.

Implications

Based on the empirical evidence reviewed in this paper and the discussion presented, I would suggest that if a goal of work experience programs for in-school youth is to improve academic achievement and self-concept, then work experiences have all but failed. There is a great need for clarification of the aims and goals of social intervention efforts. Of four studies reviewed, only one found significant changes in self-concept. Do we intend to encourage or foster poor academic performance? The evidence is conflicting as to whether or not working inhibits achievement, but relatively clear that it does not promote academic achievement. Is the purpose to help poor youth remain in school by providing them with money? Some experts (e.g., Mangum & Walsh, 1978) have argued that this is a key component of CETA sponsored work experience programs for in-school youth. If this is true, the government should provide straight income transfer or provide for educational loans much like what is offered to needy college students.

For in-school youth, important consequences of working need to be elaborated upon. Decisions must be made as to the direction intervention programs are to take in the future and an analysis of these consequences should have an important impact on decisions regarding the continuation of large scale federally sponsored work experience for in-school youth. Several issues in the literature mitigate against work experience for in-school youth. These are:

(1) Some authors suggest that work is still a place of toil, labor, and hardship. There is little to be gained from going into the jobs youth presently occupy (see Dreeben, 1974).

(2) One study suggests that in-school youth who work are more likely to have poor school attendance and lower grades than non-workers. Educational achievement is critical for these youth. Where work sabotages education, work should not be encouraged. It also reports that delinquency among those who work is higher than those who do not (Greenberger & Steinberg, 1979).

(3) There is evidence from adult programs which suggests that the CETA system is contributing to the development of a dual labor market system by channeling poor people into low paying, low skilled jobs. Youth programs are a part of the CETA system and will surely fall prey to the same problem (National Governor's Association Report, 1979).

The first two issues above raise the question of the quality of jobs and more generically the question of "are jobs per se a social good?" There have been many black leaders who have made the point that the coming generation growing up into adulthood with no employment opportunities is bad. It is critical to separate the argument here. For those youth who are both out of work and out of school, a job (any job) is a social good. For youth who are full-time students, there is much less of a critical need for employment opportunities. Work offers little that is not already provided in one form or another in school settings. What youth need (particularly poor in-school youth) are more credentials which will allow them to compete successfully in the labor market. Work, as traditionally defined, pulls youth away from school and the primary labor market.

The most significant contradiction in work experience programs revolves around the fact that occupational success in this country is strongly related to educational attainment. Work experiences lower educational aspirations, interfere with classroom time and studying, and lower the quality of the education received. This remedy (work) is being proposed for the very youth who are already at the bottom of the socio-economic ladder. We are at once faced with the situation of telling youth that education is the key to success and at the same time removing him/her more and more from the educational process through the use of various work experience pro-

grams (vocational education, cooperative education, Youth
Employment and Training Programs).

.If work does not improve academic achievement, if it in
fact interferes with schooling, and if schooling is very strongly
related to occupational success, then what is it that we are
offering the youth who qualify for federally supported work
experiences. Are we not in fact contributing to the development of a dual labor market system (issue #3)? The dual labor
market is a system which has structural constraints which pro-
hibit movement from one labor market to the other. Poor
youth are being tracked or channeled away from the primary
market which relies upon educational criteria (e.g., grades,
test scores, etc.) for admittance and channeled into those jobs
which represent the lower socio-economic strata in our society.
In commenting on this issue, the Governor's report on rural
CETA suggests that:

Because of the very strict limitations on length of participation in
CETA training, people are normally trained only for low skill, low
level occupations. This makes CETA a partner in patterns which
perpetuate economic barriers between the "primary" and "secondary" labor markets. (National Governor's Association Report, 1979).

Conclusion

In America, we have a history of encouraging upward
mobility; a history of removing the barriers to success. I fear
that this time we have been misguided. Work experiences, as
presently structured, do little or nothing to foster the kinds of
development its proponents have suggested and given the evidence that it may in fact hamper the development of that
which is strongly related to occupational success (education),
there is good reason to completely rethink the concept with
regard to in-school youth.

Future work programs should be aimed at serving those
youth who are both out of school and out of work. If there is
need for money to go to poor youth who are still in school,
then a simple income transfer program should be developed
which does not interfere with schooling. Instead of focusing
new monies on drawing drop-outs back into secondary school

settings, programs should encourage the youth to pursue their education in adult education classes and at programs which are offered at local universities. To place youth who have failed in a secondary school setting back into the same environment and expect success is sheer folly.

Finally, structural components of CETA are programmed to fail because they do not represent the basic principles upon which this country was formed. Leonard and Nelson (National Governor's Association Report, 1979) suggest that:

Official antipathy toward welfare recipients is so strong in rural areas that programs such as WIN are not likely to succeed in rural areas.

I suspect that the same is true of CETA youth programs in urban areas and any attempt to improve adolescent development by this means begins with one foot in the swamp and the other not far behind.

References

Adams, A., Mangum, G., Stevenson, W., Doniger, S., & Mangum, S. *The lingering crisis of youth unemployment*. Kalamazoo, Michigan: W. E. Upjohn Institute for Employment Research, 1978.

Barton, P. E., & Fraser, B. S. *Between two worlds: Youth transition from school to work*, (Vol. 2). Programs and Experimentation. Washington, D.C.: Center for Education and Work, National Manpower Institute, 1978.

Bernardo, P. C. The effects of a pilot work study program on the school adjustment of delinquent male youth returning from institutions. *Dissertation Abstracts International*, 1973, *34*, (4-A), 1512–1513.

Dreeben, R. Good intentions. *School Review*, 1974, *83*, 37–48.

Greeley, A. Carter's plan for dropouts doomed to fail. *New York Times*, February 12, 1980, ff.

Greenberger, E., & Steinberg, L. *Part-time employment of in-school youth: A preliminary assessment of costs and benefits*. Program in Social Ecology, University of California-Irvine, August 1979.

Hamilton, S., & Crouter, A. Work and growth: A review of research regarding the impact of work experience on adolescent development. *Journal of Youth and Adolescence*, 1980, *9*.

Illich, I. The alternative to schooling. *Saturday Review*, June 19, 1971.

Katyal, K. L. The effect of the work experience program on the self-concept, the work values, and school interest of selected Canadian high school students. *Dissertation Abstracts International*, 1977, *38*, (5-A), 2558.

LaPointe, C. Employment, group motivation, and the achievement, self-concept, and attitudes toward school of impoverished students. *Dissertation Abstracts International*, 1977, *38*, (1-A), 115.

Levitan, S., Mangum, G., & Marshall, R. *Human resources and labor markets* (2nd ed.). New York: Harper and Row, 1976.

Mangum, G., & Walsh, J. *Employment and training programs for youth: What works best for whom?* Washington, D.C.: Office of Youth Programs, Employment and Training Administration, Department of Labor, Government Printing Office, 1978.

Mayer, M. Self-concept and the dropout-prone high school student: A study of a program for potential dropouts. *Dissertation Abstracts International*, 1974, 34, (7-A), 3880.

McGowan, E. & Cohen, D. Career education - Reforming school through work. *The Public Interest*, 1977, *46*, 28–47.

National Governor's Association Report. CETA and Rural Areas, Washington, D.C., 1979, 43–104.

President's Science Advisory Committee Panel on Youth. *Youth transition to adulthood*. Chicago: University of Chicago Press, 1974.

Work-Education Consortium. *Work and service experience for youth*. Washington, D.C.: National Manpower Institute, 1978.

Work experience as preparation for adulthood: A review of federal job training, vocational, and career education programs, an analysis of current research and recommendations for future research. Prepared for the Interagency Panel for Research and Development on Adolescence by Social Research Group, the George Washington University, Washington, D.C., May 1973.

Children and Youth Services Review, Vol. 2, pp. 97–112, 1980
Printed in the USA. All rights reserved.

On the Involvement of Public and Private Sector Employers in Youth Programs

Steven D. Johnson
Cornell University

Over the years, the United States government has initiated numerous programs aimed at addressing youth unemployment problems.[1] The most recent of these endeavors is the Youth Employment and Demonstration Projects Act (YEDPA). Its predecessors include, among others, the Neighborhood Youth Corps, the Job Corps, and the Vocational Education Act.

Private industry has also attempted to address the need for youth employment opportunities through individual company programs and, perhaps most notably, via the establishment, during the mid-1960s, of the National Alliance of Businessmen. The extent to which these and other efforts have been used to address youth employment is suggested by Mangum and Walsh (1978):

The creation of job opportunities outside the normal processes of the labor market, either by direct public job creation or by subsidizing employment in private firms and institutions or public agencies

Steven D. Johnson, Youthwork National Policy Study, Cornell University, Ithaca, New York 14853.
[1] A more thorough discussion of the issues contained within this paper as well as additional topics may be found in the report *Employer Involvement: A Study of Public and Private Sector Linkages to Youth Programs.* Copies of this report are available by writing in care of the author at N-229 MVR Hall, Cornell University, Ithaca, NY 14853.

has been one of the major strategies of attempts to alleviate youth unemployment. In 1974, for example, 70 percent of all employment and training program enrollees under 22, and 90 percent under 19 years of age were enrolled in work experience programs. Since the passage of CETA, and now with YEDPA, subsidized employment for youth has been expanded both absolutely and relatively. (p. 52)

Unfortunately, for all our efforts to date, very little research on the viability of various approaches to the youth problem exists. With this being the general situation, it is not surprising to discover that even less is known about how best to involve employers in federally-funded youth programs. Mangum and Walsh (1978) note that, "Evaluative material on youth participation in public service employment and subsidized private employment is sparse" (p. 53). In the foreword to a more recent review of the literature in the field, focusing primarily on private-sector participation in federal youth programs, Ungerer writes:

The principal conclusion [of this report] is that this whole field of private-sector involvement with youth transition programs, while rich in anecdotal examples, is very poorly documented and researched in any formal sense. The result is that, in spite of substantial experimentation, we really know little about what motivates and sustains private-sector involvement and what outcomes can be expected from such participation. (Elsman, Note 1, p. iii)

The outlook for the near future may not be nearly so bleak. Numerous studies have been initiated to more systematically investigate currently unresolved questions. Entire programmatic areas have been developed with a primary focus toward knowledge development. One such instance is the Exemplary In-School Demonstration Projects, supported through Youth Employment and Training Program (YETP, a subtitle of YEDPA) discretionary funds.[2] As with other YEDPA programs, it is incumbent upon those individuals operating the Exemplary Projects to broaden our knowledge base. The first general principle of the YEDPA Planning Charter (U.S. Department of Labor, 1977) states:

[2]The Exemplary In-School Projects are subdivided into four programmatic focus areas: private sector involvement; youth operated; academic credit; and career awareness. Each focus area emphasizes a different approach to addressing the problem of youth unemployment.

Knowledge Development is a primary aim of the new youth programs. At every decision-making level, an effort must be made to try
out promising ideas, to support ongoing innovation and to assess
performance as rigorously as possible. Resources should be concentrated and structured so that the underlying ideas can be given a
reasonable test. Hypotheses and questions should be determined at
the outset, with an evaluation methodology built in. (p. 5)

This current paper is devoted to presentation of data
collected via a special sub-study of the ongoing Youthwork
National Policy Study (YNPS). More specifically, the purpose
of this sub-study was to examine how both public and private
sector employers were involved in these programs.

The data reported here were collected by YNPS field
observers at 29 programs, located in 18 states. Interviews with
program personnel, most often the program's director/opera-
tor and job coordinator, were conducted during January and
February of 1980. Of the issues discussed, those which are
briefly presented in this paper include: (1) how employers
were contacted; (2) the nature of employer involvement; (3)
incentives/disincentives to employer involvement; and (4) distinctions between public and private sector placements for
youth. The final section of the paper provides a series of
recommendations beneficial to program involvement of employers as suggested by the data reviewed.

Before proceeding with the discussion of the findings,
several caveats need to be stated.

1. The term "employer(s)" is used throughout this paper. Unless public or private sector employers are specifically identified, one may assume that the term is being used to include both employment sectors.
2. The term "work experience" as used in this paper refers to
   work experience in general, including both vocational exploration and on-the-job training. Where appropriate a
   specific form of training is identified.
3. Data pertaining to *both private and public sector* employers are
   discussed within this paper under the assumption that if
   one wishes to weigh the merits of private sector involvement over public sector involvement in youth programs,
   then both should be reviewed. As several of the reporting

programs, having a work experience phase, have used a mixture of both employment sectors, this becomes an opportune time to examine to some extent, issues contrasting these employment sectors.

4. Due to the varying nature of the reporting programs, many of the questions contained on the interview questionnaire were not applicable to specific programs. As such, responses for all 29 programs exist for very few of the following sections.

5. Only five of the 29 reporting programs were specifically designed to focus on private sector involvment. The employer-related data from many of the remaining programs reflect secondary and tertiary program components and not the major emphases of these programs.

Findings

Contacting Employers. The methods most commonly used to identify and contact public and private sector employers at all four types of Exemplary In-School Projects included: (1) face-to-face contact; (2) identification through available lists, e.g., Chamber of Commerce, NAB and the yellow pages of the telephone book; (3) letters and phone calls to businessmen; (4) presentations before local organizations; (5) word of mouth; and (6) through personal contacts/friends. Two less often used methods were through the use of advisory councils and using the program youth as locators of jobs via an outreach process (a canvassing of local employers).

Whether the involvement of the employers was or was not a primary focus of the program, similar experiences occurred. Clearly, face-to-face contact with employers was essential. Whether programs began with this method or not, they almost all ended up using this method. A job developer emphasized:

the importance of direct one-to-one contact with employers, and that it was harder for employers to say no to an appeal to community commitment to youth in a face-to-face contact as opposed to contact over the telephone or in a letter.

The weakness of introductory letters as noted above, was corroborated by information from a second program which initially identified employers via the yellow pages. The field observer noted:

A list of employers was compiled from the yellow pages of the county phone book. These employers were sent introductory letters which contained descriptions of the program, and asked if they would like to participate. They were told that if they were interested in having a student at their place of employment, they should contact the project. The response was underwhelming—not one employer called.

The familiarity of staff with the community's resources was beneficial in the identification of employers and worksites—especially more specialized work experiences. This process was enhanced when staff individuals working with employers had been a part of the community for a number of years. One field observer noted in her conversation with a program analyst, who had been in the community for many years:

After contacting an initial group of employers and getting their commitment, he waited until students had particular needs outside this group to make new contacts. "And then the secretary began to help me. She has personal friends that are doctors, people like that, so she would make the contacts for me." All of the staff credit the secretary for developing many of the professional placements in the project.

The use of program youth, at one site, was a highly successful method of locating potential employers. During the first year of this program's outreach (about 30 days in duration), program youth canvassed local business establishments. Through this process, approximately 140 youth identified over 700 businessmen interested in participating in the program. These employers provided guest speakers, business tours and work placements for all program youth.

The use of advisory councils to disseminate information about the program and help identify worksites was found by several programs to be of great value. However, a particularly critical feature to help enhance success of the councils was to follow up on these councils as well as other linkages developed by program personnel. One situation suggested what can happen if follow-up does not occur.

I should add that another component built into the original proposal which was supposed to assist in private sector placement was the Work Education Council. It would have several committees to work closely with the project, one of those being private sector employment. This committee met a few times but faded out with no personal commitments or very much interest shown from community people. The project director did not really push for it, so several months into the project it kind of died a natural death (the whole council idea).

The Nature of Employer Involvement. The involvement of employers most often took one of the following forms: (1) to provide guest lecturers; (2) to provide tours of their businesses; (3) to participate on advisory councils; and most importantly, (4) to provide work experiences. The varying foci of the programs dictated the extent to which each of these uses employers were engaged. The consensus among program personnel was that their programs had generally been successful in working toward their program's goals regarding employer involvement. This "success" may result from a highly organized program administration or smooth program implementation to simply the sheer determination by program personnel to see the program succeed.

Programs within the private sector involvement focus area as well as the other focus areas found it necessary to use public sector placements to a greater extent than had been anticipated. One reason for this is identified by a program operator:

In terms of finding job opportunities for youth we have been doing fairly well up until the last month or so. We had anticipated finding much more employment during the Christmas holidays, but we just found there were not the jobs available we hoped there would be. We are particularly finding, within the last month or so, that the employment and job openings have been the least we have seen in a long time. As you probably know there are a number of individuals laid off and at present there are not a number of jobs open. There still seems to be a lot of interest from employers. They like the idea of being able to go to the schools and find students and work with people from the schools in finding students in their community or in the area where the business is located to get students, especially those who have an interest in their type of employment opportunity. But right now there just are not the jobs available, and that has caused a problem in some of our programs in helping youth get jobs.

Another reason precipitating greater public sector involvement was the type of work available. A field observer stated:

Almost all placements are within the private sector. The few public sector placements have resulted from students requests to gain certain types of experiences, i.e., library aide, teacher aide, which are not available in private sector employment.

The implication drawn from this statement was that program operators need to be sensitive to the career interests of youth participants when identifying work placements.

Two final inhibitors to the use of private sector employers were the refusal of CETA prime sponsors to allow placements in this sector and in other instances the delay of reimbursement of youth wages to private sector employers. Both situations reflect an uncertainty as to the interpretation of CETA regulations concerning the subsidization of employment in the private sector. At certain programs, this problem was resolved via almost exclusive use of public sector work placements.

Late program start-up and understaffing were additional factors with which some programs have had to contend. The former precluded ample time to identify potential employers. The latter resulted in a variety of program modifications—or perhaps less politely, deletions. Two situations suggest what can occur when staff are expected to do more than is reasonable. A field observer at a career awareness program provided the following:

During the first year of operation (1978–79), the vocational teacher/counselor had two scheduled class periods a day. That arrangement allowed him time to develop his program, arrange field trips, job experiences, and job observations. He had arranged with several businesses to have students work part-time on a temporary basis and without pay to have a work experience and learn about that particular business. During the school year (1979–80), however, none of the above has continued. There are two reasons for this. The first is a matter of time. In an effort to keep down class size, the vocational teacher now has a class each period. The main purpose of the class is career awareness and job acquisition skills. No provision is made for individual placement or supervision. Field trips also are not possible because of continuous classes as well as transportation problems. The second reason is the assumption and feeling that YET (another local youth program) can handle the actual job placement and supervision for interested students. There is, however, no referral system between the alternative school and YET. Also, there seems to be little if any communication between the two programs despite the fact that they are housed in the same building. The vocational teacher did not know if any of his students were being served by YET. He did agree it would be helpful if he knew so that he might supplement the student's work experience in the classroom and individualize the instruction for the particular needs of the student.

The second instance of understaffing occurred where career education specialists within the schools were expected to operate a career center and attend all the employer guest lectures held in the school. The career education specialists felt their time was better spent in the career center providing "concrete career information." The field observer noted that one way these specialists resolved their mandatory attendance at lectures was by scheduling as few lectures as possible.

Incentives/Disincentives to Employer Involvement. A question which eventually every program operator must resolve is, "What can this program offer employers as incentives to participate in this program?" Resolution of this issue is imperative if in fact youth employment programs are to succeed.

Full financial subsidization of work experiences in the public sector occurs at all reporting programs. Most programs subsidize 50% of a private sector placement, though a few also use a full subsidy approach here. There were extremely few instances of an employer paying the full wages of a youth. Wage subsidization was probably the most critical factor in the acquisition of employer participation as it allowed employers the luxury to provide work experiences which otherwise would not exist. One field observer related:

Students' wages are fully subsidized by the program and this has been a major incentive to employers. Many employers have stated that they would not be able to have another person in their facility if wages were not subsidized. Most employers like the method of subsidy, since not only does it relieve them of financial burden, but also it relieves them of extensive paperwork.

Another program's operator suggested that, "possibly 20 percent of the employers might have participated in the program if they had to pay—and (that) they would be mostly in the private sector."

A wide range of non-financial incentives have further influenced employer participation. At one program the following five features were identified as important: (1) the businessman's knowledge and trust of the job coordinator; (2) good past experience (with other programs); (3) prescreening of students by the program to determine their potential for success in specific work experiences—a matching process between youth and job; (4) flexibility of scheduling—as an alternative school the youth could work any time during the day; and (5) a growing positive program reputation within the community. This last point, program reputation, should not be taken lightly. Program personnel repeatedly identified it as an important factor when addressing employers. The experience at one program suggested the value of a good reputation:

Has the program's reputation helped or hindered? The project operator felt that in the beginning, when it was a generalized CETA reputation, it hurt. But now that they had a specific programmatic reputation, it helped. "Now that we have proven ourselves, the employers are coming to us."

Added to this, are factors mentioned by individuals from other programs. One such factor being the sense of "community obligation." A job developer identified this as a "strong commitment to the future of the youth in the community." The field observer at a rural program noted that:

Some employers are concerned about community obligations. For instance, one of the questions frequently asked of the job developers is where these kids come from. The employers are much more receptive to helping high school students from their own communities. Quite a few employers have mentioned that their children, when they were teenagers, had difficulty obtaining jobs and they support this program because of their empathy for youth.

An additional factor favoring these programs was the realization by employers of the importance of work experiences for youth. Combined with this was a desire by some employers to become involved with a youth early enough that the youth may be trained properly.

Numerous reasons concerning why individual employers refused to participate were identified through the conversations with program officials. Perhaps the most common was simply that the employer had no need for additional help. Small businesses, in particular, may fall into this category. These businessmen certainly cannot justify taking on additional help—even if it is free labor—if it means that current employees will have less to do.

A second factor repeatedly noted was the age of the youth and the labor laws. One program director noted that it was not refusal on the part of employers, but that there were "so many places we cannot put students." In particular, program operators have found it quite difficult to place 14- and 15-year-olds in work experiences.

Stereotyping of the youth in these programs by employers was noted at several programs. These misunderstandings ranged from a general "distrust" of high school youth to the stereotypical ideas about programs of this nature.

The program directors stated that the main barrier to acquiring job sites has been an initial rejection of involvement with the youth program based on stereotypical ideas about programs like these. Some employers have had contact previously with youth programs and have had negative experiences. Some of these employers have complained of the time required in supervising students and of not trusting youth in general. Several of these sites, who have been persuaded to take on students anyway on a trial basis and have had some positive experiences with youths from the project, are now willing to take on what they consider to be "high risk kids."

Additional disincentives encountered can be divided into two areas: those specifically program oriented and those more generic in nature. In the first category fall such factors as: (1) jobs requiring sophisticated skills—specific training of any nature before placement is not a feature of any of these programs; (2) inexperience of job developers and/or poor presentation of the program's purposes by youth to employers—this reflects the value of staff familiar with both the program and the community and of better preparation of youth prior to identifying worksites; and (3) the coordination of cooperating agencies in the acquisition of worksites— a problem which has slowed this process at one site was reflected in staff changes and limited staff time, which would be provided the program by the agency originally identified to locate jobs.

Issues impacting on these programs but not to any great extent within their control included: (1) the current economic condition which is not terribly conducive to small business expansion—one reason why employers were pleased with the full subsidy approach of several programs; (2) a reluctance to become involved in federal programs which may lead to auditing of their books and simply the forms and "red tape" that appear generally assumed to go hand in hand with federal programs—this was another area avoided via full subsidization of youth; (3) CETA prime sponsors who have refused to allow subsidization of private sector placements; (4) unions; and (5) public sector employer fears of state aid cuts. These last two factors, noted at one program were further explained by the program director:

We haven't been able to get into places that have unions because of the union rules. And, there is also that incident I told you about with the nursing home, where they were afraid if they took our students, they would receive a cut in state aid.

Distinction Between Public and Private Sector Placement. In an attempt to address the question of whether student placement in one employment sector was preferable to the other, program personnel were asked to make distinctions between these employment sectors. Data concerning this issue were received from only eight sites. However, each of these sites had placed youth in both employment sectors. The opinions/experiences related below are varied and at times contradictory, but at the same time provide an enlightening view of this issue.

Personnel from four programs noted that public sector employers take a greater interest in helping students. One program coordinator noted:

Students receive more supervision and there seems to be more opportunity for job training and skill development in the public sector jobs. Public sector employers seem more interested in helping our students and not just getting work out of them. Private sector employers and supervisors are not quite as patient. They seem more concerned with the profit motive and don't have the student's interest at heart.

One field observer suggested that this perception may be in part due to the nature of public sector jobs—their being more person/service oriented than private sector jobs.

In contrast, data from two programs suggested that public sector employers were more likely to accept behaviors which would not be tolerated in the private sector. A job coordinator related:

Well, public sector is non-profit, and in the public sector the student is, for all practical purposes working for free. There is no pressure in the public sector to perform. Whereas, in the private sector it's a profit motive; it's sink or swim. I mean in the private sector you get fired if you are no good, I mean you are gone. That is not necessarily true in the public sector. Public sector can afford to keep their less productive employees because they are free. Whereas, private sector can't afford to keep them. As you know working in the public sector you can slide by a lot.

The field observer added:

The public sector is seen as a place where one can "get away with" certain behaviors. Therefore certain kids who couldn't make it in the private sector are placed in public sector jobs. I see a hierarchy that a student can move through. First he must show the correct attitude in job orientation class. Then he is placed in the public sector. If he shows that he is a dependable, responsible worker, he is placed in the private sector.

The greater availability of public sector jobs, even when competing with other programs was one incentive to use this sector. As one director noted, these employers "always need help in some area." However, another program director was concerned that "supervisors in the bureaucracy are too accustomed to programs like this—the students are from just one more program, like many before them." The implication being that public sector employers may not be as concerned with the experience the student receives.

Some clear distinctions between these employment sectors have emerged. They include: (1) less permanence and chance for advancement in the public sector; (2) public salaries are not as good; (3) greater turnover in the public sector; and (4) a different variety of jobs exist between these employment sectors. This last point was identified at a private sector program. It was noted that use of public sector sites should not be excluded as there are some youth who have career interests which can only be found in this employment sector.

A final issue which was brought out at virtually all sites pertains to how youth are used at their work placements. This issue was also the one which received the greatest amount of contradictory views. To begin, one job developer suggested that there was less possibility of a youth in a public sector placement to be "used." The field observer related:

One job developer feels that the public sector offers a greater opportunity to students without the temptation to "use" the students to do just any job. She feels that the public sector is more committed to offering training for youth.

These sentiments echo the first quote contained in this section. In contrast, program staff at one site, which had to rely almost exclusively on public sector placements, were of the belief that this type of work was "make work" and that the private sector reflected the "real world." Staff at another program attributed the difference between programs to the profit motive of the private sector.

Both individuals feel that the public and private placements differ, but in subtle ways. They both feel that students receive more substantial work assignments in the private sector. They think the profit motive has something to do with this—a private businessperson is more likely to put the student to good use than someone in a bureaucracy.

Conclusions and Recommendations

The purpose of this final section is to briefly summarize several issues which Exemplary In-School Project personnel have identified as important to the involvement of employers in their programs. These issues reflect critical occurrences at individual as well as multiple programs. The following observations and recommendations, as suggested by the preceding data have been placed under three headings: Programmatic Issues; Employer-Related Issues; and Distinctions Between Public and Private Sector Placements. Each category provides suggestions which may be used in the development of new youth employment programs.

Programmatic Issues. Programmatic issues reflect those program features which can be directly built into a program, i.e., planned for, or which are under the control of program staff. For example, the method of employer contact can be planned, while follow-up of possible employment sites is under the control of program personnel.

1. Although a variety of approaches were tried, the most successful means of acquiring employer involvement was through *direct face-to-face contact.*
2. The hiring of staff familiar with the community and its employers enhances a program's ability to acquire a sufficient number of worksites as well as provide greater access to more specialized placement.
3. The use of program youth to identify potential worksites was attempted at only one site. The first year's experience in which over 700 interested businessmen were identified by approximately 140 youth, suggests that this approach be seriously considered. Two obvious advantages to this approach are the reduction of the workload placed on staff and the increased number of potential worksites which may be contacted.
4. Advisory councils or other supporting bodies can be quite helpful to programs in the dissemination of information about the program as well as the identification of worksites.
5. It is imperative that any linkages with the community, be they via advisory councils or individual encounters, be followed up. Failure to do so can decrease the ability of a program to acquire community support.
6. Late program start-up, i.e., start-up after the beginning of the school year (which occurred at virtually all of these programs), and understaffing are two factors which need to be circumvented if at all possible. Each contributes to a program's implementation problem: time available vs. tasks to do. Typically the end result is an insufficient level of attention to program components. If in fact there is a concern for employer involvement in the program, then sufficient time and staff need to exist to pursue this pro-

gram aspect. A pre-program planning phase will help facilitate both worksite acquisition and other program components.

7. The reputation of the program within the community can act as either an incentive or disincentive to potential employers. It is therefore imperative that every effort be made to present the program well and for program personnel to follow up on program contacts/commitments within the community.
8. One alternative school program has found that its flexible scheduling, allowing students to work at any time during the day, has enhanced its ability to acquire worksites. If a program's design is flexible enough to allow for this form of scheduling, it should be seriously considered.
9. The age of youth participants is a factor which must be considered when developing a youth program. For example, it may be more appropriate to develop a career awareness type program if the youth to be served are 14- and 15-year-olds—an age group that is quite difficult to find work experiences for due to labor laws.

Employer-Related Issues. These suggestions speak specifically to the experiences programs have had in acquiring employer participation.

1. Program personnel repeatedly indicated that without subsidies, very few employers would have participated. This may, in part, be due to the current economic conditions. Whatever the reason, financial incentives, at present, appear to be necessary.
2. All programs placing youth in the public sector fully subsidized youth wages. This is probably the only way public sector employers would accept youth, unless they volunteered, for the need for additional help goes hand in hand with limited financial resources.
3. While half and full wage subsidization have been used for private sector placements, the latter has greater advantages for employers. First of course is the additional help at no cost. More importantly is that the full subsidy approach allows an employer to become involved in the program and at the same time, not have to leave his books open for possible government auditing. Governmental interference in one's business is a concern of employers.
4. Stereotypical ideas among employers about youth, be they a special group or just youth in general, need to be confronted and allayed as best possible. It is here that a program's reputation can play an important role.
5. The sense among employers of community "obligation" or "commitment" and the idea that they can have an impact on the development of the students work skills are two factors which program personnel can use to help "sell" the program.

Distinctions Between Public and Private Sector Placements. Clearly these two employment sectors provide different experiences for youth. Program personnel need to be aware of the experiential needs of program youth when attempting to acquire work placements. Regardless of the employment sector chosen, the following have been identified as important factors to consider:

1. It may not be entirely appropriate to focus a program on either the public sector or the private sector as each provides different types of work experiences. The career interests of the youth being served should help dictate the identification of worksites.
2. A greater-than-anticipated reliance on public sector employers has occurred in these programs. One reason for this has been the refusal of CETA prime sponsors to pay for private sector placements. A clearer understanding of CETA regulations by both program personnel and CETA personnel would alleviate these misunderstandings. Subsidization in the private sector is allowed within certain guidelines.
3. There are varying levels of worksite supervision. Whether one sector tends to be more conscientious in this regard is debatable. Most likely the level of supervision depends on the specific employer. However, this does suggest that program personnel need to closely monitor the work experiences of youth.
4. How students are "used" by employers also needs to be closely monitored. These work experiences should emphasize a quality learning experience for the youth and not a material gain for employers.

This paper has reviewed a number of findings relevant to the involvement of employers in youth programs. The concluding recommendations suggest that employer involvement can be successfully achieved and further, they suggest methods to facilitate this process.

Reference Notes

1. Elsman, M. *Involving the private sector in youth transition to work programs: A literature review and the state of the art.* (Draft), a literature review prepared by the National Manpower Institute for Youthwork, Inc., 1980.

References

Mangum, G., & Walsh, J. *Employment and training programs for youth: What works best for whom?* Washington, D.C.: Office of Youth Programs, Employment and Training Administration, Department of Labor, Government Printing Office, 1978.

U.S. Department of Labor. *Youth Employment and Demonstration Projects Act planning charter.* Washington, D.C.: U.S. Government Printing Office, 1977.

Children and Youth Services Review, Vol. 2, pp. 113–134, 1980
Printed in the USA. All rights reserved.

Awarding of Academic Credit for Work Experience: When and Why

Heather E. Wiltberger
Cornell University

The Youth Employment Demonstration Projects Act of 1977 (YEDPA) began the first national coordinated effort between the U.S. Department of Health, Education and Welfare and the U.S. Department of Labor to address the employment needs of youth. The intent of this legislation was to encourage collaboration between Local Education Agencies (LEAs) and Certified Employment and Training Act (CETA) prime sponsors in the design of youth programs sensitive to the education and labor market needs of economically handicapped youth.

Four different programmatic areas were created under the YEDPA legislation, one of which was the Youth Employment and Training Projects (YETP). A public nonprofit intermediary organization, Youthwork, Incorporated was created to channel approximately $20 million of the YETP funds into projects deemed exemplary as a means to demonstrate and evaluate the efficacy of different types of youth employment program strategies. One of the programmatic areas chosen for study by Youthwork, Inc. was programs designed to award academic credit for work experience.

The academic credit for work experience programmatic thrust exemplifies the means to coordinate the efforts of education and labor in helping economically disadvantaged youth prepare for the transition from school to the world of work.

Heather E. Wiltberger, Youthwork National Policy Study, College of Human Ecology, Cornell University, Ithaca, New York 14853.

Historically, youth unemployment rates have been high and
continue to rise (Adams & Mangum, 1978, pp. 1–3). Separate
policy and programmatic avenues developed by education and
labor have failed to adequately meet the needs of educationally and economically handicapped youths (Congressional
Budget Office, 1980, p. iv). Since 1965, the Department of
Education has spent $20 billion on compensatory programs
(through Title 1 of the Elementary and Secondary Education
Act) which have had a negligible effect on improving the reading levels of secondary school youth (Maeroff, 1980). Similarly, Department of Labor programs have been criticized as
unable to help youth in the job market as they have failed to
remediate youth to the extent that employers will hire and
retain them (Berry & Pine, 1979; Fuller, 1980).

Another critical difference in the two system's approaches
to meeting the employment needs of youth has been their
choice of target populations. Education sponsors programs
serving the whole population of school attending youth
whereas labor focuses exclusively on the economically handicapped youth. The former's work programs tend to attract
those least in need of these services (more mature and higher
socio-economic status (SES) youth). As such, those youth most
in need of labor market services do not partake of them (Graham, Note 1). As a consequence of their differences in service
populations; "One reason for urging greater involvement of
the schools in work experience, including the award of academic credit for what is learned, is to equalize educational opportunity out of school as well as in" (Graham, Note 1, p. 2).

To remedy the problems inherent in both approaches,
the Carnegie Council on Public Studies in Higher Education
recommend the teaching of basic skills through more programs that link the school and the work place (Maeroff, 1980).
It has been found that alternative education programs which
combine work experience with classroom instruction have
been most successful in encouraging youth to stay in school
and improve their basic competencies (Congressional Budget
Office, 1980, p. ii). The academic credit for work experience
programs are one means to join the concern and skills of labor
and education in meeting the employment and education
needs of youth.

The inter-institutional linkage which is a result of channeling funds through CETA to the schools to implement and operate the YETP programs is a crucial ingredient in the success or failure of these programs. As the school system has had the role of sponsoring these programs, it is important to determine how the academic credit programs are received and maintained under the auspices of the school system. The most sensitive component of the linkage between the CETA prime sponsors and Local Education Agencies (LEAs) is how and when academic credit for work experience is awarded to YETP participants.

Awarding Academic Credit—Problems and Prospects

Amid claims of a boon in experiential learning programs over the past decade (Keeton, 1978, p. 1) there are few comprehensive studies or surveys of the actual type, implementation and operation of experiential learning programs in the United States. This is especially the case for experiential learning programs which grant persons academic credit for work experience as defined by the Department of Labor. In presenting guidelines for the award of credit for work experience under the Youth Employment and Training Programs (YETP) the Department of Labor specifies:

The Congress fully intended that arrangements be made with the state and local education officials so that academic credit would be given for the skills and knowledge acquired through work experience that would deserve credit if earned through traditional schooling or in other ways. In referring to "competencies," the intent was not to limit recognition narrowly to job skills but also to basic skills of language and mathematics and to a knowledge of society and how to resume responsibility in it. The credentials that may be earned in these programs of work experience and training will recognize "competencies" in occupational skills and in the areas of traditional education as well. (U.S. Department of Labor, 1977, p. 1)

Certain types of experiential learning programs, such as cooperative education, have been in existence in the United States since the early 1900s. Sponsored experiential learning which occurs outside the classroom has been traditionally accredited by education institutions as vocational or cooperative education and more recently as career exploration. In these instances, the credit earned was an elective component of the student's degree program. Receiving academic credit for work experience in state mandated courses of study or post-secondary core curriculum is a new focus in and expansion of experiential learning programs. Although Illich (1970) and other "progressive" educators have proposed alternative out-of-school means of acquiring knowledge, the YETP academic credit for work experience programmatic guidelines are the first consistent national effort to implement joint education and work programs designed towards the acquisition of and credit for basic skills derived from work experience. Despite the novelty of this legislation, there are few existing legal restrictions on the award of credit for experiential learning across the United States.

Several different sources have the authority to sanction knowledge and skills gained by the population for competencies acquired through participation with an education institution. These include: State legislation, guidelines and standards; State Boards of Education; Local Boards of Education; Curriculum Committees (local, state and national); and Accrediting Associations (National Center for Research in Vocation and Education, 1979, p. 14). While many different institutions may be involved, the local school district has the primary legitimizing function of awarding credits for learning which occurs in their districts at the secondary level (Wurzburg, 1980, p. 9). Whether the subject area is mandated by the state or LEA, the LEA has the primary responsibility for determining the type and amount of academic credit awarded within their state's mandated minimum courses of study.

Predominantly in American schools, the local school board is the only agency authorized by legislative action to develop local policy governing the award of credit. Learning which takes place under the sponsorship of that local district, whether it is mandated by state or locally developed curricula, whether it is "in the school" or elsewhere, can be legitimately recognized by the districts through the award of credits.

There appears to be a great deal of local autonomy in the granting of credits. Building principals may have discretionary power over the awarding of credit. School districts can create courses of study and determine how many credits each is worth. (National Center for Research in Vocational Education, 1979, pp. 14–15)

At the post-secondary school level, the institution's administration has the autonomy of the LEAs in their credit determinations. Usually accreditation associations function much like the state in setting basic guidelines for the award of academic ·credits and formal recognition of learning. For both the LEAs and post-secondary institutions there are few restrictions on the award of academic credit for alternative methods of learning in mandated subject areas. A survey of state restrictions on awarding academic credit for work experience found only four states (Alabama, Kentucky, Louisiana and Oklahoma) which specifically did not allow experiential learning credit as it relates to CETA. In all but another four states (California, Florida, Minnesota and New York) post-secondary institutions were allowed autonomy in the awarding of academic credit (National Center for Research in Vocational Education, 1979, pp. 18–19). Although there are few state restrictions on experiential learning, the immense variety of state rules and regulations have been found to be confusing to LEAs attempting to implement these programs (Wurzburg, 1980, p. 6). While there has been local autonomy granted to most education institutions in the award of academic credit, the level of commitment of the various education institutions of the YETP-defined experiential learning programs is unclear. The Council for the Advancement of Higher Education (CAEL) is one of the few organizations which has attempted to discern the prevalence in the U.S. of work experience experiential learning programs.

The CAEL institution in 1977 undertook a survey of work experience experiential learning programs in post-secondary institutions to determine the differences between CAEL and non-CAEL members in the award of credit for sponsored and nonsponsored experiential learning. They found that nearly half of all institutions surveyed award credit for sponsored experiential learning, with CAEL institutions more likely than non-CAEL member institutions to do so

(Knapp & Davis, 1978, pp. 13–15). For nonsponsored experiential learning experiences, it was found that 47% of the CAEL member post-secondary institutions and 39% of the non-CAEL members have operational programs for recognizing nonsponsored learning occurring at these institutions. Over three-quarters of the post-secondary programs formally recognize the experiential learning which occurs from work experience activities through awarding academic credit towards graduation (Knapp & Davis, 1978, p. 15). Hence, approximately 35% of the surveyed post-secondary institutions award academic credit for nonsponsored learning, and about half of the institutions award credit for sponsored experiential learning. Certain types of experiential learning endeavors were more likely to receive formal recognition than others. It was found that career exploration, cooperative education, pre-professional training and internships were more likely than personal growth and development or cross-cultural experiences to receive credit.

Interestingly, it was found that although almost half of the post-secondary institutions do award credit towards graduation for experiential learning, there was a difference between what institutions said was the maximum amount of available experiential education credit and what students actually received. Non-CAEL members awarded 7–14 credits out of a maximum 26–40 credits, and CAEL members awarded an average of 15–25 credits out of a ceiling of 26–40 credits (Knapp & Davis, 1978, p. 8).[1] On the whole, this figure applies to an average of 30 students at each surveyed institution who were able to participate in the experiential learning programs. These figures suggest that despite the authors' claim of post-secondary institutions' commitment to experiential learning (Knapp & Davis, 1978, p. 15), few students participate in these programs, and the maximum potential for formal recognition of learning (credits) has not been realized. Another study (SUNY, 1978, p. 1) found that 15% of interviewed CETA participants might be able to receive academic credit from a post-secondary institution for their work experience acquired skills and knowledge. Possibly the CAEL findings are an over-

---

[1]The figures for nonsponsored experiential learning were not reported.

representation of post-secondary institutions' "commitment" to experiential learning which occurs outside the classroom, as the questionnaire response rate was 68% for CAEL members and 33% for non-CAEL members (out of a total selected sample of over 600 institutions). In summation the authors note:

The number of students assessed and the number of credits awarded vary from institution to institution sufficiently and in such a way as to indicate that there are other factors not investigated in this study that determine the acceptance and state of nonsponsored experiential learning at an institution. (Knapp & Davis, 1978, p. 21)

Wurzburg (1980) undertook one of the few studies which compared the acceptance of awarding academic credit for work experience between post-secondary and secondary institutions. He found that post-secondary institutions were more likely than secondary institutions to be receptive to granting experiential learning credit to YETP participants. Although he did not suggest why there was a difference between the two educational institutions, he did find that two-thirds of the studied prime sponsors reported that it was available in 1979, and that the majority of YETP programs had it as a regular program feature serving some participants. Similar to the CAEL study, Wurzburg found that while experiential work experience credit was available, only about 5% of the YETP participants were receiving academic credit for work experience (Wurzburg, 1980, p. 9).

Several reasons have been proposed as to why there is hesitancy in operating academic credit for work experience programs. One factor the CAEL study found to be related to a post-secondary institutions' commitment to experiential learning was whether there existed a centralized structure for administering the programs (Knapp & Davis, 1978, p. 19). Part of the reason this may have been an important factor in an educational institution's experiential learning commitment was that centralized administration was a means to assure the "quality" of the learning which received credit. Craft (1978) found in his study on assuring the quality of education in experiential learning programs that location of the program was an important determinant in the acceptance of experien-

tial work experience education programs. He suggested that
internal monitoring and control of programs was more difficult for institutions when the programs or learning occurred
off the institution's campus, and hence it was harder for institutions to determine the learning which was acquired (Craft,
1978, p. 38). Control of the learning situation as the means to
assure quality was also found in the National Center for Research in Vocational Education study (1979) to evoke hesitancy in educators' acceptance of awarding credit for out-of-
class work experience.

Most educators contacted express a genuine concern for the economically disadvantaged unemployed or under-employed persons
which CETA seeks to help. However, there is some despair over
whether, realistically, it was possible to develop and maintain standards in areas outside the direct purview of the school. "Would not
the credibility of credit be diluted, or even the high school diploma
itself be downgraded?" (p. 120)

Assurance of quality relates to the difficulties educators
have with determining measurements of competencies acquired outside the traditional classroom. Past studies of the
awarding of academic credit for work experience have not
been specific about how to award credit, other than to caution
against awarding credit solely on time-based measures (Graham, Note 1, p. 2). Further, few programs exist nationally
which have developed performance evaluation techniques for
work experience learning as it relates to traditional core curriculum (SUNY, 1978, p. 3).

An integral part of the problem is that educators do not
know what can, or is learned at the work site. In 1979 a pilot
study of the applicability of CETA jobs to educational credit,
one of the educators interviewed noted:

Perhaps more CETA workers could be granted credit for on-the-job
experience if we understood a little bit more about what is happening on various jobs and about policies and practices of our institutions in granting academic credit for work experience. (University of
Wisconsin-Green Bay, 1979b, p. 1)

Beyond confusion over how experiential learning techniques relate to traditional in-class academic credit course-

work, there are different interpretations concerning the type and amount of credit which could be awarded for work experience derived learning. As Craft (1978) found in an earlier survey of post-secondary institutions:

Faculty assessors in 24 different institutions were given a common body of evidence concerning student performance on certain interviewing skills. The assessors were asked to state what credit awards, if any, they would recommend at their institutions for the learning achieved. Although in agreement as to *what* had been learned, the assessors differed significantly among themselves as to whether the achievement deserved academic credit, undergraduate credit, or no credit. Though all the institutions were educating students for professions in which interviewing skills would be important, they were not in agreement as to whether it was their task to develop those skills as part of the intended outcomes of their degree programs. (p. 40)

In sum, although a number of studies have suggested that educational institutions are receptive to experiential learning programs, it appears that only a minority of youths actually receive academic credit for work experience despite the availability of these programs. Acceptance of awarding academic credit for work experience has been found to be contingent in part on what type of educational institution sponsors the learning, and where the program is located. Another concern which has been found to affect the acceptance of experiential learning credit programs has been the lack of understanding on the relationship between the work experience and academic subject mastery. Intrinsic in this argument is disagreement between educators on the meaning of formal education; when, and how much academic credit should youth receive for nontraditional experiences?

A Research Assessment

Eight of 11 projects funded by Youthwork, Inc. for 1980 in the focus area of academic credit for work experience as Youth Employment and Training Projects Exemplary In-School Demonstrations were selected for study. Three of the Youthwork, Inc. projects in the focus area of academic credit work experience were excluded from study because incomplete data was obtained from these sites. Three of the projects are extensions of previous programs, whereas the remaining five projects are new programs. The projects are located primarily on the East Coast ($n=4$) and the South ($n=2$) with the remainder in the North Central ($n=2$) region of the United States. Areas of location of the projects ranged from population densities of major metropolitan proportions to rural areas with populations of less than 10,000.

Program Characteristics. The academic credit projects are designed to help economically disadvantaged youth make the transition to the work world by providing youth with work exploration and placement in the public and private job sector. As an incentive to participate, to help them economically, and to stimulate real work experiences, they receive minimum wage payment for their job placements. Additionally, the participating youth are awarded academic credit for their participation. This second dimension is an inducement for the target population, potential dropouts, or dropouts to remain/return to school and to earn credits towards graduation. The projects offer a gamut of services to youth: psychological, educational and vocational testing; career education guidance counseling; remedial education; job readiness skills classes, career exploration; and job placement.

The academic credit projects vary greatly although they have in common the basic feature of awarding credit for work exploration/experience. Two of the projects are post-secondary programs (one is affiliated with a community college and the other with a state university) and involve young adults aged 18–21 years old. The remaining projects serve a 14–19-year-old population. These latter six projects are located in a variety of settings: three are in self-contained alternative schools, and three projects are physically located in school buildings. Two of the projects also cut across these categories. One has seven high school sites and a community college site and another has both an alternative school and a public nonprofit site. The size of the target population to be served ranged from 38 to approximately 700 youths.

Methodology. A number of different data collection methodologies were implemented at the eight project sites to provide information for this analysis. Trained participant observers, located at the eight Youthwork, Inc. projects provided three forms of data for this report. The first method used by the participant observers was transcription of their program's operations and interactions based on a focused analysis packet concerned with issues of program operation. Over 500 pages of focused on-site observation data were generated in the form of protocols by means of this method. This information was cross-validated through a comparative analysis of several thousand pages of protocol data provided by the on-site observers at these projects during the fiscal year 1979. The second data collection methodology used by on-site observers was unstructured questionnaires which followed the outline of the analysis packet on issues of program organization. The third method employed by seven of the on-site observers was narrative summaries of observers' perceptions of the characteristics of their project's program organization. This third data methodology was especially useful as a means of triangulation of findings, as it provided a means to cross-validate the researchers' conclusions from the protocol data by comparison with the on-site observers' impressions.

Findings: The Determination of Academic Credit— Organization

Whether academic credit is granted, what type and how much credit is awarded to YETP academic credit program participants is determined by three different organizations: the LEA, state, or post-secondary institution. Depending on the population served and the project location, the academic credit for work experience project staff negotiated with these organizations to determine the award of academic credit to participants. Table 1 summarizes the relationship in the granting of credit between the eight projects and the accreditation institutions. The credit negotiation process between the projects and the educational institution varies contingent upon which education organization has authority over the recognition of academic credit.

TABLE 1
Relationship Between Programmatic Model and Education
Organization in the Granting of Academic Credit

Programmatic Project Model	Education Organization		
	State	LEA	Post-secondary Institution
In-school	0	3	0
Alternative school	2	1	0
Post-secondary	0	0	2
Total	2	4	2

The state has discretionary power over the granting of academic credits at two of the alternative schools and is involved in setting minimum competency levels for graduation at one in-school project. The accreditation process at the two alternative schools took place before the inception of this study, and hence cannot be documented here. Aside from annual curriculum and program checks, the state appears to have allowed these two projects to decide for themselves the design of courses, curriculum and competencies (within state-mandated course minimums). The states allow more autonomy and local project authority in credit arrangements to the alternative schools than do the LEAs to their affiliated youth-work programs. The most stringent requirements are set by post-secondary institutions.

The LEA is involved in deciding curriculum, courses, and competencies at four of the studied academic credit projects (three in-school and one alternative school). Determination of credit arrangements between project staff and the LEA occurs on an individual-by-individual student basis at three of the four projects. At the LEA-affiliated alternative school, whose participants come to the program from a number of different public schools, the credit process is described by the on-site observer as follows:

Academic credit is granted in subject areas defined by the public school in which the student is formally enrolled. English, math, social studies and physical education are common to all local public schools. Other subjects may differ from school to school. Credits are granted in accordance with the policy of the individual school . . . In other words, all granting of credit must be handled on a school-by-school basis.

Two in-school projects negotiate with the LEA on a similar basis, where participants' credit arrangements are made through interactions with the public school (LEA) teachers or guidance counselors and project teachers. This is particularly the case for state minimum courses of study (i.e., basic skills), as opposed to electives. A learning coordinator at one in-school project said:

For some academic courses where the students are to get YETP credit, I have gone to the regular high school teachers of the courses and found out what teachers expect of their students and what activities occur in regular classes. If I feel the YETP student cannot meet the regular course objectives, then I modify the course and call it independent study.

Academic credit and course work is predetermined by the LEA curricula for the project participants in the area of basic skills. Project teachers work with LEA teachers to assure that participants meet the LEA course and competency criteria. This negotiation process occurs when project academic credit plans for a youth are being designed between the LEA teacher or counselor and the project staff. Once a youth becomes a program participant, the LEA is no longer involved in the participant's project educational experiences. The LEA does not actively monitor the "quality" of the youth's educational services or academic credits at these two in-school projects.

The final in-school project is organized differently than the other two in-school projects. Instead of reporting directly to the LEA, they have been integrated into a special education program at the school site and negotiate with that program. Indirectly they are involved with the LEA as their teaching staff are teachers from the school system assigned to the Youthwork program. Credits and courses are determined by the other alternative program at the school, although essentially the credit coursework is the same as the site's public school curriculum. The on-site observer explains:

Up until now the public school's department heads have not been involved with the YETP program because the school's alternative program has made the decisions as far as what was taught without input from the department heads. Most of the teachers in the YETP project were assigned to it from the public schools because they were lowest in seniority, not because they were ideologically committed . . . the teachers run their classes as they please. The YETP program is a lot of extra work for them as they are supposed to make sure students do not work in class on competencies they are assigned to learn on the job. The teachers ignore this and do not treat the YETP student's curriculum any differently than the regular alternative education program student's curriculum.

In this instance, the public school alternative program is responsible for monitoring the academic credit arrangements for participants although they have allowed more autonomy in the initial choice of competency levels than the other two in-school projects. In part this may be because the project teachers are from the school system and know the traditional curriculum well enough to match learning contracts and competencies with the public school's measures of subject mastery.

The post-secondary-affiliated projects are similar to the LEA-affiliated projects in the determination of credit for Youthwork participants. Credit is awarded to Youthwork participants at the two post-secondary projects when they meet the standards outlined in the institution's core curriculum. Independent study courses do not have to meet such rigid competency requirements. A post-secondary observer explains:

The post-secondary institution would not approve the awarding of credit for direct work experience, so through curriculum design the project staff attempted to circumvent this problem. None of the academic credit is granted in lieu of taking a traditional curriculum course. The complete course of study includes basic courses and program courses, much like a traditional college program with a major subject.

The two post-secondary projects differ in the process of obtaining credit for Youthwork participants. At one project the students enroll in the institution's regular courses, and at the other project the project teaching staff teach the class material themselves from the post-secondary course syllabus. Both projects rely on tutoring of participants in core curriculum, with credit determination negotiated between project and the post-secondary teaching staff. The post-secondary administration decides the basic guidelines, such as whether participants get credit for work experience, and rely on their teaching staff to negotiate with the project staff and individual participants on the acquisition of academic credits. Regarding credit arrangements, the post-secondary institution is the least flexible of the project-affiliated educational institutions.

Where projects have to negotiate with several different schools (which includes three projects) problems emerge. Aside from being time consuming and limiting in the types of credit awarded and for what type of mastery, there is confusion over how much credit can be awarded. An LEA-affiliated project observer discusses some of the problems of granting credit to Youthwork participants:

The awarding of credit varies from one school system to another. One school may say, "Because we assume the students will learn English in school and at work we will give them full credit for English." Another school in the same situation may say "We will give the student half a credit for work and half a credit for English." Each school determines its own requirements for distribution of credits. Each school can make whatever it wants into an academic credit.

There is evidence from the observational data that the process for determining academic credit is changing. This is particularly the case for those projects affiliated with an LEA or post-secondary institution. Originally, these projects (three in-school and two post-secondary) were stymied by the education authorities in the granting of credit to Youthwork participants.[2] Over the past year, negotiations have led to greater acceptance of the projects. One post-secondary Youthwork project teacher said:

I think what is going on is that we have had some successes with the students. The faculty sent us some students they thought were real losers and they are turning out well. They are getting jobs now. I think that helps a lot.

[2] See (Rist, 1979a, pp. 74–80) Youthwork National Policy Study *Interim Report #1*, for start-up problems of projects and the lack of commitment by LEAs to the Youthwork academic credit projects in awarding both basic skills credit and work experience competency-based credit.

The process of institutionalization of the academic credit projects and their evolving relationships with the LEAs will be examined in a forthcoming report. At present, the relationships are having clear ramifications for the functioning of the projects, especially in regard to credit arrangements for the student participants.

The Determination of Academic Credit—Competencies

Negotiating with the LEA or post-secondary institution for accreditation of learning or skills acquired by youth, the Youthwork Academic Credit projects have designed several means to ascertain the level and type of achievement of their participants. Contingent on the credit arrangements made with the LEA or post-secondary institution, the projects "measure" youth performance or learning through the use of learning contracts or competency tests. Learning contracts are individualized and are designed by either project teaching staff by themselves or with input from LEA teachers or guidance counselors. The contracts are designed to measure youth mastery of skills or knowledge through matching objectives with behavioral indices of achievement. Competency tests can be part of this process, or indirectly related by means of acquiring credits through passage of LEA, state or post-secondary standardized competency tests. A standardized competency test, the GED, can also be employed to quantify and accreditate knowledge acquired by project participants.

Seven of the eight observed academic credit for work experience projects were granting academic credit to participants during the Fall 1979 school term. Credit was awarded to participants for both elective or work-study and basic skills (core curriculum) coursework. The one project which was not granting credit was unable to do so because of problems in developing learning contracts and measuring competencies.

This project exemplified a process that six of the eight studied projects were undergoing. As the projects entered their second year of operation, they began to develop new procedures or refine old ones so as to determine measurement of competencies or acquired knowledge skills. Why projects are trying new methods is discussed by the observer at an alternative school:

The program coordinator feels that they are getting closer to a working system of awarding academic credit by trying new ideas to see if they work. She felt that they would develop a theory later. No one seems to know exactly how to do it.

In the effort to develop new procedures so as to enhance program services, one project rendered itself incapable of granting credits. As was explained by the on-site observer:

This fall they decided to pretest students on their curricula for the entire school year, not just for the competencies the student might acquire at the worksite. Pretesting began in October 1979 for math and English subjects, and it took the students two-three weeks to complete these tests. For the social studies component, most students took five-six weeks to complete the pretest. The xeroxing of these pretests alone cost $500. The tests are still not marked as of mid-December, as the two aides who were supposed to mark the tests quit. It took one aide, before she left, one full day to mark the math tests for one student: Hopefully, contracts will be established for the students once the tests are marked.

Five of the other projects are also working on their learning contracts or means of determining credit, although they have not become paralyzed by this process. One in-school project has not changed its credit procedures as the project staff are satisfied with the process which was developed last year. The other project which has not changed is a post-secondary project which has its course competency levels set by the faculty. In both cases educational institutions defined competency levels so projects did not need to try innovative approaches. Otherwise, six projects (including the stalemated project) have devised new or refined competency determinations and learning contracts.

The ways these projects are changing their measurement of competencies and expectation of participants differ. Thus far, employers have not been observed to be involved in ascertaining youth's competencies at any of the eight projects. Employers are asked to report on attendance and general attitude of the participants, which is factored by project teachers into the youth's course grade or award of credits. Competencies and receipt of credit, for the most part, are determined by passage of written tests, turning in products and for all but three projects, attendance records.

Involvement of work site supervisors in ascertaining competencies is one means of relating the work experience learning and skill attainment into the youth curriculum and academic coursework. Two post-secondary projects and one alternative school have begun to involve work site supervisors in the measurement of youth competencies and teaching of youth skills.[3] The observer at an alternative school reports:

Right now they are attempting to involve more employers in the awarding of credit through a reading and writing workshop that is planned for the near future. The program is going to insist that all employers attend this workshop and try to pressure them to become involved in integrating teaching skills on the job.

Seeking input from supervisors is in response to problems encountered at the work site where students were not properly supervised. Without proper supervision youth participants were not able to integrate the skills gained through work experience with their academic and educational needs. At an alternative school:

Some of the employers have not been able to provide the close supervision some of the students need. The director hopes to be working with employers to help them develop techniques for supervision that require minimal time, yet provide the students with the attention and directions that they need to have.

One post-secondary project beginning to involve the employer more in the process of evaluating and teaching youth participants at the job site has encountered problems in doing so. The change in procedure was requested by the prime sponsor and entailed having work site supervisors sign a paper acknowledging their responsibilities to the youths. This has

[3]This is beginning to occur at one other in-school project, but has not been as active a process. The other projects do not involve the employer in the competency criteria and objectives, although the project staffs do integrate work experience gained skills and knowledge into the contract or competency criteria.

not proved to be successful in integrating the work experience into the youth's competencies plans or in making supervisors more responsive to youth's skill and knowledge needs. This procedure has been documented to frighten potential supervisors from employing youth at their work sites. One teacher at this project said employers responded to signing the document and paperwork by saying:

"I will be happy to take the kids, but I am not going to fill out any papers." The teacher then commented, "So what am I going to do?"

Not only are employers hesitant to become involved in this documentation process, the teachers at this post-secondary project themselves have not been committed to this mandated procedure. They have had to respond to faculty pressure in designing their curriculum and have had to conform to the institution's competency determinations. As one teacher explained:

We have to make sure the school system's objectives are met first. I have to see, for example, that a student covers all units of a sociology syllabus first.

This project has been thwarted in its efforts to develop work experience related competencies because of this lack of curriculum autonomy, and also because they have been unable to define the objectives of the post-secondary curricula. When asked why they have been unable to develop objectives and measures of attainment in their learning contracts, one teacher responded:

My problem with the college faculty is that they know nothing about education. I think if you asked them for the objectives of their courses they would say "each student has to write a paper." Academicians are concerned with memorizing facts, not real learning. They want students to memorize facts; not learn the basic sociological principles.

The other three projects (one in-school and two alternative schools) are refining their competency/learning contracts in several ways. The in-school project is in the process of making several changes: (1) increasing amount of credit possible to obtain, (2) streamlining competency related paperwork, and (3) focusing more on the intent of the coursework and less on the course (specific) objectives. One of the alternative schools is trying to individualize competency criteria for coursework and more thoroughly analyzing each youth participant's economic and social background. The other alternative school is in the process of discerning participants educational and course needs as a means to assure participants meet graduation credit requirements. This process is beginning to entail a pre- and post-test of participant's competency levels in math, English, social studies, and science.

Discussion

Previous research (see Knapp & Davis, 1978; Wurzburg, 1980) has suggested that post-secondary institutions are receptive to experiential learning programs. In fact, Wurzburg found that post-secondary institutions were more likely than secondary education institutions to grant academic credit for work experience under the provisions of YETP. The findings of this research are the opposite; LEA secondary schools were less stringent than post-secondary institutions in the award of academic credit for work experience to program participants.

The literature (see Craft, 1978) has suggested that where the experiential learning program is located may be partially responsible to the reception alternative education programs receive. The difference between the secondary and post-secondary programs cannot be explained by this phenomena. Only one of the five programs in the categories of secondary and post-secondary YETP programs is located off the school grounds. As such, the location of the program does not seem to be a crucial barrier to the reception of experiential learning programs. Monitoring the programs and assurance of "quality" appears to go beyond direct institutional control.

One reason why the secondary schools have been more receptive to granting credit for experiential learning YETP participants is that these institutions have been found to not have been as concerned about the quality of learning which occurs in their institutions as the post-secondary institutions have been. Assurance of quality and monitoring of learning has not been present at the LEA secondary institutions possibly because of the difference in client population. An earlier Youthwork National Policy Study (Rist, 1979b, p. 49) found that secondary schools were receptive to the YETP programs in part because "troublemakers" and other educational "failures" were taken out of the regular classroom and separated from the mainstream into the YETP programs. Secondary schools are mandated to serve all youths until their sixteenth birthday; which is a difficult undertaking given the difference in educational aptitude and motivation of the total youth population. Post-secondary institutions, on the other hand, select their client population in a manner to achieve as homogeneous a group as possible. With a client population selected on their ability to perform at the post-secondary level, there is neither the need nor the desire to sponsor or create special programs for their clients. More research is necessary to explore this proposition.

Developing competencies and learning contracts to "measure" youth achievement in receiving academic credit for work experience is an ongoing process at all the studied YETP projects. To date, employer involvement has been minimal in the assessment of youth's accomplishments and design of tasks specialized to meet youth education and employment needs. Because of the individual needs of YETP participants and the lack of applicable experiential credit guidelines, projects have had to evolve their own credit awarding procedures. Integration of the work experience into academic subject and curriculum areas is just beginning to be systematically undertaken at several projects. An important area of inquiry, the procedures and outcomes developed by projects which award academic credit for work experience will have to be longitudinally studied in the future. How much credit, and for what type of subject mastery needs to be further explored.

Reference Notes

1. Graham, R.A. *Youthwork projects having to do with academic credit for work experience.* Unpublished manuscript, Washington, D.C.: Youthwork, Inc.

References

Adams, A., & Mangum, G.L. *The lingering crisis of youth unemployment.* Kalamazoo, Mich.: W.E. Upjohn Institute for Employment Research, 1978.

Berry, J.M., & Pine, A. Black teenagers fear "deadend" jobs. *Washington Post,* December 8, 1979.

Congressional Budget Office. *The federal effort for high schools—A preliminary analysis.* Washington, D.C.: Human Resources and Community Development, Government Printing Office, 1980.

Craft, W.M. Overcoming the problems of accreditors with experiential learning. In M.T. Keeton & P.J. Tate (Eds.), *Learning by experience—What, why, how.* San Francisco: Jossey-Bass, Inc., 1978.

Fuller, B. Carter's program for youth. *New York Times,* February 12, 1980.

Illich, I. *Deschooling society.* New York: Harper and Row, 1970.

Keeton, M.T. Assuring the quality of educational programs. In M.T. Keeton & P.J. Tate (Eds.), *Learning by experience—What, why, how.* San Francisco: Jossey-Bass, Inc., 1978.

Knapp, J., & Davis, L. Scope and varieties of experiential learning. In M.T. Keeton & P.J. Tate (Eds.), *Learning by experience—What, why, how.* San Francisco: Jossey-Bass, Inc., 1978.

Maeroff, G.L. Slow reading youths are focus of a $2 billion education-jobs plan. *New York Times,* February 18, 1980.

National Center for Research in Vocational Education. *Work experience and academic credit: Issues and concerns.* Columbus, Ohio: Ohio State University, 1979.

Rist, R.C., et al. *Forging new relationships: The CETA/school nexus.* Ithaca, N.Y.: Youthwork National Policy Study, Cornell University, 1979. (a)

Rist, R.C., et al. *Strategies for coordinating education and employment services: A preliminary analysis of four in-school alternatives,* (Occasional Paper #1). Ithaca, N.Y.: Youthwork National Policy Study, Cornell University, 1979. (b)

SUNY. *Guide for awarding academic credit under the Youth Employment and Demonstration Projects Act.* Albany, New York: The State Education Department, 1978.

United States Department of Labor. *The awarding of academic credit under the Youth Employment and Demonstration Projects Act of 1977.* Washington, D.C.: Employment and Training Administration, U.S. Department of Labor, 1977.

University of Wisconsin-Green Bay. Results reveal "creditable" learning on CETA jobs. *Update,* (Vol. II, No. 1). Wisconsin: Office of Educational Research and Development, 1979. (a)

University of Wisconsin-Green Bay. Study of credit for CETA work underway. *Update,* (Vol. 1, No. 4). Wisconsin: Office of Educational Research and Development, 1979. (b)

Wurzburg, G. *Youth and the local employment agenda.* Washington, D.C.: National Council on Employment Policy, 1980.

Children and Youth Services Review, Vol. 2, pp. 135–157, 1980
Printed in the USA. All rights reserved.

0190-7409/80/010135-23$02.00/0

A Case Study of the Implementation of In-School Employment and Training Programs: The Functions of Program Administration

Mary Agnes Hamilton
Cornell University

Implementation, as it is addressed here, is about the metamorphosis of policy framed by legislators in Washington, D.C. into programs belonging to communities across the country. Involved in this transformation are inevitable discrepancies between a policy's intent and the eventual program actualities, between the vision and the reality, the theory and its application. The tensions are real. Any consideration of the implementation process must include the interaction between both poles as critical determinants of what eventually occurs.

This paper describes the implementation of 14 exemplary in-school programs funded through the Youth Employment Demonstration Projects Act (U.S. Congress, 1977).* Two functions related to program administration emerged as critical to implementation. The first function involved program delivery to the youth, especially the nature of staff roles and the staff

Mary Agnes Hamilton, Youthwork National Policy Study, College of Human Ecology, Cornell University, Ithaca, New York 14853.
* I wish to thank Ray C. Rist and Stephen F. Hamilton for helpful advice and criticism on an earlier draft of this paper.

relationships to the local educational institution. Negotiations, funding, compliance with regulations, and reporting to the program sponsor constituted the second administrative function. The ability of program administration to respond to both policy guidelines and community norms when carrying out these functions directly enhanced or impeded the implementation of the projects.

Pressman and Wildavsky (1973) state that it is not too surprising or useful to predict that the implementation of new programs will be difficult. Rather, they say that the helpful questions center on identification of unexpected obstacles to implementation, and an understanding of implementation as an evolutionary process.

Implementation is evolution. Since it takes place in a world we never made, we are usually right in the middle of the process, with events having occurred before and (we hope) continuing afterward. At each point we must cope with new circumstances that allow us to actualize different potentials in whatever policy ideas we are implementing. When we act to implement a policy, we change it. (pp. 190–191)

Once accepting implementation as an evolutionary process, policy makers and researchers can no longer expect new programs simply to be enacted according to detailed planning from Washington, D.C., or according to proposals accepted from local sites. New programs and research must then acknowledge the limits of experimental manipulation. The study of "planned variation" in follow-through revealed that local programs did not necessarily embody the distinctive approaches of the sponsors. The intended comparison among contrasting models for compensatory education were impossible because the models were not implemented consistently. As one reviewer of this effort has noted: "The underlying reasons for this result, of course, are that volunteerism was and is a major American political tradition and decentralization a central fact of United States' political life, especially in education" (Cohen, 1975, p. 155).

Studies of school innovation in the early 70s found that frequently school innovations were not implemented at all (Goodlad & Klein, 1970; Gross, Giacquinta, & Bernstein,

1971; Smith & Keith, 1971). The extent of the innovations ranged from curricular changes to new roles and organizational structures for staff and students. Sarason (1971) and Guskin and Guskin (1970) convincingly explain that most innovations are not implemented because they fail to take into account the cultural norms and practices of the existing institutions within which they are to be integrated. The problem set for this paper is to explain the functions of program administration that enhanced or impeded the implementation of federally funded programs.

Career Awareness Projects and Models

Youthwork, an intermediary non-profit corporation, was established in January 1978 through the discretionary funds of YEDPA (Sec. 348, a.1.) to assist the Department of Labor in exploring the dynamics of the in-school programs and their effectiveness in addressing issues in the transition from school to work for poor youth. (See U.S. Department of Labor, 1977, 1978; Youthwork, Inc., 1978 for information about the translation of YEDPA legislation into program guidelines.) Twelve career awareness projects began in 1978–1979 as part of the initial 48 Exemplary In-School Demonstration Projects funded through Youthwork. Two of these 12 completed their contracts in June and August 1979 respectively. Meanwhile three additional Non-Competitive Projects joined the career awareness area in the Fall of 1979 because of similarities in purpose to projects already in that area.

Five types of educational organizations operate the career information projects (see Table 1). The two local education agencies (LEAs) are school districts; one is in a metropolitan area (over 500,000 people), the other in a small city (between 50,000 and 100,000). Two consortia (CONS) represent joint efforts among school districts. One consortium links three separate districts in a rural area (population under 50,000), while the other involves 36 districts in a large metropolitan area. A third consortium in another large metropolitan area attempts to unite a board of education and a community college. One CETA prime sponsor operates a career information project in a medium-size city (between 100,000 and 500,000 people).

TABLE 1
Program Models at Career Awareness Sites

Program	Operator[b]	Alternative School	Employment Training	In-school Career Awareness	Work Experience
1	LEA				x
2	LEA	x			
3	CONS	x		x	
4	CONS			x	x
5	CONS			x	x
6	CETA		x		
7	COLL			x	
8	COLL		x		
9	COLL		x		
10[a]	COLL				
11	NPR			x	x
12	NPR				x
13	NPR	x		x	x
14	NPR				x
15	NPR				x
Totals		3	3	6	8

[a]Program 10 did not provide data.
[b]LEA = Local Education Agency. CONS = Consortium. COLL = College. NPR = Non-Profit Organization.

Four community colleges (COLL) operate projects: two in metropolitan areas, one in a medium-size city, and one in a rural area. Five non-profit organizations (NPR) also sponsor projects: two in rural areas, two in medium-size cities, and one in a metropolitan area.

Projected enrollments have ranged from 15 to 2,000. Two sites have served between 800 and 2,000 youth, seven sites served between 100 and 400 youth, and six sites were under 100 youth. Five programs have had more than one operational site. In sum, four projects have been located in rural areas, one in a small city, four in medium-size cities, and six in large metropolitan areas. The geographic distribution has been three projects on the east coast, five in the south and southwest, four in the midwest, and three in the west and northwest. Career awareness projects have been operational in 14 states.

Each of the 15 projects has emphasized one or a combination of learning situations for the participating youth.

These have included job-seeking skill training, personal awareness counseling sessions, information about different careers, training in group dynamics, on-the-job work experience, and counseling about personal directions for the future.

An analysis of service delivery at the various sites suggested four programmatic models. The four include (1) alternative school, (2) employment training, (3) in-school career awareness, and (4) work experience. A distinguishing feature for each of the four program models has been the context within which the learning experience took place, be it at the alternative school, at the employment training program, within the curriculum of a traditional school, or at the job site. Five exemplary project operators have administered two or more models under the same administrative umbrella.

Alternative School. Three projects have operated career information programs through alternative schools affiliated with the regional public school systems. The project operators (a consortium, a LEA, and a non-profit organization, respectively) have sponsored an alternative junior high, one staff member in an alternative high school, and two staff membersand a day care program in a school for teenage mothers and mothers-to-be. Students have frequently categorized their alternative school as the final option within the educational system by which they might achieve a high school diploma.

Employment Training. One prime sponsor and two community colleges have operated the employment training strategy. This approach has featured planned sessions on job-seeking skills, employment opportunities, and personal awareness. Clients have actively sought the program because of these attractive features, hoping that it would help them make the transition from school to work. Two programs have extensively trained peers, preparing them for the role of future trainers. The sessions have been independent of the school curriculum, meaning that the students have come outside of class hours. In the third instance, the students participated in an all-day, two month long program.

In-School Career Awareness. The in-school career awareness strategy introduced career information into the existing
services already present at traditional high schools. Six operators have sponsored such projects. The efforts consisted of
either setting up career information centers in district high
schools (two projects) or conducting workshops for high
school teachers, hoping that these teachers will incorporate
this information into their curriculum (four projects). In contrast to the alternative school and employment training approaches, the programs have been non-intensive, of short duration, and targeted toward large numbers of youth. Students
participated in projects by entering an information center or
by attending regular class periods taught by their teacher who
attended a project training workshop.

Work Experience. Eight projects have operated on the basis of a work experience strategy. The extent and form of
career information, guidance, and job-seeking skill training
that accompanied the actual work experience varied among
projects. Placements included both private sector and the public sector, large bureaucratic organizations, and small owner-
operated businesses.

The Study

Data for this study have been gathered by on-site observers at 14 career awareness sites for the Youthwork National Policy Study team at Cornell. The research method is
ethnographic because of its ability to report qualitative data
that capture the process involved in implementing programs
and describing the day-to-day life in those programs. The on-
site observers interviewed key informants and project participants at the settings and observed project activities. Interviews
and observations were supplemented by project proposals,
project newletters, third party evaluation reports, and standardized descriptive data of youth participants collected
through a Management Information System (MIS) and submitted to Youthwork. Such a triangulation of data helped to
develop a clearer understanding of actual program implementation as it developed in these settings (Denzin, 1970).

Findings

Section I describes the trends in program delivery within each of the four models. Staff roles and their links to the local educational establishment often determined enhancements and impediments to program implementation.

Section II addresses the administration of relations with the funding source which significantly affected projects in all four program models. Resolution of stressful relations depended upon the presence of organizational mediators, ideological commitment, and/or the lack of friction between bureaucratic norms of CETA and the local educational establishments.

I. Program Delivery

Alternative School Model. It appears impossible to separate the administration of career information projects within the three alternative schools from the overall administration of these schools. Narratives of staff meetings, and interviews with teachers lead one to the conclusion that administrative decisions by staff—be they principals or teachers—are made in accord with how the school operates and the particular identity it chooses to carve for itself. Decisions about discipline, teaching styles, and curriculum content stem from the administration and teachers' interpretations of what their approach should be. Program implementation of these decisions succeeded in part because of administrative structures that allowed this high degree of teacher participation, a crucial feature missing in the innovative school studied by Gross, Giacquinta, and Bernstein (1971).

Teachers at one alternative school actively pursued questions about the school's identity throughout the first fiscal year (1978–79) of the school. The principal at one staff meeting advanced clarification by introducing a two-page listing of unique characteristics of an alternative school, posing the question about differences between their being or becoming a "mini-traditional school" or a real alternative. A field trip to another alternative school provoked comments by teachers to the on-site observer about startling differences between "us and them." This continuing dialogue among staff indicated a conscious effort to keep their school from becoming a place of license for behaviors that caused the students "trouble" at their former school. The assumption among this staff was that a temporary refuge for such behavior would not help them re-enter and succeed in the traditional school. A second assumption was that an alternative school is only a temporary shelter, rather than a permanent one. Students have and will leave the alternative junior high school to enter the traditional high school. Emphasis on school success is partially evidenced by the yearly report from this school which stated that student attendance rates increased as their suspension rates decreased.

The teachers and principal at this alternative school designed the program to concur with their educational philosophy. Current levels of program staffing would not allow them to create an individualized program for the original projection of 200 students. Therefore, they lowered the target to 150. However, the maximum they still felt they could serve at one time was 50 students. With the complete support of the CETA prime sponsor, and the school administration, they were able to merge the program with an extended day school, and thereby increase the numbers served at any one time to 100 students by providing counseling services to the extended day school students. Actual school enrollment did not exceed 50 students. Thus this administrative link to another school in the district provided a resolution to the conflict between intensive individualized services and target numbers.

A teacher at a second alternative school explained how he did not separate his career information activities from what he did as a teacher in his alternative school:

He said that he would like the target youth to be able to identify with him and be able to stay in school. He wants them to stay around long enough so that he can get some career information to them. He said he has had to be extremely careful so that he is not just outright saying: "Hey, we're going to talk about careers." He indicates that they just turn off to very straight approaches. He said he had to go through the back door to reach them and so, in essence, his goal was to keep them in school, to keep them in contact, to build a relationship with them so that he could have some influence in their decision making relative to jobs and careers. Mentioned as a vehicle to build a relationship with these youth was a back-packing trip that he had just been on the past weekend.

In this instance, the teacher's primary concerns were the needs of the individual youth in his school and how the school's program responded to them. The project and the school allowed him this freedom to integrate materials and activities to the extent he saw compatible with their needs. Mangum and Walsh (1978), citing from a recent evaluation, *An Experiment in Career Education that Worked* (1977), suggested that these teachers' behaviors contributed to improved school conduct and employability skills in career planning and decision-making ability on the part of the youth.

Conclusions were that the success arose from a supportive atmosphere, ready availability and dedication of teachers, counselors and other staff, dealing with the intern as "a whole person" treating the school and program as a tool rather than an entity, providing a school experience congruent with realistic life goals and expecting the interns to make their own decisions and to perform. (pp. 101–102)

What makes such teacher behaviors possible are administrative structures within these alternative schools that support individualized instruction, planning, and creation of a responsive program. Sarason (1971) has noted it is remarkable that people who advocate innovations frequently do not allow teachers the time to work out, develop, and internalize those ideas for themselves (p. 207). Innovations reduced to simple "how-to-do-it" manuals or teacher-proof curricula are not likely to be implemented.

The third alternative school receives support from the director of the sponsoring organization in delivering services. The parent project administrator is viewed by the project staff and director at the alternative school as a mediator who facilitates their task of implementing the program. The director of the school elaborated:

The project administrator has helped the job placement person in letter writing and organizing her time better. The job placement person was a very good PR person but needed some guidance from him with her. He is is always there when a problem comes up. The high school had had funding problems with various aspects of its program. Specifically, the high school had problems with the equipment for the child care center. They wanted to get good equipment. It was expensive equipment, and he came up with more money through a local city university in getting a grant for them. He seems to, therefore, play the role of a trouble shooter, of a liaison person who helps out with specific problems when asked.

The strength of the links between the alternative schools and the local educational systems makes it possible for the alternative schools to operate. Two of the alternative schools receive additional staff members through the exemplary project, but rely primarily on the school system for their funding support. The other alternative school was able to negotiate an arrangement with the school system that allowed it to meet its target members without diluting its services to the core group.

Employment Training Model. The two employment training centers have been hampered by a time-consuming decision-making structure that continually necessitated the involvement of their sponsoring community colleges in program decisions. Partly because of this situation, the project director at one site resigned, while the second college project experienced a delayed start-up but did succeed in involving the college when hiring staff and when recruiting peer counselors and students.

The third employment training center sponsored by a local CETA office never gained the full support of the school system. The project encountered difficulty recruiting youth and teachers to its after school program. The program administration was often at loggerheads with the school administration, as both institutions wanted control over the program.

Deciding what to do with the students was never considered at the college centers, as that was straightforwardly described in the curriculum packets. However, the curriculum at one site involved 18 time-consuming steps in career awareness where the counselors trained peer counselors and then the other students. The counselor/trainer staff spent considerable time deciding their roles in service delivery; i.e., who would do what, and how that should be decided.

Low morale increased as the project did not reach any students during the first semester of operation, and lowered its projected target from 2,000 to 800, and then to 500 students. The lack of clearly defined staff roles in service delivery persisted as a problem. These problems became more visible and perhaps comprehensible as staff expressed concern about being "stretched" and the project being understaffed. Consequently the staff developed a coping strategy during the project's second and third semester by limiting their own personal involvement and by rotating the position of counselor coordinator among three counselor/trainers during the Fall and Winter of 1979–80. The on-site observer describes a conversation where the project director related his perception of the implementation problems:

He noted that the main problem evolved from a misperception on the part of DOL as to where the project was at the time of funding. His opinion was that when DOL/Youthwork funded the original project, they thought that all the planning had been completed and that the project was ready to be implemented. This, in fact, was not true, because a great deal of additional planning was still needed. In other words, the college submitted the proposal with the intent that it (if funded) would be a developmental project. DOL, however, funded the project with the understanding that the program was already operational.

Service delivery by project staff at the other college employment training center contrasted vividly with the above example. Staff worked with the students as "trainers" and "counselors" for eight hours during a four week period. The lack of role conflict or role ambiguity by staff members in addition to the time available for and required by the training curriculum contributed to implementing the program for 178 of the 200 targeted students in six months.

In-School Career Awareness Model. The four reporting in-school career awareness programs have serviced four to 20 traditional high schools each within populated areas of over 500,000 people. All four have attempted to reach youth while they were yet within the school building.

The administration of service delivery of this model has been strongly affected by the fact that the programs operated within the schools. Program deliverers, be they high school teachers or new project personnel, were constrained in what they could do because of the organizational context, i.e., the school, within which the programs operated.

When projects relied primarily on teachers within the schools for service delivery in their existing classes, the crucial element for project implementation became the identification or recruiting of potential target teachers who could receive training. Once trained, it was assumed that the youth in classes where teachers integrated the career awareness into their lessons received the service. Project implementation is then relatively easy, in that large numbers of students can be reached by distributing curriculum or demonstrating career awareness topics at workshops in the summer or during the school year. Here the implementation process does not attempt to integrate new structures within an existing school setting, but rather to confine the innovation to the structures within which youth and teachers already operate. The project is implemented as long as students attend classes of the target teacher even if the classes do not change significantly in content or in teaching style.

One such project encountered start-up problems when entering the schools the first year, especially in negotiating the training time of teachers and the collection of confidential data about the students using the Blackstone forms. It appeared from reports of early negotiations that project staff had to spend unanticipated time and energy in order to comply with regulations and procedures of the school system. Adjustments were made to relieve the problem of confidentiality and use of substitute teachers. Arangements were worked out school by school to satisfy the requirements of different headmasters. The result was greater variety in the implementation of the program than originally anticipated.

When the service deliverers are hired by the project and located within the schools, successful implementation must attempt to link project staff and organization with that of the school.

The project director of one site was located at a community college and one career specialist was located at each of five high schools. During the first year the specialists received little program direction as the director found himself tackling the many paperwork and reporting tasks for the project. Several specialists reported at that time that they took the initiative and established their own directions. During the Fall of

1979 the project director found more time to deal with program format, but by then the specialists had already established programs and were into the rhythm of their particular schools. The following account describes the dilemma experienced by a specialist who tried to integrate her program into the life of a school, yet found such behavior in conflict with the organizational needs of the overall project.

I arrived and as we (on-site observer and project director) started to talk the phone rang. It was the specialist from one of the high schools who was calling to tell the project director that she could not attend a staff meeting scheduled for that afternoon. The project director was visibly angry, reminding the specialist that the meeting had been arranged a while ago and part of her responsibility was to report back to these staff meetings so that some degree of coordination could be effected. The specialist had, however, scheduled a school activity for that day and could not postpone that activity (administration of career awareness inventory tests) to come to the meeting.
      After hanging up, he explained that one thing he had learned was that this arrangement of coordinating 5 specialists out in the schools and who had divided loyalties to the college and to the high schools was not an effective way to provide services. "Next time, I will let the schools supervise them and we will just have a liaison coordination arrangement."

This observation vividly portrays the delicate balance of membership in two organizations that the career specialists straddled in this project. Yet maintaining a balance is the essence of project implementation in this model that is so tenuously related to the school system.

      Work Experience Model. The eight work experience programs have attempted to provide career information along with an on-the-job experience for under 100 youth per site. Staff roles for program delivery at the five sites that reached (or nearly so) their projected student population were clearly defined and contributed to project implementation.
      One site has operated in five high schools with a staff of three persons in each school. These career information specialists have constituted a support team for the in-school career awareness component in the schools. Recruiting for the work experience component took place in career awareness

classes. For the work experience component the specialists conducted student training sessions before and during the work experience. Staff from the project administration offices of the non-profit organization developed the job sites. They also served as a liaison between the student and the high school support specialists by making site visits. In addition, they developed a manual that served as the basis for the curriculum used in training sessions by the support specialists. A picture of role clarity begins to evolve when describing the program administration of service delivery at this site. People were able to depend on others to contribute to the functioning of the project. An examination of one situation that may have impeded the project implementation furthers our understanding of the key dynamic that role clarity played. Two support teachers were interviewed by the on-site observer and shared their opinions about the role of work site liaison.

Support Teacher #1. The supervisors at work did not want to deal with the problems that came up; they thought we should do it and so they would tell the two liaisons and the two liaisons would tell us, and we would deal with the student. If I only had the job of vocational education coordinator, then I would deal with the situation right when it arose on the job. That was a problem that I had with this.

We were too far removed. We were there as a support system but were too far removed. And I would like to have been right in there when things were happening and not get the message two days later and track down the kid. I would like to go get in my car and go right out there and you know, talk about it right there.

Support Teacher #2. I am not sure how I feel about that because I think it is difficult to go out and get the job, find the job sites, and sell the employers and then still be the student's advocate. The communication would be a whole lot easier, but structurally, it would be much simpler, a much stronger hold on it, but I really feel it would be more difficult, on one hand, to have sold the employer into taking a student and then still be the student's advocate. I found that both school liaisons, almost out of necessity, had to take the employer's side in any of the small things that came up because they would come back and tell us, listen, we got these job sites, we promised this, this, and this. It is your job to make sure that the kids perform.

Alternative staffing structures were available to the program. But instead, a course was set by the program's operator at the beginning and staff complied with the master plan. While the above interview acknowledges these alternatives, the support team also knew that the project had a set goal to train and place 100 students within a given time frame. Accepting the planned roles allowed an efficient implementation at the expense of the participation of the support team in overall program design.

The trade-off of efficiency versus participation in program design explains the difficulty another work experience project had in project implementation. Staff hired to instruct and supervise placements for youth on an Indian reservation had a skeleton plan from which to work. Problems arose concerning the relevance of work for these youth, and how to create strategies for increasing their motivation. During this process new roles for staff and a new program design emerged, that would create two types of work experience responsive to students with different degrees of motivation and commitment to learning. This process of recasting the program took almost a year, and saw the resignation of the first set of service deliverers. The project continued to have the support of the reservation and the school district because of their belief that youth unemployment was a grave problem to which they had no solution, but were willing to support another group that might create solutions.

Another program created a unique solution to communication problems between the exemplary staff and training center staff. Project staff entered a sheltered workshop as a team so that similar but separate services could be extended to the CETA eligible youth, a new population of the training center. Initial months of parallel delivery caused organizational conflict over training center norms and expectations. As a resolution, exemplary project staff members joined the regular staff on equal service delivery lines. This meant that rather than create separate but equal services for the CETA youth, the capacity of existing staff to work with this new population was strengthened by the addition of exemplary project staff.

This kind of linking the exemplary project service delivery roles closely to existing roles in an organization lessened the competition among staff members, as well as increased

understanding and the ability of those staff members to provide services for the new target group. The stage has also been
set for the sheltered workshop staff to continue integrating
this group into its program after project monies are depleted.

The inability to clear the roles in service delivery with the
educational institutions—a school system and a community
college—explains slow implementation at another project.
After 12 months of funding, the site had placed 17 high
school students at work experience sites. The original projected total of 240 placements was lowered in the late summer
of 1979 to 91 high school students and nine college students.

The coordination problems experienced when trying to
bring the college peer counselors together with the high
school work experience students illustrated the almost impossible demands that had to be addressed before starting the
project. The Board of Education had 200 student applications
processed for work slots in Spring 1979. However, the college
had not yet trained the peer counselors for counseling these
students during their work. Over the summer, peer counselors were paid, but not for counseling the high school students. The project was placed on probation by the funding
agency. In the Fall of 1979 the on-site observer reported multiple unexpected decision making steps involving placement of
peer counselors in the high schools.

The stages of decision making about peer counselor roles
included discussions by the Board of Education and the Department of Employment about the academic and financial
qualifications of the 15 peer counselors. The unanticipated
number of decisions that had to be made surrounding the
unique feature of this project, the peer counselors, added to
the array of individuals with input into the decision-making
process. These included:

—The Department of Employment feared that acceptable academic ratings would eliminate most applicants from CETA
  eligibility.
—A college student group inquired about the minority representation of the peer counselors.
—The Board of Education coordinator, the college counselor,

the high school liaison contact, and the peer counselors had to coordinate schedules before peer counselors could visit high schools.
—The Board of Education and the college counselors changed the peer counselor role description three times: (1) counseling high school students in career plans; (2) sporadic counseling and filing applications; and (3) recruitment and intake of high school students.

Consequently, the multiple decisions necessary for project implementation hindered the project implementation from being efficient and effective (cf. Pressman & Wildavsky, 1973 for a similar situation).

II. Relationship with the Funding Source

The second function of program administration, the relationship with the funding source, affected implementation across all four models. The degree to which projects suffered delays in start-up, poorer program quality, or administrative "burn-out" depended upon three variables affecting the success of the relationship with the funding source: the presence of a mediator; the ideological commitment of the staff; and/or the degree of conflict between CETA/DOL organizational norms and those of the educational system to which the project was linked. Wurzburg's *Analysis of Prime Sponsor Experience Implementing the Youth Employment and Demonstration Projects Act* (1980) used the metaphor of "carrots and sticks" to describe the attractiveness of the grants and the ensuing enforcements (p. viii). Sticks for the in-school demonstration projects included reporting, MIS intake forms for project participants, CETA eligibility requirements for participants, and contracting a third party evaluator and an on-site observer.

An interesting commonality existed between the two alternative school sites, where one or two staff members were funded by project monies. In both cases, the overall project administration served the role of mediator, i.e., handled financing and paperwork for the alternative school project staff as well as for other activities that operated under the auspices of the project. This assumption of reporting and financing by the project administration freed the teachers from these responsibilities, allowing them time to plan curriculum, formulate goals, and work with students. It also meant that the YEDPA funding did not help a new alternative school get started, but rather, that project monies supported additional staff to work with the target group at an alternative school already under way.

The principal at the third alternative school served as the mediator. The on-site observer reported:

She feels in order to "get the job done" it is important to go "straight to the source." She frequently contacts the prime source directly through phone calls and letters— mostly the latter for clarification and information—so records can be more easily kept. The prime sponsor has been very helpful in explaining, clarifying, and interpreting various guidelines and regulations.

This project director perceived her behaviors as mediator as the most efficient way of handling questions on paperwork for this project. She managed the competing demands of her various roles, but also volunteered that separate people in the roles of principals and project director would have made "the program more ideal." One might speculate that her commitment to the alternative school's ideals enabled her to tolerate the competing demands and overload of both roles.

Projects working closely with school systems experienced difficulties when project start-up dates did not synchronize with those of the school year. For example, one project had chosen students for work experience but a delayed contract approval resulted in an eight-month postponement. In another case, a large project was not funded in August 1978 as expected. The project administrators insisted upon the importance of synchronizing the project start-up date with that of the school year and supplied their own organization's funds to begin the in-school career awareness component. They operated for two months in good faith that the funding sponsor would respond. The ability of the project operator to mediate with the funding source, as well as advance funds to cover costs before contract approval, allowed the project to hire staff to provide services at the start of the school year.

The long-term impact of such operating procedures invites skepticism and diminished enthusiasm about the glamour of YEDPA grants.

Uncertainty about funding levels, regulations, and the law itself is a distinguishing characteristic of the entire CETA federal/prime sponsor partnership. Habitual as such uncertainties are, and continue to be under YEDPA, they still exact an enormous toll . . . these factors have reduced the planning and development time for new programs, and hurt the credibility of sponsors with other local agencies. They have also created a difficult work climate and seriously undermined prime sponsor staff stability. In the end, they have almost certainly lessened the effectiveness of the programs. (Wurzburg, 1980, p. ix)

The prime sponsor experience reported above is similar to that of project operators. The CETA operating procedures have necessitated a firm ideological commitment and consequent energy and enthusiasm. Projects without the ideological support or mediator were seriously jeopardized by difficulties in contract negotiation as well as in meeting reporting requirements. These problems raise questions about what types of organizations are able to endure the strains encountered when operating projects through federal sponsors.

CETA eligibility requirements such as verification of age and income level have caused many site problems. Identification of youth by income level proved a difficult task in two metropolitan areas, because such procedures were in direct opposition to school policies respecting the privacy of the youth, and the lack of discrimination by income. Another site project director spent most of the project time attempting to comply with and understand the regulations with the result that the project staff did not receive direction about project goals. Two college projects had difficulty meeting age requirements because most of their students were over 21-years-old.

Another factor influencing the slow start-up rested in the difficulty identifying CETA eligible youth, i.e., youth under 21 years of age in the proper income category. An on-site observer elaborated on the difficulty in the following memo concerning an adjustment in the income eligibility category:

The guideline change for peer counselors referred to the fact that the college was using an obsolete income criteria scale. The more current scale from the prime sponsor allowed for a higher family income, thus, potentially qualifying more students since the students applying to the program tended to be in a higher family income bracket than was allowed under the obsolete scale. Meeting the income criteria of CETA is a problem in terms of getting enough eligible students, but it is not the only consideration. Other related problems in this area include age, the number of daytime students available, interest, etc. The 48 others were ineligible for many of the above reasons as well as such reasons as securing employment elsewhere and not meeting training standards. The bottom line of the problem is that the composition of this community college population tends to be over the age of 21.

The poor fit between the eligibilty guidelines of CETA and the actual college population contributed to low enrollment figures. The original plan (January 1979) to provide services to 2,000 youth was reduced to 800 in August 1979, and then to 500 in October 1979.

The receipt of YEDPA grants required schools to identify students according to income and age. Selection procedures that assured correct targeting resulted in separate services for the CETA eligible group at some sites in the alternative school, employment training and work experience models. Schools are not accustomed to distinguishing among students on the basis of family income. However, given the limited resources available, targeting is one way of meeting the employment training needs of these youth, needs that are not being met by conventional schools (Barnes, 1978).The danger of targeting is that it identifies a certain group of young people as "needy," and isolates them from their peers.

Conclusions

This case study of 14 in-school employment training programs explained how two functions of program administration—facilitating service delivery, and carrying on relationships with the funding source—related to successful implementation. Facilitating service delivery included especially helping define the roles of program staff in delivering the program to youth, and the relationship of staff to the local educational institutions. The study found that the four models tolerated or encouraged different degrees of role ambiguity, and experienced varying dependencies on the educational institutions.

The alternative school model allowed staff members to develop roles and programs consistent with the school's ideology. This development happened in part because of administrative supports that encouraged and facilitated staff in that process. Links to the local educational institutions operated as necessary supports toward these goals of individualized instruction for small numbers of students.

The employment training model depended upon the educational institutions for decision clearances regarding staffing or programming at two projects, yet these clearances proved time-consuming. One project where staff members had unclear roles, did not have the mechanisms to help overcome ensuing problems and failed to be implemented.

The in-school career awareness model operated within the schools, subject to the organizational structures of classes, schedules, teaching roles and curriculum. This model was the easiest model to implement as it depended either upon identification of target teachers who then delivered career awareness in some form to their existing classes or upon students entering an information center. Scheduling, space, and the confidentiality of students surfaced as the loci of implementation problems, as these may be the only areas where the schools could exert control over this model. Because of the reliance of this model on the on-going structure of the school, it appears that staff, other than teachers who are hired to deliver the services, must be keenly attuned to, and aware of, these structures, and project operators must likewise allow these staff to relate first to the school.

Successful project implementation at the work experience model tolerated little role ambiguity. Five projects that delivered services to almost all the projected numbers of youth, hired staff to accomplish set tasks. One of the five encountered initial conflicts between project staff and training center staff, and subsequently resolved the conflict by changing their administrative structure. Two projects encountered delays in servicing youth; one because of ineffective staff roles and a quest for more relevant solutions to programming, and the other because of coordination difficulties when several bureaucracies were involved in deciding what the roles of peer counselors should be.

Program adminstration also fulfilled a second function that affected program implementation: carrying on relationships with the funding source. All four models negotiated with the funding source for the grant and then received the funding, submitted reports and MIS forms on participants, filed CETA eligibility requirements for participants, and contracted observers and evaluators. The degree to which projects experience delayed start-ups, suffered administrative burn-out, or had poorer program quality depended in part upon: (1) the presence of a project mediator who would devote energy to these problems; (2) the staff's ideological commitment to what they were doing; and/or (3) the degree of conflict between the CETA/DOL organizational time lines and reporting procedures and those of the educational organization to which they were linked. The CETA rhythm and that of the schools were not always synchronized with each other. CETA needs to respond to some of the rhythms inherent in the school's organization, with particular regard to school-year scheduling, and in some models, the disadvantages of targeting only CETA-eligible students.

The degree of change incurred through the in-school career awareness model is on the order of a curricular supplement or an instructional modification, leaving the basic school structure intact. At the other extreme, incorporation of the work experience model into the school would mean a radically new program for some schools. One program succeeded in implementing such a project within the school, but services were delivered by project staff. No work experience programs relied on regular school teachers to supervise students.

In all of the programs, attempts to integrate the goals of the YEDPA's in-school career awareness component with the needs of local communities and the structure of local education institutions required administrative initiative and support. Successful programs transformed the abstract policy and guidelines framed in Washington into workable programs responsive to their own situations. The flexibility of the national guidelines made this local adaptation possible.

References

Barnes, W. Target groups. In *CETA: An analysis of the issues*. (A special report of the National Commission for Manpower Policy. Special Rep. No. 23). Washington, D.C.: U.S. Government Printing Office, May, 1978, 63–104.

Cohen, D. K. The value of social experiments. In A. Rivlin & P. M. Timpano (Eds.), *Planned variation in education: Should we give up or try harder?* Washington, D.C.: U.S. The Brookings Institution, 1975.

Denzin, N. *The research act*. Chicago, Illinois: Aldine, 1970.

Goodlad, J. I. & Klein, M. F. *Behind the classroom door*. Worthington, Ohio: Charles A. Jones, 1970.

Gross, N., Giacquinta, J. B., & Bernstein, M. *Implementing organizational innovations*. New York: Basic Books, 1971.

Guskin, A., & Guskin, S. *A social psychology of education*. Reading, Mass.: Addison-Wesley, 1970.

Mangum, G. & Walsh, J. *Employment and training programs for youth: What works best for whom?* A report to the Office of Youth Programs Employment and training Administration, U.S. Department of Labor. Washington, D.C.: National Council on Employment Policy, May 1978.

Pressman, J. L., & Wildavsky, A. *Implementation* (2nd ed.). Berkeley: University of California Press, 1973.

Sarason, S. B. *The culture of the school and the problem of change*. Boston: Allyn and Bacon, 1971.

Smith, L. M. & Keith, P. M. *Anatomy of educational innovation: An organizational analysis of an elementary school*. New York: John Wiley and Sons, 1971.

U.S. Congress. *Employment and Demonstration Projects Act of 1977*. (Public Law 95-93), August 5, 1977.

U.S. Department of Labor. *A planning charter for the youth employment and demonstration project act of 1977*. Office of Youth Programs, Employment and Training Administration. Washington, D.C.: U.S. Government Printing Office, August, 1977.

U.S. Department of Labor. *A knowledge development plan for the Youth Employment and Demonstration Projects Act of 1977*. Office of Youth Programs, Employment and Training Administration. Washington, D.C.: U.S. Government Printing Office, 1978.

Wurzburg, G. *Youth and the local employment agenda: An analysis of prime sponsor experience implementing the Youth Employment and Demonstration Projects Act*. Washington, D.C.: National Council on Employment Policy Youth Evaluation Project, January 1980.

Youthwork, Inc. *Youthwork knowledge development plan*. Washington, D.C., 1978.

Children and Youth Services Review, Vol. 2, pp. 159–183, 1980
Printed in the USA. All rights reserved.

The Part-time Employment of High School Students: A Research Agenda

Laurence D. Steinberg
Ellen Greenberger
Program in Social Ecology
University of California, Irvine

The high rate of unemployment among out-of-school youth in the United States—a problem in several other western nations as well—has attracted the concern of economists and policy makers at the highest governmental levels. At the same time, however, a related phenomenon has gone largely unremarked and unstudied. This phenomenon is the *increased* participation of in-school youth in the part-time labor force.[1] More American teenagers are working today, in absolute as well as relative numbers, than at any other time in recent years. Since 1940, the proportion of teenagers who work part-time while attending high school has skyrocketed: for 16-year-old males, for example, part-time employment has increased on the order of 500%; and for females of the same age, it has risen by a factor of 16 (U.S. Bureau of the Census, 1940, 1950, 1960, 1970). Current estimates indicate that about 50% of all high school juniors and seniors and about 30% of all 9th- and 10th-

Laurence D. Steinberg, Program in Social Ecology, University of California, Irvine, California 92717.

Preparation of this report was supported by a grant from the Ford Foundation. The authors share equal responsibility for this report. We wish to thank Laurie Garduque, Mary Ruggiero, and Alan Vaux for their helpful comments on earlier drafts of this paper.
[1]The populations of out-of-school and in-school youths are, of course, by no means identical. Out-of-school youths, who are so often the subject of youth employment policy discussions, are typically between the ages of 16 and 24, whereas in-school youths are primarily between the ages of 15 and 18.

graders are employed at any one time during the school year. The proportion of high school students who have any paid work experience before graduating is, naturally, much greater, since many teenagers move in and out of the labor market frequently.

Not only are proportionately more school-going teenagers working now than 30 years ago, but those who do work are doing so for greater amounts of time than did their counterparts in earlier years. For instance, only 44% of all 16-year-old, in-school male employees worked more than 14 hours per week in 1960, whereas 56% did so in 1970. The increase was equally dramatic for 16-year-old females: from 34% in 1960 to 46% in 1970. The percentage of younger employees (14- and 15-year-olds) working more than 14 hours each week increased between 1960 and 1970 as well (U.S. Bureau of the Census, 1960, 1970). In fact, we may be witnessing the end of a relatively brief historical period during which children went to school to the exclusion of work.

Are these trends cause for celebration or concern? What sorts of economic, political, social, and legal policies should we adopt with respect to teenage employment? And what kinds of information would policy-makers concerned with these issues need in order to make informed decisions? Our purpose in this paper is to lay out a research agenda pertinent to the study of adolescent part-time employment. This agenda involves examining: (a) the effects of working on the individual; (b) the place of part-time adolescent employment within the larger social structure; and (c) the significance of work in terms of cultural definition of adolescence.[2]

The Impact of Part-Time Employment on the Individual

A multidimensional conceptualization of adolescent work environments is critical to an understanding of the impact of employment on development. Curiously, social critics, policy-makers, and researchers alike typically discuss adolescent work as if it were a unidimensional phenomenon, i.e., as if all jobs were essentially equivalent in their activities, roles, and inter-

[2]The structure of our agenda is based, in part, on the theoretical framework provided by Bronfenbrenner (1979).

personal relations (Bateman, 1949, 1950; Douvan & Adelson, 1966; National Panel on High School and Adolescent Education, 1976; Panel on Youth of the President's Science Advisory Committee, 1974). The indiscriminate perspective on adolescent work seems especially remiss in light of a vast literature substantiating the multidimensional nature of *adult* work environments (Duncan, 1961; Holland, 1973; Kohn & Schooler, 1969, 1978; Lofquist & Dawis, 1969; Temme, 1975) and demonstrating that working in different types of environments has different developmental consequences (Kohn & Schooler, 1969, 1973, 1978). If working does affect the development of the adolescent, it stands to reason that different kinds of jobs may have different kinds of effects. Although numerous social critics have suggested that holding a job will teach responsibility, engender positive attitudes toward working, provide opportunities for the application of skills learned in school to "real-world" situations, and facilitate interaction with non-familial adults (Goodman, 1971; Illich, 1971; Panel on Youth of the President's Science Advisory Committee, 1974), recent research on prototypic adolescent work settings indicates that jobs differ considerably in behavioral opportunities relevant to these assumed outcomes (Greenberger, Steinberg, & Ruggiero, Note 1).[3] For example, the percentage of time adolescent workers in six commonly-held part-time jobs spend in reading, writing, and arithmetic computation differs significantly: young people employed in food service, manual labor, and cleaning jobs spend almost no time on these activities, while those in retail, skilled labor, and clerical jobs have far more opportunities to use school-taught skills.

The effects of working are likely to be mediated not only by what the adolescent actually does on the job but also by characteristics of the individual worker and by the amount of time he or she spends in the work setting. In addition to the demographic variables customarily included in studies of young people (age, sex, social class, and ethnicity), research on

[3]This, and all subsequent references to our research on adolescent work, refer to a project funded by the National Institute of Education (U.S.D.H.E.W.) to examine the nature and effects of part-time work among high school students. The findings are based on a survey of over 3000 10th- and 11th-graders at four Southern California high schools and an intensive study of approximately 500 working and non-working youngsters.

early work experience should examine the possible mediating effects of occupational expectations, academic ability, previous work experience, and various personality and attitudinal dimensions. Steinberg, Greenberger, Garduque, and McAuliffe (Note 2) have found, for example, that school performance is affected more by how many hours a youngster spends in the workplace each week than by whether the youngster is or is not employed and that youngsters of relatively lower academic ability show a larger relative gain in "practical knowledge" as a consequence of working than do their academically more talented counterparts.

Our discussion thus far calls for future research that addresses differences among jobs, differences among workers, variations in the amount of time adolescents work, and the interactions among these factors. We turn now to potential outcomes of working that need further empirical study. These domains are the effect of work on the individual adolescent's (1) educational performance and plans, (2) family relations, (3) peer relations, (4) consumer behavior, (5) delinquency, (6) occupational development, and (7) health.

Work and Education. Interest in the relationships between work and education derives from a concern that working should supplement, rather than detract from, the young person's formal school experience. It is presumed not only that the adolescent will learn different skills through working than through attending school (specific job skills as well as what are often referred to as "real-world" skills), but that these skills can be acquired without compromising school-based learning. Despite the scarcity of research on either of these assumptions (see also Ingoldsby & Adams, 1977), educational policies and programs have been developed in order to facilitate the placement and maintenance of high school students in jobs. These efforts range from locating youth employment services within high schools, to modifying school schedules to free blocks of time for work, to actually giving educational credit for job experience (Interagency Panel for Research and Development on Adolescence, 1973; National Panel on High Schools and Adolescent Education, 1976; Panel on Youth of the President's Science Advisory Committee, 1974). Research on the effects of work on schooling indicates that working long hours is associated with lower grades in school (Bateman, 1950), and recent research (Steinberg et al., Note 2) suggests that lower grades result from, rather than precede, working, even when social class and other demographic factors are controlled.

One would want to know more, however, about the relation between work and education than simply the effects working has on students' academic achievement. In particular, it is important to know whether skills acquired in the work setting are utilized in other settings (e.g., the school or family); whether time commitments to one setting affect commitments to the other; whether working and involvement in school life are related; and finally,whether early experience in the world of work has any effect on educational aspirations or expectations. But, we would argue, none of these questions can be answered without adequate information on the nature of the work experience itself. Working in a job that requires arithmetic computation may have a positive impact on certain aspects of school performance whereas working as a manual laborer may not. Moreover, the structure of the relationship between school and work will shape, in part, the impact that work experience has on the adolescent's educational development.

Work and Family Relations. In recent years, the field of family impact analysis has grown rapidly. Those working in this area study the effects of various social changes, planned or otherwise, on the quality and nature of family life (Family Impact Seminar, Note 3). Although the impact of adolescent employment on the family is a virtually unstudied issue, one can assume that when a teenager takes on a job, the time that the person spends with members of his or her family changes in both quantity and quality. Furthermore, the employment of adolescents may have important consequences for family finances.

Changes in the sheer amount of time available for family activities would be expected to occur when a teenager takes on a part-time job. School occupies most of the youngster's day, leaving only late afternoons, evenings, and weekends available for working. These are the times that might otherwise be spent, at least in part, in family activities. Adolescents' work schedules, for example, are such that their jobs may interfere with the family dinner hour, one of the few times during the day when an entire household can interact together. Family sociologists and developmental psychologists have recently voiced concern over the dissolution of the American family and have drawn attention to those forces that appear to impinge on the time that family members have for each other (Bronfenbrenner, 1978). Whether the part-time employment of teenagers is another disruptive force is an important social question. Our own studies indicate, in fact, that adolescents who work *do* spend less time in family activities than their non-working peers (Greenberger, Steinberg, Vaux, & McAuliffe, 1980).

Aside from examining the effects of teenage employment on the *quantity* of time adolescents spend with their families, researchers should also focus on changes in the *nature* of family relationships as a result of working. The development of autonomy has special significance during adolescence, and research has shown that the family plays a critical role in the teenager's development of various types of emotional and behavioral maturity (Hill & Steinberg, 1976). Working may affect the development of autonomy through its impact on family relationships. Holding a part-time job could encourage a young person, treated as a responsible person on the job, to seek more autonomy and behave more independently at home, or correspondingly, induce an adolescent's parents to grant more autonomy to a working child who has shown him or herself as capable of handling greater responsibility. The well-documented, reciprocal relationship between adolescent autonomy and parental independence-granting (Baumrind, 1975) may, then, be accelerated by a teenager's taking on a part-time job. Thus, in addition to the direct positive impact that work is presumed to have on psychosocial maturity, it may also promote autonomy indirectly, by provoking changes in parent-adolescent relationships.

Finally, an adolescent's part-time employment may have a financial impact on the family. Depending upon the young person's earnings and the family's relative financial situation, an adolescent worker may be able to make a significant contribution to the family's income, either directly, by turning over a portion of his or her salary to the family, or indirectly, by assuming expenditures which previously were parental responsibilities. The part-time employment of adolescents may function as an indirect form of family assistance. Alternatively, a young person's employment might have a net negative effect on the family's finances if the family is forced to spend money for services that were once provided by the teenager but are no longer available (such as child care). Apart from these short-term costs and gains, a teenager's part-time employment during high school could have a positive long-term impact on the family's financial situation if a substantial proportion of the youngster's earnings were saved in order to finance the student's further education. It is therefore important to determine whether and to what extent adolescent workers save their earnings for this purpose.

Work and Peer Relations. The third set of outcome variables we discuss concerns the adolescent's relations with peers. Like time with family, time with friends may be jeopardized by holding a job, since the times during which an adolescent would be likely to be engaged in social activities are those when youngsters are most likely to be working (i.e., weekday afternoons and evenings, and weekends).

In other respects, however, working may facilitate interaction among teenagers, since many common adolescent work sites are staffed chiefly by young people. For some students, work actually may be a source of friends, and these adolescents may have just as much, if not more, contact with peers as their non-working counterparts. The nature of these workers' peer groups may differ from that of their non-working schoolmates, in that friends made through work need not necessarily be similar with respect to age, socioeconomic status, ethnic background, or area of residence (as is generally the case with school-based friendships).

Whether working in fact does bring youngsters into contact with persons from different backgrounds is a question that ought to be investigated empirically, given the frequency with which work is suggested as a means of social integration. We know very little about the types of people adolescent workers are likely to encounter on the job, the amount and type of social contact workers have with others while at work, or the degree to which meaningful relationships develop among co-workers. It would be interesting to know, for example, whether holding a job provides a teenager with additional close friends and sources of social support.

Not only might work affect the amount of time an adolescent has available for friendships and the pool of persons from which potential friends can be drawn, but holding a job during the high school years may also alter the quality of the young person's relations with others. First, the economic power and independence that working affords a young person may increase that individual's popularity and status with peers. Second, working may provide the adolescent with the economic means to engage in various activities with peers that were previously unaffordable. And finally, if social skills such as cooperation were acquired on the job, working could have a positive impact on relations with others.

Working and Consumer Behavior. Part-time employment is to most adolescents, above all, a source of money. An adolescent working for 20 hours each week at the present minimum wage earns about $250 monthly. While out-of-school youths may have to support themselves and even dependents, in-school workers generally do not have these sorts of obligations. Thus, an important set of issues concerns financial aspects of adolescent employment, in particular, how and for what purposes adolescent workers use their earnings. The policy-related ramifications of these issues—ranging from considerations of the effects of teenage employment on income distribution to its impact on consumption patterns—should not be overlooked, and we raise a number of these issues in later discussions of the social structural aspects of teenage work. In the section at hand, we limit our discussion to the effects on the individual worker.

A part-time job provides the young person with a regular and substantial income. Adolescence is an impressionable age period, and it is important to know whether and how attitudes toward spending and saving and toward the importance of material goods are shaped by early work experiences. Working, of course, is often extolled as a means by which adolescents learn "how to handle money." Although this notion is widely accepted and is frequently used to justify youth employment efforts, to our knowledge, it has never been examined empirically. Is it a fact that adolescents who work have a greater understanding of personal finance that those who do not hold jobs? If so, what does this understanding consist of? Do youngsters who work open their own bank accounts, develop and maintain personal budgets, or plan for large expenditures in the future? Does working help students acquire knowledge about credit terms, interest rates, tax deductions, or personal loans? Are youngsters who work more informed or critical about purchases as consumers than their non-working peers? And what role, if any, does the working adolescent's school, family, and peer group play in socializing consumer behavior and attitudes?

We feel it is also important that information be collected on how adolescent workers use their earnings. As noted earlier, teenage workers may indirectly benefit their families, by assuming financial responsibility for items (such as clothing) that were previously parental expenses, or by setting aside money for further education. But it also may be that many workers spend most of their money on luxury items which they and their parents would not buy if not for the adolescent's job. Some of these so-called luxuries are quite innocuous—records, extra clothing, recreational expenses, and the like—but others are far less desirable: alcohol, drugs, and cigarettes. Because we suspect that considerable amounts of workers' earnings are, in fact, used to purchase items such as marijuana and liquor, we think that knowledge about the uses of adolescents' earnings is essential to the formulation of youth employment policy. It would be ironic, indeed, if well-intentioned programs designed to place students in part-time jobs were actually serving to finance teenagers' alcohol and drug use.

Work and Delinquency. The assumption that employment deters youth from delinquent behavior has inspired a number of different attempts to place adolescents in jobs (Benjamin, Lesh & Freedman, 1965; Cassell, 1966). Ostensibly, (1) working occupies youths' time, and therefore reduces time available for

delinquency; (2) working serves to integrate otherwise alienated and frustrated youths into the adult world, thereby raising
youngsters' feelings of self-esteem, attachment to society, and
purposefulness (Burchill, 1962; Cloward & Ohlin, 1960); and
(3) working provides youths with income to obtain material
goods which otherwise might be acquired through illicit means
(cf. Elliott & Knowles, 1978). (Whether delinquency results at
all from idleness, alienation, or avarice remains to be seen, of
course.) What research does exist on the relation between work
and delinquency is inconsistent and of generally poor quality.
To date, no clear relation between working and the deterrence
of delinquency has been established.

There is, of course, a possible connection between work
and delinquency that is seldom discussed in the youth employment literature, namely, that working may *increase* delinquent
behavior by providing new opportunities for delinquency and
by inspiring new forms of illicit activity (Ruggiero, Note 4).
Four possible links between part-time employment and increased delinquency can be suggested: (1) working provides a
new setting in which such acts such as theft, vandalism and
sabotage are possible; (2) working provides the financial
means to engage in illicit activities such as drug and alcohol
use; (3) working engenders a desire for materialistic goods in
excess of the adolescent's financial means, thereby providing
the impetus for theft; and (4) working brings the youngster
into contact with adults who regularly violate the law at work,
thereby communicating to the adolescent the notion that certain behaviors, while illegal, are acceptable. (Our research, in
fact, provides support for all four propositions.)

Work and Occupational Development. Early part-time work
experience may have an impact on the adolescent's future as a
full-time, adult worker. How does holding a job during high
school affect occupational attitudes and values, aspirations and
expectations, and subsequent employability? Do youngsters
who gain work experience early have an advantage over those
who do not?

It is often suggested that work experience during adolescence fosters responsibility, teaches the value of hard work,
instills pride in the completion of tasks, and shapes attitudes

and values believed important to success as an adult worker. Although we can find little empirical support for this claim, it is so widely accepted that it seems almost sacrilegious to question this wisdom. Yet, these propositions are used frequently to justify various youth employment programs. With all due respect to Benjamin Franklin, we feel it time to research these assumptions systematically.

There are also lessons to be learned from working that may be less desirable. Given the menial nature of most adolescents' jobs and the minimal demands for responsibility, it is not unreasonable to speculate that, as a result of early part-time work experience, young people may develop cynical attitudes about working and the belief that work ought to be done as quickly as possible and with the least amount of effort expended. Findings from our recent studies, in fact, suggest that both positive *and* negative attitudes toward work are developed as a result of part-time job experience (Ruggiero, Note 4).

Whichever the kinds of attitudes and values a youngster may acquire as a result of early work experience, they are likely to depend largely upon the type of introduction to the world of work that the individual has had, both in terms of the nature of the work itself and in terms of the reactions of parents, peers, and teachers to the adolescent's work experience. Jobs which are highly routinized and low in the extent to which they require autonomy and decision-making could hardly be expected to foster creativity, industry, or responsibility. We call attention once again to the importance of future research which is sensitive to differences among jobs and among the adolescents who hold them.

As well as shaping values and attitudes, early work experience may affect a young person's plans for the future, primarily through exposing the individual to the workplace and to other adult workers. One of the benefits of early experience in an unpleasant, low-status job is that it may teach the adolescent what types of jobs *not* to seek as an adult. It is important, from a human capital perspective, to determine whether youngsters who work develop occupational ambitions that are higher, or more realistic, or more carefully planned than their non-working peers.

Finally, one would want to know whether part-time work experience during high school significantly enhances the future employability of the young person. This issue has been the focus of a number of extensive investigations, most notably, the National Longitudinal Surveys (Parnes, 1974) and is viewed by many to be the single most significant issue in the study of adolescent employment.

The results of longitudinal investigation into the subsequent (young adulthood) occupational experiences of individuals who had worked as adolescents are mixed. Out-of-school 16- to 19-year olds who are employed during these years are less likely to be unemployed as young adults than are those who were both out of school and out of work during late adolescence. Along similar lines, young adults who were unemployed and out of school as late adolescents earn less than young adults with early employment experience (Stevenson, 1978).

Early employment concomitant with school appears to have far fewer benefits, however, with respect to employability and earnings during young adulthood. "Only for women is teenage unemployment while in school related to later participation rates," (Stevenson, 1978, p. 103), and even then only marginally. For example, 67.8% of the young women surveyed who had been in school and employed as adolescents (16 to 19 years of age) were employed as young adults (23 to 26 years of age), as compared with 67.4% of those who had been out of the labor force, but in school, during late adolescence. When young adulthood earnings are examined as a function of adolescent work experience, a similar picture emerges: Being out of the labor force *as a student* is not associated with lower earnings later on.[4] Furthermore, regardless of adolescent work experience, those students who are in school between the ages of 16 and 19 fare better as young adults than do those who are not.

These findings, taken together, suggest that part-time

[4]It is important to differentiate, however, between those students who are *out of the labor force* during high school (who do not seem to be adversely affected by this), and those who are *unemployed* during the school years (i.e., unsuccessfully looking for work). The latter group appears to suffer in terms of subsequent earnings, although not nearly as much as youths who were not in school and not working during late adolescence.

employment during adolescence may attenuate some of the occupational difficulties that out-of-school adolescents typically face as adults, but that such employment does not substitute for formal education. To the extent, therefore, that part-time employment may interfere with successful high school completion (an unresearched issue), it may, in fact, have a deleterious effect on long-term occupational development. This is a critical research and policy question.

Work and Health. Finally, we raise the issue of the relationship between early work experience and adolescent health. High school students who are working 20 hours each week at a part-time job in addition to attending school may be exposing themselves to stress which could conceivably entail costs to physical and psychological health. Such youngsters have, at an early age, time and energy commitments which exceed those of many adult workers. Many adolescents, because of their job schedules, work evenings and nights during the week and must be in school early in the morning on the following day. There is virtually no research on whether this sort of daily routine takes its toll, either immediately or in the long run, on the person's health, but self-report data from our studies do not show increased illness, fatigue, psychological difficulty, or injury among workers.

Adolescent Part-Time Employment in the Larger Social Structure

In this section, we raise a number of questions which examine adolescent work from a broader perspective. These questions have generally been raised by economists and lawyers. In many respects, more is known about various social structural aspects of teenage employment than about the effects of employment on the individual adolescent. We raise four issues here which we feel are timely and important: adolescent work and minimum wage; the employment of in-school versus out-of-school youth; adolescent work and the child labor laws; and adolescent work and the economy.

Adolescent Work and the Minimum Wage. Critics of the minimum wage have argued that it causes large numbers of adolescents to be excluded from the labor force (Mincer, 1976;

Moore, 1971; Ragan, 1977; Welch, 1978). They show that if wages were permitted to fall below present minima, more jobs would open up. Presumably, these jobs would be acceptable to teenagers, who are thought to be more willing to work for lower wages. (Although the majority of studies on this subject show that the minimum wage does indeed have a disemployment effect on young workers, when wages drop below a certain point, even teenagers may be reluctant to accept employment.) Nevertheless, on balance, when all existing studies are considered as a group, it does appear that setting the minimum wage at or near its present level has a significant disemployment effect on teenagers, and particularly on non-white youngsters. If the minimum wage were nonexistent, lower, or differentially lower for young workers, more adolescents would be working than presently are. Recently, many policy makers have argued for the removal of such minima so that youngsters' employment opportunities would not be constrained.

Few studies have looked carefully, however, at *which adolescents* would be likely to enter the labor force if the minimum wage were lowered and *which jobs* they would be likely to enter (see also Welch, 1978, for a discussion of this topic). It may be the case, for example, that in-school adolescents, and not their out-of-school peers, would move into the labor force if the minimum wage were lowered. This would be likely if the effect of lowering the minimum wage were to create more part-time positions in the service and retail sectors. These sorts of jobs are acceptable to individuals working primarily for extra pocket money but probably not to those in need of full economic support for themselves and in some cases, their dependents. Thus it could be the case that economic policies designed to combat youth unemployment would affect only a particular segment of the youth population. Any proposals to alter the minimum wage to stimulate the hiring of young workers must therefore draw on research which takes into account how different groups of adolescents may be differentially affected by this economic policy. It would be unfortunate if a policy designed to reduce the unemployment of out-of-school youths did little to help these individuals and instead, made it easier only for in-school teenagers to work. Moreover, we question the wisdom of taking measures to increase youth employment (such as creating separate minima for youths and adults) in the absence of empirical data on the effects of work experience on adolescent development.

In-school versus Out-of-School Workers. It is ironic that the proportion of in-school adolescents in the labor force should have risen so dramatically concurrent with the equally dramatic rise in unemployment among youths who are not in school (see Kalachek, 1969 for a discussion of youth unemployment). Yet, within the last 20 years, because of growth in the number of jobs in the retail and service sectors of the economy, it has been relatively easy for high school students to find acceptable jobs, and virtually impossible for their out-of-school peers to do so. All too often, differentiation is not made between these two very different groups of young people, and policies which might benefit one group may well have deleterious effects on the other.

Current economic and social conditions clearly favor the employment of students rather than out-of-school youths, despite the higher costs of unemployment among the latter group. Few out-of-school youths would be willing to accept the low-paying, part-time jobs that high school students typically hold, because they are more likely to have to support themselves and, in many cases, dependents as well. Not only are one's earnings from these jobs limited by both the wage rate and the weekly hours, but rarely do these jobs offer security or company benefits. They do permit employers, however, to hold down labor costs considerably, since part-time workers are relatively cheaper to employ.

The expansion of the economy in recent years has been chiefly in the secondary labor market, which is comprised mostly of part-time, low-paying jobs (Ginzberg, 1977). This expansion has benefited students and others looking for part-time work (among the latter, married women seeking supplementary family income), but has relatively little impact on those interested in full-time employment. Hardest hit have been unskilled, out-of-school youth.[5]

[5]Once again we note that the out-of-school, unemployed youth we refer to here range in age from 16 to 24, whereas the in-school youth who are the focus of this paper generally are between 15 and 18.

Although these out-of-school youth could not work in the part-time positions presently held by their in-school counterparts due to the limited economic pay-offs these jobs offer, there is no doubt that most unskilled non-students could successfully perform the work involved. It is therefore important to recognize that many unemployed, out-of-school youth could be working if some of the part-time jobs presently held by high school students were combined into fewer full-time positions. Implementing this transformation (including, perhaps, some form of subsidy to employers in order to provide an economic incentive for the conversion) may well be less expensive than creating full-time jobs anew, which has been the usual approach in this country to the problem of youth unemployment.

Adolescent Work and the Law. Present child labor laws restrict the types of jobs which teenagers can hold as well as the amount of time, both daily and weekly, that they can work. These laws have come under attack recently, both by those who would strengthen them and by those who would relax them (Sanderson, 1974; Taggart, 1972; Trattner, 1970). Proponents of more stringent laws and enforcement point to widespread violation of child labor statutes, rampant exploitation of youngsters in certain industries, and unsafe working conditions to which many adolescent workers are exposed. These who would relax the laws also point to their widespread violation, claiming that this is an indication of their uselessness and of their antiquated and superfluous nature. Nonetheless, both sides agree that revisions in the laws are long overdue.

What kinds of information would be necessary in order to make intelligent and realistic revisions in the child labor laws? First, one would want to know the extent and nature of present labor law violations. Our survey data indicate, by conservative estimate, that one-third of those under 16 are working in violation of the hours-time provision of the California state labor law. (This figure does not take into account youngsters who may be working in compliance with the hours-time provision but are violating different provisions, which refer to the type, rather than the amount, of work.)

Many of the existing restrictions on the employment of teenagers were formulated initially because it was assumed that certain types of work, or work in excessive amounts, would have an adverse impact on the young person's development (Trattner, 1970). Certain jobs were viewed as being likely to result in accidents; others, as bringing impressionable youngsters in contact with adults of questionable moral character. Additionally, it was argued that *any* work in doses which were too large would lead to school and health difficulties. To our knowledge, these assumptions seldom have been tested, much less verified, empirically. A second type of research is needed that examines the effects of working in different types of jobs, and for various numbers of hours, on health, school performance, and delinquency. Without this type of information, there are no firm grounds upon which to base revisions in the child labor laws. (To those who suggest common sense, let us point out that the common sense behind the present Illinois child labor laws prohibits teenagers from working in and around skating rinks—which of course, are used nowadays almost exclusively by teenagers.)

Adolescent Work and the Economy. Adolescent workers contribute to the economy in two important ways. As suggested by the figures on employment given at the outset of this paper, adolescent part-time workers are in considerable demand. We wish to emphasize here the fact that certain industries rely almost *exclusively* on teenage labor, and substantially, on the labor of in-school youth. In the fast food industry, for example, the majority of employees are young people. One wonders whether the industry could survive, with its current price structure for goods more or less intact, were the base of adolescent part-time employees to vanish. (We shall refrain from entering any value judgments on this matter!)

Another way in which in-school adolescent workers affect the economy is as consumers. The combined economic impact of millions of adolescent wage-earners, with a considerable degree of control over how they spend their money and relatively few financial obligations, is substantial. Just as certain industries depend on adolescents as employees, others rely on young people as the primary market. Any policies which encourage or discourage employment of in-school teenagers will therefore affect the economic well-being of a number of industries.

Work and the Nature of Adolescence in American Culture

The questions we raise here concern the place and significance of adolescent work in contemporary American culture. At this level of analysis, we consider historical variations in teenage employment patterns and differences between teenage work in America and other Western countries. These considerations are at the heart of the issue of adolescent part-time employment.

Teenage Employment and Historical Change. As noted earlier, this past quarter-century has been characterized by a dramatic increase in the proportion of in-school youngsters employed part-time. It should not be overlooked, however, that the proportion of teenagers in the labor force varied considerably from decade to decade prior to 1950 as well. In general, from around the beginning of the 20th century (when labor force participation is first reported by age) until 1940, the proportion of youths in the labor force declined (U.S. Bureau of the Census, 1910–1970). This decline, of course, is confounded by the fact that the proportion of young people enrolled in secondary schools rose dramatically during the same period. It was not until 1940 that labor force participation rates were reported separately for in- and out-of-school youths, and it is therefore difficult to tell to what extent the labor force participation rate of in-school teenagers varied during the years prior to 1940.

Historians have noted that the employment of teenagers has waxed and waned with changes in the need for cheap, unskilled, part-time labor (Carlson, 1971; "Children at Work," 1944; Sanderson, 1974). Thus the rise of teenage employment during the post World War II period is undoubtedly related to the tremendous growth of the retail and service sectors of the economy, both of which thrive on minimum-wage, part-time employment. It also may be the case that child labor laws and their enforcement vary, too, as the need for cheap labor rises and falls: during times when the supply of this kind of

labor exceeded the demand, social critics and "protectors" of
the young called for more stringent laws and more thorough
enforcement; when demand exceeded supply, "champions" of
the young pointed at the laws as exploitative and discriminatory, and demanded their relaxation (Sanderson, 1974). In
any case, it is impossible to look at the issue of adolescent
employment and to make policy recommendations without
considering the nature of the labor market, both at the present time as well as in terms of projections for the future. If,
for example, the demand for part-time, minimum-wage labor
were expected to decrease over the next decade, it would be
fruitless to implement policies encouraging in-school youth to
seek jobs.

We do not intend to suggest that economic changes alone
have accounted for variations in adolescent labor force participation. Historical events, cultural transformations, and value
shifts also have played important parts. One only has to look
at changes in educational philosophy over the past twenty
years to see a case in point. As more and more social critics
accused the educational system of failing to meet the needs of
adolescents, more and more educators (with the critics' bless-
ings) developed programs designed to place youngsters in the
"real world" (e.g., the workplace) where, theoretically, education is more relevant. During the early 1970s, increasing numbers of high schools began giving academic credit for job experience, adjusting school schedules to make them more compatible with work schedules, and offering employment and
placement services in the schools themselves.

This push toward the workplace as a learning context for
adolescents, however, was perhaps more motivated by dissatisfaction with secondary education than by any real knowledge
that the work setting was a valuable context in its own right.
Prior to 1950, when universal secondary education was hailed
as the great democratizer, equalizer, and socializer, attention
was turned away from the workplace (which, of course, had
previously played a critical role in educating the young) and
toward the comprehensive high school. Because the comprehensive high school failed to deliver on many of its creators'
promises, dissatisfaction with the institution grew over the
years, and now it is the workplace that is the "new" solution to

the problems of socializing adolescents. Thus, one should recognize that our present fascination with the workplace as a
learning environment is to a great extent not due to any philo-
sophical awakening but rather is a reaction to historical and
economic changes that have taken place in recent decades.

Existing problems in the comprehensive high school may
not be permanent and, as some demographers have warned,
may have resulted not from deficiencies in the institution, but
from the dramatic and sudden increase in the youth population during the 1960s. Social policies of the 1980s should fit
the demography of that era, not of one twenty years previous.
In point of fact, for all the heralding it now receives as a
potential learning environment, the work setting has *never*
been evaluated so carefully, thoroughly, or critically as the
high school. One wonders how well it would hold up under
rigorous scrutiny.

It would be interesting to know whether the recent rise in
adolescents' interest in employment signals some sort of widespread devaluation of formal education or whether most young
people who hold jobs still appreciate the value of schooling. We
must ask ourselves if, by encouraging youngsters to take on
jobs, we are (as is hoped) communicating the idea that the
workplace can be a source of learning and not (as is feared) that
time spent in the classroom is wasted time. The immediate
gratification of a paycheck can be quite strong for someone
who is relatively inexperienced and impressionable. Thus, if
policies which encourage youth to work are enacted, they
should be designed so as to reinforce, rather than undermine,
the value of education. It is still the case that the completion of
high school is a better predictor of later occupational attainment than is early, part-time work experience.

Adolescent Work in America and Abroad. The employment
of in-school youngsters is a distinctively American phenomenon among countries in the West, although it has recently
begun to appear in a number of European nations. In
Sweden, particularly, there has been a dramatic rise in the
labor force participation of high school students, and, as in the
States, these youngsters are employed primarily in retail and
service positions. But for the most part, the typical European

youngster spends the first part of adolescence as a full-time student with little regular experience in the world of work and makes a rather abrupt transition into full-time work after the end of formal schooling. (The custom of working during the school week is far less familiar in Western Europe than in the United States.) In contrast, the typical American youngster spends the early adolescent years in full-time school without any work experience, enters into a period of combined full-time school and part-time work, and continues this pattern until the end of high school, at which time he or she either enters the workplace full-time or goes on in the educational system (perhaps working part-time once again).

It is interesting to ask whether the period of part-time work during mid-adolescence facilitates the transition from adolescence to adulthood or whether, as we have argued elsewhere (Steinberg & Greenberger, 1980), the job experiences of the young are themselves distinctively "adolescent" in nature and have little bearing on the young person's entrance into adult occupational roles. Interestingly, work experience during the high school years is presently being discussed in the United States and in most of Western Europe as a remedy to the "transition" problems of young people. Countries vary, however, in the extent to which they view *naturally-occurring* youth employment (rather than deliberately designed employment programs) as a potential facilitator of the transition to adulthood.

It is instructive to examine the reasons for the absence of working high school students on most European countries, since these factors help to explain why it is so prevalent here. First, and perhaps most important, are the more numerous job opportunities available to American adolescents than to their European counterparts. In most European countries, retail shops are generally not open late on weekday evenings and they are typically not open on Sundays (two times during which many American students work). Fast-food restaurants, also staffed chiefly by teenagers, are not prevalent in Europe, either.

Second, Europeans claim that their youth spend considerable amounts of time outside of school on their studies, a practice apparently not so common among American teenagers. On a recent trip abroad, we had occasion to ask about the adolescent work situation in other countries and to describe the current situation in the United States. Our European colleagues in England, Belgium, Italy, and Sweden were surprised to hear of the numbers of American students working for so many hours each week, and wondered how these students found the time to do so. (It is not uncommon for adolescents in their countries to spend three or four hours on homework *nightly* and to have, therefore, little time or energy for working.)

Third, many European countries, faced with higher rates of unemployment than ours, are highly sensitive to the political costs of permitting or encouraging students to hold jobs that are needed by out-of-school youth and adults.

A fourth reason for the relative absence of adolescent work in Europe concerns values and attitudes. It was suggested to us that most parents would be embarrassed if their child obtained employment while the youngster was in school: The parents' responsibility is to support their children while they are still students. As a Polish colleague joked, "In Poland, a good father is a father who takes care of his son until his son retires." (In contrast, our survey revealed that an overwhelming majority of parents of working students are pleased with their youngster's employment. American parents appear to place a greater emphasis on fostering responsibility and independence in their youngsters and believe that work contributes to this end.) We imagine, therefore, that in Europe, most parents would dissuade their children from working or working many hours per week while in school.

Summary

A social phenomenon of great potential significance has appeared on the American scene over a period of years and has gone largely unremarked and unstudied. This phenomenon is the employment of an increasing proportion of high school students in part-time jobs for increasing numbers of hours each week. The acknowledgement of this phenomenon raises a number of fundamental issues concerning the nature of adolescent jobs, the development of adolescents, the impact of adolescent work on the labor market and the economy, and the value of work experience in the preparation of young people for the transition into adulthood. The purpose of this paper has been to set the phenomenon of adolescent employment in a broad framework and to outline an agenda for future research. The agenda we propose involves research on the individual, societal, and cultural levels of analysis. It is our view that the examination of these issues necessitates a multidisciplinary perspective. To view the problems and promises of early adolescent employment at any one level of analysis to the exclusion of others, or as the exclusive domain of educators or economists, or of persons in any one discipline, would be to distort its implications for adolescent development and for society as a whole.

Reference Notes

1. Greenberger, E., Steinberg, L., & Ruggiero, M. *A job is a job . . . or is it? Behavioral observations in the adolescent workplace.* Submitted for publication.
2. Steinberg, L., Greenberger, E., Garduque, L., & McAuliffe, S. *High school students in the labor force: Some costs and benefits to schooling and learning.* Submitted for publication.
3. *Family Impact Seminar.* Interim report. Washington, D.C.: The George Washington University, 1978.
4. Ruggiero, M. *Adolescent occupational crime: A psychosocial analysis.* Paper presented at the annual meeting of the Western Psychological Association, Honolulu, May 1980.

References

Bateman, R. The effect of work experience on high school students as revealed by the Bell Adjustment Inventory. *Journal of Educational Research,* 1949, *43,* 261–269.
Bateman, R. The effect of work experience on high school students' scholastic achievement. *Occupations,* 1950, *41,* 129–148.
Baumrind, D. Early socialization and adolescent competence. In S. Dragastin and G. Elder, Jr., (Eds.), *Adolescence in the life cycle.* Washington, D.C.: Hemisphere, 1975.
Benjamin, J.G., Lesh, S., & Freedman, M.K. Youth employment programs in perspective. Washington, D.C.: Office of Juvenile Delinquency and Youth Development, U.S. Department of Health, Education, and Welfare, 1965.
Bronfenbrenner, U. Who needs parent education? *Teachers' College Record,* 1978, *79,* 74–94.
Bronfenbrenner, U. *The ecology of human development.* Cambridge, Mass.: Harvard University Press, 1979.

Burchill, G.W. *Work-study programs for alienated youth.* Chicago: Science Research Associated, 1962.

Carlson, E. More companies turn to illegal child labor in cost-cutting drive. *Wall Street Journal,* March 20, 1971.

Cassell, F.H. New dimensions in employment services for youth. *Employment Service Review,* May, 1–6, 1966.

Children at work: War-time needs for labor causes 26 states to relax rules on employment. *Business Week,* June 17, 1944.

Cloward, R.A., & Ohlin, L.E. *Delinquency and opportunity: A theory of delinquent groups.* New York: Free Press, 1960.

Douvan, E., & Adelson, J. *The adolescent experience.* New York: Wiley, 1966.

Duncan, O.D. A socioeconomic index for all occupations. In A.J. Rees, Jr. (Ed.), *Occupations and social status.* New York: Free Press, 1961.

Elliott, B., & Knowles, D. Social development and employment: An evaluation of the Oakland Youth Work Experience Program. In M. Davidson & R. Taggart (Eds.), *Conference report on youth unemployment: Its measurement and meaning.* Washington, D.C.: U.S. Government Printing Office, 1978.

Ginzberg, E. The job problem. *Scientific American,* 1977, *237,* 43–51.

Goodman, P. *Compulsory miseducation.* London: Penguin Books, 1971.

Greenberger, E., Steinberg, L., Vaux, A., & McAuliffe, S. Adolescents who work: Effects of part-time employment on family and peer relations. *Journal of Youth and Adolescence,* 1980, *9,* 189–202.

Hill, J., & Steinberg, L. The development of autonomy during adolescence. In *Jornadas Sobre Problematica Juventil.* Madrid, Spain: Fundacion Faustino Orbegozo Eizaguirre, 1976.

Holland, J.L. *Making vocational choices: A theory of careers.* Englewood Cliffs, New Jersey: Prentice-Hall, 1973.

Illich, I. The alternative to schooling. *Saturday Review,* June 19, 1971, pp. 44; ff.

Ingoldsby, B., & Adams, G. Adolescence and work experience: A brief note. *Adolescence,* 1977, *12,* 339–343.

Interagency Panel for Research and Development on Adolescence. *Work experience as preparation for adulthood.* Washington, D.C.: Social Research Group, George Washington University, 1973.

Kalachek, E. *The youth labor market.* Washington, D.C.: National Manpower Policy Task Force, 1969.

Kohn, M.L., & Schooler, C. Class, occupation, and orientation. *American Sociological Review,* 1969, *34,* 659–678.

Kohn, M.L., & Schooler, C. Occupational experience and psychological functioning: An assessment of reciprocal effects. *American Sociological Review,* 1973, *38,* 97–118.

Kohn, M.L., & Schooler, C. The reciprocal effects of the substantive complexity of work and intellectual flexibility: A longitudinal assessment. *The American Journal of Sociology,* 1978, *84,* 24–52.

Lofquist, L.H., & Dawis, R.V. *Adjustment to work.* New York: Appleton-Century-Crofts, 1969.

Mincer, J. Unemployment effects of minimum wages. *Journal of Political Economy,* 1976, *84,* 87–104.

Moore, T. The effect of minimum wages on teenage unemployment rates. *Journal of Political Economy,* 1971, *79,* 897–902.

National Panel on High Schools and Adolescent Education. *The education of adolescents.* Washington, D.C.: U.S. Government Printing Office, 1976.

Panel on Youth of the President's Science Advisory Committee. *Youth: Transition to adulthood.* Chicago: University of Chicago Press, 1974.

Parnes, H.S. *The National Longitudinal Surveys.* Columbus, Ohio: Center for Human Resources, 1974.

Ragan, J.F., Jr. Minimum wages and the youth labor market. *Review of Economics and Statistics,* 1977, *59,* 129–136.

Sanderson, A. Child-labor legislation and the labor force participation of children. *Journal of Economic History,* 1974, *34,* 297–299.

Steinberg, L., & Greenberger, E. The transition from adolescence to adulthood: The contribution of part-time work. In F. Monks (Ed.), *Ontwikkelings—psychologische bijdragen (Developmental issues).* Nijmegen, The Netherlands: Dekker & van de Vegt, 1980.

Stevenson, W. The relationship between early work experience and future employability. In A. Adams & G. Magnum (Eds.), *The lingering crisis of youth unemployment.* Kalamazoo, Michigan: W.F. Upjohn Institute for Employment Research, 1978.

Taggart, R. The case for less restrictive regulations. *Education Digest,* 1972, *37,* 6–8.

Temme, L.V. *Occupation: meanings and measures.* Washington, D.C.: Bureau of Social Science Research, 1975.

Trattner, W. *Crusade for the children.* Chicago: Quadrangle Books, 1970.

United States Bureau of the Census. *Characteristics of the population 1910 through 1970.* Washington, D.C.: U.S. Government Printing Office.

United States Bureau of the Census. *Characteristics of the population* (United States Summary, Table XV). Washington, D.C.: U.S. Government Printing Office, 1940.

United States Bureau of the Census. *Characteristics of the population* (United States Summary, Table 122). Washington, D.C.: Government Printing Office, 1950.

United States Bureau of the Census. *Characteristics of the population* (United States Summary, Detailed Characteristics, Table 179). Washington, D.C.: U.S. Government Printing Office, 1960.

United States Bureau of the Census. *Characteristics of the population* (United States Summary, Detailed Characteristics, Table 215). Washington, D.C.: U.S. Government Printing Office, 1970.

Welch, F. *Minimum wages: Issues and evidence.* Washington, D.C.: American Enterprise Institute for Public Policy Research, 1978.

Children and Youth Services Review, Vol. 2, pp. 185–208, 1980
Printed in the USA. All rights reserved.

0190-7409/80/010185-24$02.00/0

$185 - 208$

A Multi-Method Approach to Research on Youth Employment Programs: A Case Study of the Youth Conservation Corps

Stephen F. Hamilton
Steven K. Stewart
Cornell University

This paper examines the issue of what kinds of work programs are most desirable for youth. It has three parts. In the first part, we present some findings from our study of five Youth Conservation Corps programs (Hamilton & Stewart, 1978). These findings were based primarily upon interviews and observations. The second part presents findings based on similar data from some other studies and identifies those program characteristics that are widely seen as desirable. In the third part, we attempt to relate these findings, based on our own and other investigators' qualitative data, to some of the quantitative data collected in our study. In doing so, we hope to demonstrate both the importance and the challenges of this kind of effort.

The term "project" will be used to designate a particular work activity, such as maintenance of a park, in which a group of young people are engaged. "Program" will refer to the administrative entity that is responsible for planning and supervising one or more projects in a particular community. A given program, therefore, might operate one or many differ-

Stephen F. Hamilton, College of-Human Ecology, Cornell University, Ithaca, New York 14853.

ent projects employing youth. A given work crew might engage in one project or in several.

Findings from the Youth Conservation Corps Study

The objectives of the Youth Conservation Corps are to:

1. Accomplish needed conservation work on public lands;
2. Provide gainful employment for 15- through 18-year-old males and females from all social, economic, ethnic and racial backgrounds;
3. Develop an understanding and appreciation, in participating youths, of the Nation's natural environment and heritage (Federal Register, 1975, p. 100).

Conspicuous in its absence is the objective of income redistribution. The Youth Conservation Corps (YCC) has no income eligibility requirements. Applicants are selected randomly to assure that they represent a cross-section of youth.

YCC is jointly administered by the Departments of Agriculture and Interior. One set of programs is administered directly by these Departments on land under their control. Another is administered by the states on non-federal public lands. New York State, the location of the five programs studied, subcontracts most of its YCC funds to local sponsoring organizations, which plan and operate individual programs and provide the 20% matching funds.

The five YCC programs we studied employed 180 youth for six to eight weeks during the summer of 1977. One local sponsor also administered a summer youth program funded by the Comprehensive Employment and Training Act (CETA), in which 80 additional youth did the same kinds of jobs as YCC participants. Youth worked in parks, school grounds, and a camp, doing work such as routine maintenance, brush clearing, nature trail building, wildlife habitat improvement, timber stand improvement, and light construction work.

Two programs were investigated more intensively than the other three. One was a large rural program that included the CETA program patterned after YCC. The other was located in a city of about 200,000 people. These will be desig-

nated the large rural and the urban program. The remaining
programs studied were a small rural one with 20 youth, a suburban program employing 40 youths, and a residential program in which 20 youth from all over the state lived near the
work site all summer. Our sample from the large rural and the
urban programs included 200 YCC and 33 CETA enrollees.
Forty-five of these youth were interviewed at the end of the
summer, after being identified by their crew leaders as having
benefited the most or the least from the programs. Crew
leaders in all five programs were interviewed. Each program
was visited at least four times, twice in connection with pre- and
posttesting and two more times solely for observation. The two
intensively investigated programs were observed weekly. The
paper-and-pencil instruments used in pre- and posttesting will
be described below.

   Analysis of the interview and observation data led to the
identification of three factors as being particularly important
in these programs: the nature of the tasks, the competence of
the adult leaders, and the presence of organizational support
for individual work crews. More specifically, *we recommended
the following as criteria for high quality programs:*

1. Tasks
   a. Provide opportunities for cooperation and decision mak-
      ing;
   b. result in lasting improvements to the community;
   c. provide visible benefits to many people;
   d. are varied; and
   e. require high-level skills.
2. Leaders
   a. Are authoritative (neither permissive nor authoritarian);
   b. have sufficient power to change unsatisfactory task and
      discipline workers;
   c. are good teachers; and
   d. develop warm relations with participants.
3. Organization
   a. Unites control of tasks and responsibility for education;
      and
   b. gives crew leaders adequate support, especially commu-
      nication, planning time, supplies and equipment.

The derivation of these recommendations is described in the following paragraphs.

1. Tasks. Two frequently observed tasks that illustrate the strengths and weaknesses of the kinds of work projects undertaken in YCC are brush clearing and the construction of wooden footbridges along trails. Although brush clearing is an important task in some situations and is not without its rewards, when it was the major activity of the summer, morale problems were almost always serious.

The first problem with brush clearing is that it is boring, as reported in an observer's field notes.[1]

> Louise is working hard dragging out saplings but managing to carry on conversations as she does so. "This work doesn't seem too bad," I allow. "You'll get tired of it after two days," she chuckles.

Swinging a sickle, raking, and dragging brush are tedious activities. Furthermore, they are accurately seen by participants and leaders as short-lived. Interview responses of participants revealed that work seen as lasting was much more highly valued than work that would make no difference in six months or a year. About brush clearing, the most common complaint was, "It will all grow back." The benefits of clearing brush at all were also questioned.

Harry (crew leader) explained that the group was doing brush clearing, which he did not like doing. He said he thought the work was senseless and that the bank was less attractive cleared than overgrown. It had been cleared last year and become overgrown, so the whole thing was destined to happen all over again next year. Harry said the work was particularly ridiculous since you couldn't see the bank too well from the road and nobody would notice it.

This statement presents another criterion, along with permanence, that participants cited frequently as a determinant of a task's value: whether people would see and make use of it. This factor was highlighted in the one site where brush clearing was not associated with low morale, a state-owned golf course, where a YCC crew spent most of the summer clearing brush from the woods lining the fairways. The participants frequently talked about whether their work was

[1]Pseudonyms are used here and wherever else individuals are named in field notes or in the text.

worthwhile, and some argued that they should not be employed to make it easier for golfers to find mis-hit golf balls. But frequent compliments from golfers reduced these misgivings considerably and inspirited the group. An observer experienced the same phenomenon.

As I was walking the half mile from the work site back to the parking lot, wearing my hard hat, two different groups of golfers stopped me to ask questions or comment on the YCC crew. All said they were impressed with the work. The same thing had happened previously when I was with the crew. I think I've come to understand how so boring a job could leave the crew members with high morale. There's nothing like high visibility of work coupled with regular praise to boost spirits. I left the golf course feeling pride in being associated with YCC.

The enthusiasm and competence of the crew leader also served to overcome the limits of brush clearing in this case.

Building footbridges, in contrast to brush clearing, seemed universally to inspire enthusiasm, pride, and hard work. Moreover, building bridges required a degree of cooperation and group decision making that was unnecessary, if possible at all, in brush clearing. Since no one in the crews, including the leaders, had any previous experience in building bridges, all had to discuss design and construction features. Completion of many of the steps in actually building the bridge required two or more people working together. The relative permanence and utility of bridges were viewed by participants as important. Another advantage to this sort of activity was highlighted by participants' responses to questions about the kinds of tasks they liked best and those potential tasks they might have preferred. They uniformly chose tasks calling for complex skills. We also observed an informal hierarchy in tasks within crews based on the amount of skill each required. Using an ax was more desirable than using a grass whip; using a mason's trowel and level was more desirable than using an ax.

Fortunately, there were other tasks like building bridges that appealed to participants and appeared to afford valuable work experience. Any construction work, whether of picnic tables, shelters, or finished buildings, enhanced skill development and elicited enthusiasm. Projects in which the participants were actively involved in planning also seemed effective, for example, laying out nature trails and deciding what points of interest to call attention to, and then making signs or trail guides. The digging of a simple drainage ditch provided an opportunity in one program for instruction and practice in the use of surveyors' instruments. One young woman, whose crew was developing a park in a previously unused area, asserted that she would proudly bring her future children to see the park when she was older. She was not alone in projecting her pride far into the future when work was of this nature.

2. Leaders. We expected that exposure of youth to "authoritative" adults would be beneficial, because of the work of Baumrind (1968), who describes the ideal parental style as authoritative, in contrast to either authoritarian or laissez-faire styles. She has since (1978) elaborated this typology, but we expected that the most effective leaders like the most effective parents, would actively use their knowledge and skills to promote the learning of participants, reserving some matters for decision by the young people but also stating and enforcing boundary conditions within which those decisions could be made and offering guidance and support when necessary. This general ideal for adult behavior is consistent with the ideals espoused by educational philosophers such as Dewey (1938) and Peters (1959).

In YCC programs, effective adult leaders also combined knowledge of the natural environment with manual skills related to the tasks at hand. None of them claimed to know everything related to the work, but all had a foundation for their authority which made it possible for them to rely on participants for some knowledge and skills without feeling threatened. They were also able to act as teachers and counselors and yet engage in joking and teasing with participants.

Of course, no leader exhibited all these positive qualities all the time, but some were very impressive. George, whose crew created a park, described how he exerted his authority a lot during the first two weeks, but that subsequently the participants were "self-motivated," getting right to work upon arrival and knowing just what to do. He was observed working alongside the young people and going along good-naturedly with their kidding. An observer's characterization of another crew leader provides a contrast to George's effective leadership style.

He doesn't suggest one way or another of working. He doesn't set time-bounded goals. He doesn't ask for crew input. He doesn't try to impose any order on the disorderly fashion crew members have chosen to work in. He didn't require crew members working near poison ivy to wear gloves (despite the fact that several people had been incapacitated by it). He was oblivious to kids who were not really working.

3. Organization. The nature of the organizational structure in which the YCC project was embedded and the amount of support it provided each crew was the third major factor affecting the quality of the projects. The simplest organizational framework was one in which the organization sponsoring the YCC controlled the land on which work was being done. In the suburban and the small rural programs, the persons responsible for planning and carrying out the YCC program either had authority themselves or were in close contact with those who did to decide what work would be done and to secure adequate tools and materials. These programs had varied tasks that were educational and interesting and they generally had the tools and materials required. The residential program was conducted on state park land, but staff appeared to have excellent communications with park staff. One park employee worked closely with the program throughout the summer. This program also ran smoothly and seemed effective.

The large rural program had a complex organization because of having two different funding sources, YCC and CETA, with different eligibility requirements and guidelines, and because the work sites were scattered throughout the county. Some crews even moved from one site to another. Problems in communication and in delivery of supplies sometimes occurred, but the availability of many work projects allowed the abandonment of projects that did not work out, as happened in one case when the organization controlling the property failed to provide materials needed to do the job.

The urban program was planned and coordinated by one

office, participants were hired and paid by another, and the jobs, tools, and supervisors were provided by a third. The result was that crew leaders felt powerless to change work assignments even though they soon realized that they were neither interesting nor educational. They were also deprived of authority when one crew leader "fired" a participant for insubordination and he was immediately reinstated at another site. The absence of pre-program planning time and the late hiring and high turnover of assistant leaders also hampered their program.

Findings from Other Studies

Recent reports on youth employment programs have largely agreed with these recommendations regarding YCC programs. Rist, Hamilton, Holloway, Johnson, and Wiltberger (1979) explored participant perceptions of 40 exemplary in-school employment training programs funded by the Youth Employment and Demonstration Projects Act of 1977 (YEDPA). On-site observers at each of the programs conducted interviews with participants or administered questionnaires. Analysis of the resulting reports revealed three critical program characteristics:

(1) adequate adult supervision;
(2) a close fit between education and work activities;
(3) a match between work activities and participants' career interests (p.xv).

Summarizing 10 case studies of YEDPA programs, Wurzburg (1978) emphasized two aspects of program quality:

(1) the integration of education with work experience;
(2) high quality supervision (pp. 13–22).

He noted that the goal of relating work experience to career aspirations had proved to be elusive in many programs because participants had vague and easily changed notions of future careers, a problem also discovered in the programs studied by Rist et al. (1979, p. 161).

The ideal of matching work site demands and opportunities with characteristics of the learner has also been advanced in connection with unpaid experiential learning. Miguel (1979) chaired an advisory panel that developed "Experiential Education Policy Guidelines," which include this ideal. Graham (1975) has provided the most extensive treatment of factors to consider in making this match, emphasizing the implications of differences in participants' developmental levels.

Although some of the programs studied by Rist et al. and Wurzburg place youth in work projects with other youth, most are of the type in which youth individually enter adult workplaces. In contrast, Lesh, Newman, Jordan, and Cash (1979) specifically addressed the issue of what makes a good work experience for youth who work in groups on community improvement projects, as the YCC participants did. From a review of literature and consultations with program staff, they derived the following "checklist" for public service work experience projects:

(1) Does the project meet an identified community need?
(2) Is the work experience appropriate for the age and sex of the youth?
(3) Is supervision provided by highly skilled workers?
(4) Are supportive services available to those youth who need them?
(5) Does the work experience teach real skills?
(6) Does the project provide a variety of work experience?
(7) Are the necessary supplies and equipment readily available?
(8) Are youth paid on time?
(9) Does the work experience provide appropriate degrees of challenge and responsibility?
(10) Is the project flexible enough to provide for individual differences in skill and ability?
(11) How cost effective is the project?
(12) Will the project provide access to regular jobs, education, and/or training?

From all of these findings and recommendations, it appears that several desirable characteristics apply equally to both types of programs. The most universally identified is high quality supervision. Supervisors should be competent and reliable, there should be adequate numbers, and they should behave in a supportive manner. Second, a good match between individual participants and their work placements was widely cited. Participants should see future benefits to their work in terms of planned or potential careers, and placements should be matched to participants' age, sex and developmental level. Third, there should be close links between the work experience and both education and services. Participants should have access to educational opportunities related to their work and to supportive services designed to help them benefit from it.

In addition to these common needs, community improvement programs have some special requirements. Lesh et al. (1979) described desirable characteristics of the work being performed. That work should be challenging, satisfying, require skills that are useful in future jobs, and entail real responsibilities. Because these are usually projects that would not be undertaken if young workers were not available, they run a greater risk than placements in existing adult workplaces of being "make work." It is important both from the perspective of justifying costs and in order to engage the interest of youth that these projects result in some real benefits to the community. Lesh et al. (1979) point out that in these projects there is danger that adequate supplies and materials will not be provided, undermining the effort and the morale of the workers.

Because community improvement projects are done by groups of young workers, the process of matching participants and job sites is different from the one used in placing individual youth in ongoing workplaces. Precise matching, which may be desirable for individual placements, is impossible because many youth must be placed in generally similar projects. Furthermore, within each project, there is likely to be, and should be, a wide range of tasks that may be divided or shared among participants in both formal and informal ways. Chief concerns regarding matching youth with community improvement projects should be, first, making it clear to applicants what kind of work will be involved so that they may make informed choices and, second, assuring a variety of tasks within each project.

The reports cited agree with our own YCC recommendations most strongly with regard to the importance of adult leaders. The issues of matching placements with participants and of linking work with education and services are absent from our recommendations because of the distinctive features of the Youth Conservation Corps. Unlike YEDPA programs, it is short-term and its educational goals are predominantly information about and respect for the natural environment rather than job skills and career education. YCC participants volunteer for the program, we have found, first because it is a summer job that pays better than most of those open to youth and second because they are interested in outdoor conservation work. In other words, participants do their own matching.

More Specific Questions Raised by these Findings. The convergence of our recommendations with those from other reports makes us more confident of their validity and importance. Their principal value is in providing a sketch of what good programs look like, which is useful to both policy makers and program planners. However, agreement about desirable general characteristics of programs also allows researchers to move on to more specific questions.

One question that may usefully be asked is whether other types of data corroborate these findings. For example, are participants' perceptions as expressed in questionnaires consistent with the findings derived from interviews and observations? Another question is whether there is evidence that the effects on participants are more positive in programs demonstrating these characteristics. This question leads into a complex, controversial, and extremely difficult domain, the assessment of program effects. Yet in the absence of evidence relating program characteristics and program results, recommendations about what makes a good program may be dismissed as nothing more than a matter of taste.

A third question that arises once general characteristics of good programs have been identified is, what can program directors and policy makers do to assure high quality programs? For example, if good staff are important, how can the best staff people be recruited, trained, and maintained? Research leading to recommendations on these more specific issues would be of great value; the need for such research is established by agreement among previous studies that high quality staff is important.

In the next section, we present and analyze additional data from the 1977 YCC study as a means of exploring the first two questions posed above. We did not collect the kind of data required to respond to the third question. Our purpose in elaborating on the YCC study is to illustrate the process of combining qualitative and quantitative methods to substantiate program recommendations. Both benefits and difficulties are revealed by this effort.

Cross-Method Validation of Findings from the YCC Study

Several sources of quantitative data are introduced in this section. We also move from attention to the set of five YCC programs to comparisons among the programs and then to comparisons among work crews within a single program. Our "unit of analysis," in other words, changes from all five programs together to each program taken individually and then to separate work crews within one program as we ask different questions of the data.

Hoping to assess the impact of YCC on participants' maturation, we administered the Psychosocial Maturity (PSM) Inventory at the beginning and end of the five programs. According to its developers, Greenberger, Josselson, Knerr, and Knerr (1975) the PSM Inventory is designed to measure:

three general capacities, which correspond to three general demands made by all societies on individuals. They are (1) the capacity to function effectively on one's own, or individual adequacy; (2) the capacity to interact adequately with others, or interpersonal adequacy; and (3) the capacity to contribute to social cohesion, or social adequacy. (p. 128)

Although PSM scores can be used in the form of three summary scores corresponding to these three capacities, we saw no advantage to this practice and maintained separate scores for each of the nine subscales.

One form of evidence that the program characteristics we identified as important had an impact on participants would be that programs we judged to be superior in terms of those characteristics would yield greater gains among participants on the PSM inventory. After statistically controlling for the pretest score and personal background characteristics of participants we found main effects for program membership on the adjusted posttest scores for three subscales: the self-reliance subscale [$F(4, 67) = 2.97, p = .026$]; the communication subscale [$F(4, 67) = 3.26, p = .017$]; and the social commitment subscale [$F(4, 67) = 2.77, p = .034$]. Table 1 shows the comparative adjusted posttest scores, which are not consistent with our judgments of the relative quality of the five programs, based on staff, work projects, and organization. The key element distinguishing the program that proved most effective in raising participants' PSM scores was that it was residential. Furthermore, the rankings of the other four programs change from one subscale to another and do not reflect our judgment of their relative quality. Although we performed tests of the interactions of the YCC participants' personal background factors with program membership, few of these effects were significant and they were considered spurious.

We found the differences in apparent quality of the five programs to be striking, especially comparing the urban program, which seemed to be plagued with low morale on the part of both staff and participants and to offer little of value, and the other four, which seemed to have some very positive features. The inconsistency between our judgments and this measure of impact called into question both our basis for judging programs and our chosen indicator of impact.

One possible complication, we reasoned, was that, with the exception of the residential program, there might be more variation within programs, at least regarding staffing and work projects, than between programs. What if we changed our independent variable from program to work crew? This could be most readily done in the large rural program, where crews worked quite autonomously and where we had frequent observations of work crews in operation. We shifted our attention, therefore, to 10 YCC and CETA crews in the large rural program, each having from 4 to 8 participants and an adult leader. This change held the program organization factor constant, since all 10 crews operated under the same organizational umbrella.

TABLE 1
**Comparisons among YCC Programs of Adjusted Posttest Scores of
Selected Psychosocial Maturity Inventory Subscales**

		Self-Reliance Subscale		
Urban	Suburban	Small Rural	Large Rural	Residential
(2.99)	(3.02)	(3.06)	(3.28)	(3.39)

		Communication Subscale		
Small Rural	Suburban	Urban	Large Rural	Residential
(2.93)	(2.95)	(2.96)	(3.08)	(3.40)

		Social Commitment Subscale		
Suburban	Small Rural	Urban	Large Rural	Residential
(2.95)	(2.98)	(3.01)	(3.10)	(3.38)

Note: Lines are drawn under subsets of groups for which no pair of groups have significantly different means. The Newman-Keuls test for multiple comparisons was used with $p = .05$ for each set of comparisons. Numbers in parentheses indicate each group's mean posttest score adjusted for the pretest and several personal background factors. Subscale scores may range from one to four, where the higher score indicates maturity.

The observer who was familiar with these crews rated each one either high or low in terms of leader and task quality. The principal investigator also rated each crew on the basis of observation notes and information about work projects contained in crew leaders' journals. There was complete agreement on these ratings, which will be referred to as project quality ratings or PQR.

Given the small changes in PSM scores and the small sample sizes in an analysis by crew, we did not expect and did not find overall differences between crews. However, we had three other measures that could give us some indications of program impact. Two were questionnaires we had developed and administered at the posttest: the program satisfaction questionnaire (SQ), asking participants to evaluate both the quality of the work experience and its impact on themselves; and the leader questionnaire (LQ), about what crew leaders were like and what they did. The third indicator was attendance records, derived from payroll forms on those who had been enrolled in the program for at least half of its duration.

Our analysis of these measures was an effort to check our own judgments about project quality against the perceptions of participants. Tables 2 and 3 show Pearson correlations between each questionnaire item and the PQR. The PQR correlated significantly ($p < .05$) with five of 21 items from the SQ: appropriate tools and materials were available ($r = .34$); the work accomplished was worthwhile ($r = .29$); the projects were well planned and coordinated ($r = .31$); a lot was learned about the environment ($r = .28$); and staff did not take out their frustrations on workers in unpleasant ways ($r = .33$). These correlations suggest that the PQR was reasonably consistent with participant perceptions. PQR was not correlated with other items regarding more general learning (how to use tools, how to work as a team, how to activate a community about environmental problems), with two items assessing how interesting projects were, or with an item indicating participants' wish to be more involved in decision making. The remaining SQ items with which the PQR did not correlate were less directly related to our conception of project quality.

The PQR correlated significantly with only three of 21 items from the LQ: the leader is well organized ($r = .39$); the leader teaches us how to do things ($r = .32$); and the leader sets goals for the group ($r = .34$). The first two reinforce the consistency between observers' and participants' perceptions of planning and of staff teaching ability. However, the absence of significant correlations with items regarding the authoritative behavior of leaders and regarding leaders' involvement of participants in decision making suggests that these aspects of high quality programs were not as important as other factors.

Attendance records served as indirect behavioral indicators of participant satisfaction with their leaders and work projects. Most of the research literature on employee absenteeism and turnover has focused on adult populations in more traditional work settings (e.g., the review by Porter & Steers,

TABLE 2

Correlations of Project Quality Ratings and Attendance with Program Satisfaction Questionnaire Items among Participants in the Large Rural Program

Program Satisfaction Questionnaire Items	PQR ($n = 49$)	Attendance ($n = 53$)
1. I really liked the YCC summer program.	.11	−.19
2. Boys seemed more capable than girls on most of the jobs.	.06	.15
3. We had all the tools and materials we needed to get our work done.	34*	−.20
4. This job was good experience for future jobs.	.07	−.08
5. We had interesting projects to do on rainy days.	.15	.08
6. I learned a great deal about how to use tools.	.02	−.05
7. I think the work we accomplished was worthwhile.	.29*	.41***
8. When I didn't know how to do a job, staff members always offered ideas to help me do the job better.	.16	.06
9. Our work projects and assignments were well planned and coordinated.	.31*	−.09
10. The work was boring much of the time.	−.17	−.11
11. I think I learned quite a bit about the environment in our group's environmental education program.	.28*	.10
12. Workers from different family backgrounds got along very well here.	.20	.06
13. I have developed quite a few friendships with other workers in the program.	.04	−.21
14. Staff members would sometimes take out their frustrations on the workers in unpleasant ways.	−.33*	−.08
15. I have learned a great deal about how to work on projects that require teamwork.	.20	.22
16. I feel more comfortable around adults now than I did before the program.	.05	.16

17. I have learned a great deal about how I can help people in my community become active in working on environmental problems.   −.02   −.24

18. I have learned a great deal about how to get along better with people who are different from myself. (Different in any way—racially, ethnically, personality, etc.).   −.07   −.12

19. I think we were underpaid.   −.18   −.16

20. As a result of this program I have begun to think more seriously about looking into educational or career opportunities in environmental conservation or related areas.   −.18   −.14

21. I wish I could have had more to say about planning the work and making rules.   −.08   −.11

Two-tailed significance: $*p < .05$
                          $**p < .01$
                          $***p < .005$

1973). Ilgen and Hollenback (1977) argue that the relationship between absenteeism and job satisfaction is not necessarily direct but may be moderated by other factors. However, there is support for the contention that job satisfaction is usually inversely related to both absenteeism and turnover rate. Furthermore, either absenteeism or turnover has been found to be related to many aspects of the work environment, including the consideration and authoritarianism of the job supervisor, perceived inequity of treatment among workers, perceived importance of the work, receiving feedback and recognition, job variety, and opportunities to utilize one's abilities.

For our purposes, attendance was expressed as a percentage of the total number of hours a participant was on roll, thus allowing us to include participants who were not enrolled for the entire summer. Tables 2 and 3 show Pearson correlations between these attendance scores and items from the two questionnaires discussed above. It is important to note that attendance scores had a highly skewed distribution, with most

TABLE 3
Correlations of Project Quality Ratings and Attendance with
Leader Questionnaire Items among Participants in the Large Rural
Program

Leader Questionnaire Items	PQR ($n = 51$)	Attendance ($n = 57$)
1. He/she is someone I can talk to.	.17	.20
2. He/she involves us in decisions.	.00	.29*
3. He/she praises us for a job well done.	.21	.14
4. He/she is poorly organized.	−.39***	−.13
5. He/she can be counted on to do what he/she says.	.20	−.19
6. He/she works along with us.	.09	−.02
7. He/she knows what's happening on the job.	−.17	−.08
8. He/she gets along well with the workers.	.15	−.05
9. He/she lets us loaf.	.23	.17
10. He/she is open to disagreement.	.13	−.09
11. He/she knows when someone is trying to get away with something and does something about it.	−.04	−.15
12. He/she jokes with us.	.20	.37***
13. He/she is respected by the workers.	−.04	−.15
14. He/she gives special treatment to some workers.	−.02	−.01
15. He/she calls attention to interesting things in the environment (like animal and plant life).	−.02	.25
16. He/she teaches us how to do things if we don't know how.	.32*	−.18
17. He/she explains his/her actions to the group.	.20	.12
18. He/she does not help us with problems.	−.19	.06
19. He/she comes up with new ways to approach a problem.	.13	.23
20. He/she sets goals for the group.	.34*	.13

Two-tailed significance: *p < .05
                          **p < .01
                         ***p < .005

attendance scores clustering in a small range above 90%. This makes interpretation of analyses using these scores problematic. Even with this in mind, it is still surprising that attendance correlated significantly with only three of the 41 items from the SQ and LQ. There were significant correlations between attendance and participant feelings that the work accomplished was worthwhile ($r = .41$), that their leader involved them in decisions ($r = .29$), and that their leader joked with them ($r = .37$). The correlation with the worthwhile work item is particularly interesting, since that item also correlated significantly with the project quality rating. There is a clear tendency for most participants to attend work most of the time regardless of perceived shortcomings in the work projects or in their leader, but the perception of doing worthwhile work stands out as an important factor in participant attendance. The convergence of participant perceptions that work is worthwhile with both attendance ($r = .41$) and observer ratings of project quality ($r = .29$) reinforce our recommendation that the quality of work is an important characteristic of program quality.

Of course, attendance is not only a function of the participants' perceptions of their camp experience, but may also be associated with certain personal background factors of the participants. Porter and Steers (1973) listed little research of general interest in this area. Freeberg and Reilly (1971), in a study of the Neighborhood Youth Corps, found the number of work site absences to be correlated with, among other things, global ratings of participant quality from work supervisors and counselors. Ilgen and Hollenback (1977) in their study of clerical workers found absenteeism to be correlated significantly with a value system scale containing items concerning commitment to perform one's job. To help determine what personal background factors were predictive of good attendance in this study, Pearson correlations were computed between attendance and pretest scores on the nine PSM subscales. Attendance scores correlated significantly with only the social commitment subscale ($r = .27$, $n = 61$, $p < .05$). This subscale was designed to measure feelings of community, readiness to form alliances, and interest in and willingness to work for social goals. It might well be expected that attendance would correlate well with this type of measure, especially among participants of a project dedicated to the betterment of the community, as the YCC is. However, there was a notable absence of a significant correlation between attendance and the work orientation subscale, which was designed to measure standards of competence, pleasure in work, and general work skills. Attendance also did not correlate significantly with other personal background factors such as age and sex.

Our efforts to use the PQR and its interaction with participants' personal background factors such as pretest PSM scores to predict attendance yielded complex and unreliable results, unreliable since they changed dramatically with small changes in the sample which resulted from differing patterns of missing data. Similar analyses using participants' perceptions of worthwhile work (SQ item 7) in place of the PQR also led to contradictory results. The PQR also was not a good predictor of gains in psychosocial maturity, as measured by adjusted posttest scores.

Summary and Conclusions

Perceptions of participants in 10 autonomous crews within one program supported our identification of staff quality as an important component in youth employment programs. We also found support in the participants' perceptions and attendance behavior for our contention that work projects must be worthwhile; however, this support was not so strong in the other four programs. Our principal measure of program impact, the PSM Inventory, was not related to our ratings of program quality in terms of crew leaders, work projects, and overall organization. The inclusion of quantitative data, that is to say, has indicated some agreement between participants and observers regarding the nature of the work, but the attempt to relate those criteria to measurable effects on participants revealed the greater impact of another program characteristic that was not included in our recommendations, residency. The residential program was the only one in which participants consistently showed gains on the Psychosocial Maturity Inventory that were statistically significantly greater than those in the other programs.

There are at least two explanations for this set of results. One is that our recommendations, despite their consistency with those from other studies, are simply invalid. Those characteristics may be desirable esthetically, but they make no difference in the programs' impact on participants. The other explanation is that they do make a difference, but not on program effects measured by the PSM inventory.

We incline toward the second explanation. Maturation is a slow process. The extent to which an eight week summer work program can hasten it is quite limited. Furthermore, it is a complex process that may be sampled by a paper-and-pencil instrument but cannot be comprehended by one. Other measures might have been more directly related to the program characteristics we identified.

This raises one of the key questions regarding the assessment of program impact, "How do researchers decide what sorts of effects to measure?" A second question quickly arises, "What are the most valid and reliable measures of those effects?" Unfortunately there is an inverse relation between the importance of effects and the ease with which they may be measured. Well-developed measures to assess the acquisition of facts are readily available, for example, and one is routinely given to YCC participants, but YCC programs can certainly not be justified on the grounds that participants know a little more at the end about the natural environment. If that was the purpose, classroom instruction would be far more cost-effective.

Some of these problems have to do with test construction, but some go deeper, to questions about what sorts of effects might reasonably be expected of youth work programs and where those effects might be sought. In most such programs the ultimate desired effects are on participants' adult careers, and these effects cannot be known in less than several years. Under such conditions another inverse relation operates. The longer the time between the program and the intended effects, the more difficult it is to attribute those effects to the program rather than to events occurring between the program and the measurement of its effects.

Work programs are, after all, brief and weak influences

on the lives of young people. Family, peers, community, schools, racial identity, and available job opportunities exercise far more influence. The best that can be hoped for is that work programs will either counteract some negative influences or reinforce some positive ones from these and other sources. Measuring program effects, therefore, must be viewed as attempting to identify and quantify the marginal contribution of one set of experiences to lives that are almost entirely determined by other influences.

These reflections suggest that a generous amount of modesty is in order about what youth employment programs can accomplish. Modesty is equally appropriate when considering how adequately those accomplishments can be measured by research, and how powerfully research can shape policies and programs.

Even after valid indicators of program effectiveness have been selected, the attribution to programs of changes in participants requires the use of experimental or quasi-experimental designs. And the most useful information, that certain characteristics of programs are associated with certain changes in participants, can only come from systematic comparisons among programs that vary in those characteristics (Hamilton, 1980).

These challenges can become overwhelming, especially in view of Cohen and Garet's (1975) warning that policy decisions are based on many considerations outside the realm of social science. Even the most carefully controlled and scientifically sound study affects policy only as one influence among many, and not even as one of the most powerful influences.

While we would urge that both researchers and consumers of research temper their expectations with modesty, we also challenge both parties to make the most of what can be done. This means attempting to bring together knowledge from many sources and then to identify critical questions that can profitably be explored. The nature of the questions dictates appropriate modes of research. Some questions might best be addressed by reference to the professional literature or surveys of practitioners. Others are amenable to the qualitative approaches represented in previous parts of this study. But some questions are specific enough that they would repay controlled comparisons and a combination of qualitative and quantitative data.

This process of identifying critical questions and then matching the questions with appropriate research designs and methods is best done collaboratively, with policy makers, practitioners, and researchers all involved. It demands of policy makers that they be willing to set aside some questions that are important in order to concentrate research resources on other questions to the extent that useful information results. They cannot raise dozens of questions and then dismiss the findings as being too shallow. Practitioners must be willing to share their common sense if this process is to work, and to submit to extensive probing about what their judgements mean and how they arrived at them. They must also be willing to subject some of their opinions to empirical testing and to cooperate with modifications of their programs for research purposes. Researchers need to be open to knowledge generated in many different ways to participate in this process. They must be able to make difficult decisions about how to reconcile the ideals of their research traditions with the constraints of program evaluation and policy research.

The recommendation that good staff are important in youth employment programs provides a starting point for one example of this process. If that aspect of programs is agreed upon as critical, then one question that suggests itself is how to train staff so that they will be optimally effective. The notion of optimally effective staff implies some criteria for staff effectiveness and these criteria would have to be clearly stated. Even if the criteria were not as "objective" as a researcher might wish, a research design could be developed that carefully compared two or three approaches to training staff so that one or more could be identified as improving staff effectiveness.

We believe there is enough agreement about what good youth employment programs look like in general that more specific questions should now be formulated and then explored with more narrowly focussed research that is appropriate in design and methodology to those questions. Our own study is one in what must be a series of steps in this direction.

References

Baumrind, D. Authoritarian vs authoritative parental control. *Adolescence*, 1968, *3*, 255–272.

Baumrind, D. Parental disciplinary patterns and social competence in children. *Youth and Society*, 1978, *9*, 239–276.

Cohen, D.K., & Garet, M.S. Reforming educational policy with applied research. *Harvard Educational Review*, 1975, *45*, 17–43.

Dewey, J. *Experience and education*. New York: Collier Books, 1938.

Federal Register. 1975, *40*, 100.

Freeberg, N.E., & Reilly, R.R. *Development of guidance measures for youth work-training program enrollees: Measurement of program objectives and the development of criteria*. Unpublished report, Princeton, N.J.: Educational Testing Service, 1971.

Graham, R. Youth and experiential learning. In R.J. Havighurst & P.H. Dreyer (Eds.), *Youth: The seventy-fourth yearbook of the National Society for the Study of Education*. Chicago: University of Chicago Press, 1975.

Greenberger, E., Josselson, R., Knerr, C., & Knerr, B. The measurement and structure of psychosocial maturity. *Journal of Youth and Adolescence*, 1975, *4*, 127–143.

Hamilton, S.F. Experential learning programs for youth. *American Journal of Education*, 1980, *88*, 179–215.

Hamilton, S.F., & Stewart, S.K. *Youth development in the Youth Conservation Corps: An exploratory study of personal and social development in participants*. Unpublished report, Cornell University, 1978. (ERIC Document Reproduction Service ED 173–719)

Ilgen, D.R., & Hollenback, J.H. The role of job satisfaction in absence behavior. *Organizational Behavior and Human Performance*, 1977, *19*, 148–161.

Lesh, S., Newman, J., Jordan, K., & Cash, C. *Youth serving the community: Realistic public service roles for young workers*. R&D Monograph 68, Washington, D.C., U.S. Department of Labor, 1979.

Miguel, R.J. (Project Director). *Experiential education policy guidelines*. Research and Development Series No. 160, Columbus Ohio: The National Center for Research in Vocational Education, The Ohio State University, 1979.

Peters, R.S. *Authority, responsibility and education*. London: George Allen and Unwin, 1959.

Porter, L.W. & Steers, R.M. Organizational, work, and personal factors in employee turnover and absenteeism. *Psychological Bulletin*, 1973, *80*, 151–176.

Rist, R.C., Hamilton, M.A., Holloway, W.B., Johnson, S.D., & Wiltberger, H.E. *Education and employment training: The views of youth*. Unpublished report, Cornell University, 1979.

Wurzburg, G. *Improving job opportunities for youth: A review of prime sponsor experience in implementing the Youth Employment and Demonstration Projects Act*. Unpublished report, Washington, D.C.: National Council on Employment Policy, 1978.

Children and Youth Services Review, Vol. 2, pp. 209–234, 1980
Printed in the USA. All rights reserved.

PART IV: A CRITICAL REVIEW OF CURRENT LITERATURE

Education for Employment: Knowledge for Action. (A Report to the
National Academy of Education)
By the Task Force on Education and Employment, Clark Kerr,
Chairman
Washington, D.C.: Acropolis Books, 1979, 274 pp.

The Task Force on Education and Employment was convened by
the National Academy of Education with a grant from the Ford
Foundation to review what is known about the education-employment connection. The charge was to comment on the "utility" of that
knowledge and to suggest an agenda for future research and experimentation. Like most commission reports, this one includes a series
of recommendations—to educators; to employers and worker organizations; to government policy makers; to students, parents, and the
public at large; and to the community of researchers interested in
matters of work and schooling. As one might guess, then, there is
something in this report for everyone. There is more discussion of
past and future research than of utility, and the recommendations to
various audiences offer little that is new. But the report collects in
one volume the state of knowledge and thought on this public policy
issue.

This is the volume's main contribution, and it's an important
one. As one appendix reports in some detail by education and age
level, federal agency, and categorical concern, $9.1 billion dollars of
federal money was spent in 1977 for training and employment programs, and another $20.4 billion for education and education-
related purposes. While we aren't told what portion of these monies
were used to support research on school and work issues—or how
much of the research is any good—we all know that there has been
an avalanche of research on the subject in recent years, and no
systematic way to keep track of it. This report makes a start. In so
doing, it suggests another line of inquiry not included among its
recommendations—a catalogue of past and current research efforts
on schooling and work and related programs. And we could also use

a "consumer guide" to such research, one which would not only tell us who is doing research on what programs and related issues, but also differentiate statistical or quantitative studies from the comparatively few qualitative or ethnographic studies. With several federal agencies supporting research on this subject and many academic disciplines bringing their perspectives to bear, it is nearly a full-time job to stay informed about what's going on outside one's particular area of inquiry. How many economists know what educators or psychologists or sociologists are doing, for example? There might be more cross-fertilization if it were easier to find out.

But there also might be more confusion. The literature review in *Education for Employment* presents findings of some disciplines using their preferred methods, and as one might expect, the findings frequently conflict. Much of the research reported was conducted with quantitative methods or was based on projections derived from conventional economic models. As the authors note, aggregate findings are of little use to personal or administrative decision-making, and past projections have frequently failed to materialize, which hardly inspires confidence. In theory, this is one reason for task force recommendations: they sift through the research findings, and, presumably based on them, suggest an appropriate course of action. In this report, action is suggested, but it frequently is not based on the weight of the findings reviewed.

For example, much of this report centers around manpower projections, reflecting the professional backgrounds of many members of this Task Force. The report reviews many of the theoretical and practical limitations of these projections, and also discusses several ways in which they can be useful—i.e., "to allow adjustments in the education offerings of schools and colleges, and in admissions criteria" (p. 35). We are not told of instances where manpower projections have shaped decisions; rather we are told where they have not. The report cites the Drewes and Katz study (1975) on the use of manpower data by vocational educators for program decisions. They found that "the prevailing philosophy seems to be that as long as students continue to enroll in a program, the program will be offered." Discussing this study, the Task Force tells us (p. 37): "On the basis of interviews in ten states, the authors found that student interests, faculty suggestions, advisory committees, and employer or professional associations generally prompt considerations of new programs. If manpower data support these new programs, the data are used. If not, local surveys and other data are brought to bear. Once initiated, few if any programs are terminated. Low cost, high likelihood of placement, and student interest appear to determine program continuation. Drewes and Katz observe: 'Several local directors told us of programs in their schools which had high placement rates while manpower projections showed little or no need for additional trained personnel coming from such a program.' " The Task Force goes on to say: "The fact is, there are several valid reasons for limited use of national manpower forecasts in local program decisions" (p. 37). Yet, oddly enough, it then supports the development of more sophisticated—and presumably more useful—forecasting models (p. 45).

In a similar vein, the report reviews the research on career guidance for young people and its effectiveness. The chapter devoted to this subject reveals nearly unanimous findings on the limited effectiveness and utility of formal career guidance approaches and of guidance personnel in helping youth make career choices. Indeed, the report cites the work of Holland (1975) which points out that "surveys of high school and college students present a consistent picture of friends, family, schoolwork and work experiences as the most potent influences [on vocational choice], whereas counselors and tests are usually at the bottom of these listings." But then the Task Force adds that "there is room, of course, for structured, purposeful intervention. Indeed one argument for professional guidance and counseling is that people with special training and skills are in a better position than most parents and friends to enhance decision-making skills and to provide useful information and advice" (p. 108). The Task Force then recommends that the federal government continue to support the strengthening of guidance and counseling and the development of occupational information systems for states and local districts.

The irony here is that the policy recommendations of the Task Force seem not to reflect the findings of available research. Policy analysts increasingly bemoan how little their research is used to inform federal, state, and local decisions, and there is a growing literature on just this subject. Here we have the same phenomenon, with the analysts ignoring their own research in formulating their policy recommendations.

This is not peculiar to the work of this Task Force, nor is it hard to find in the reports of many national commissions. But one wonders why it is so. One reason may concern the purpose of such reports, which is often largely symbolic. Particularly when the issue at hand is confusing, enormously complex, and of major public concern—such as the connection between education and employment in these times of high youth employment and anxiety about the quality of education—the convening of a task force comprised of acknowledged experts provides visible evidence that public and private agencies concerned with the national welfare are working on the problem. The intention is partly to provide reassurance and to build public trust.

But another reason for the divergence of research and recommendations may have to do with the difficulty of extrapolating clear recommendations from social science findings. Social science research presents stories of "how things are" at the individual or the aggregate level. It therefore permits diagnoses. Sometimes these conflict, as this report demonstrates, but even when they do not, they do not suggest clear prescriptions to correct the diagnosed problem. The recommendations which result are only abstract and not very useful. Thus, research informs us of a basic-skills problem among many young people, but it can't tell us what to do about it—beyond prescribing that more energy and resources be directed toward improving basic skills, which is one of the recommendations of this Task Force. In other instances, recommendations may diverge from research findings on the effectiveness of some established activity because it isn't clear what else to recommend. In the absence of an alternative activity or idea for one, the recommendations revert to the old prescriptions. Thus, in the face of much evidence on the limited rationality of youngsters making career choices, many, including this Task Force, nevertheless recommend the development of rational guidance information systems, for example. But the guidance systems are being developed anyway, and no one knows how to make youth behave in a more rational manner—nor is there consensus that they ought to.

The failure of policy recommendations to reflect policy-oriented research or to be useful to decision-makers may in part be a matter of overly ambitious aims for social science. One hope is that such research will converge in the direction of a central diagnosis, which as this report reveals, often does not occur. Research on one issue from the perspective of different disciplines may produce contrary findings, which does not help decision-makers. Another hope—or wish—is that social science will provide a prescriptive capability, the knowledge of what works, upon which decision-makers can act. But social science is a diagnostic tool; it is capable of providing descriptions, but it cannot tell how to create programs that work on the basis of description. In the face of these real limitations, policy recommendations are likely to remain general.

This is not to suggest that all recommendations fall by the wayside. Over time, repeated recommendations of various commissions may come to influence public opinion about the nature of a problem and what should be done to solve it. And the weight of some recommendations may then be reflected in federal policy, which will further influence public opinion. But as this Task Force report demonstrates, the recommendations often do not fairly reflect what is known. That being the case, it may be a blessing that policy recommendations are of limited use to decisionmakers.

Eleanor Farrar
The Huron Institute

The Lingering Crisis of Youth Unemployment
By Avril V. Adams, Garth V. Mangum, with Wayne Stevenson,
  Stephen F. Seninger and Stephen Mangum.
Kalamazoo, Michigan: WE Upjohn Institute for Employment Research, 1978, 152 pp., $4.00.

Over the past decade, we have been constantly reminded, in the popular press, of the growing magnitude of the unemployment problem. For youth, particularly those from the inner city, the problem has been even greater. Specifically, 15% of the nation's youth 16 to 24 years of age were unemployed in 1976. For black teenagers, the rate is 37% and for blacks from urban areas, the rate is 43%. These figures, however, do not indicate those youth who are not actively seeking work and are, therefore, not counted as unemployed. The problem of youth unemployment, therefore, is truly staggering and has many implications for the current as well as future well-being of the society. What are the causes of this growing problem? Will demographic shifts reduce the problem in the 1980s? What are the solutions to the problem and should priority be given to reducing the problem?

In *The Lingering Crisis of Youth Unemployment*, Adams, Mangum, and their colleagues undertake a reassessment of the youth unemployment problem by trying to answer these and other major questions. Through analysis of published census and other federal data and new analyses of the young men and women from the National Longitudinal Surveys (NLS), the authors explore recent historical trends in youth employment and unemployment, examine some of the causes of this problem and then look at the prospects for the coming decade.

The Lingering Crisis consists of seven chapters with different authors credited for each chapter. What emerges are seven chapters sewn together only by a common topic thread. Except for parts of the first and last chapters, which try to bring all the pieces together, each chapter could stand on its own. As a result, a continuity is lacking and there tends to be repetition of many of the facts, points, and assumptions. Despite this, *The Lingering Crisis* is a book which should be read by anyone concerned with the problem of youth unemployment or its solution.

In the first chapter, the nature of the problem is set into perspective by reviewing the relevant literature on youth employment and unemployment. This review centers around the labor market economics literature and could have been strengthened by looking into the status attainment and mobility literature of sociology. Chapters Two and Three look at trends in youth unemployment post world war two through the mid-1970s. Using census and other government-published data, the authors of Chapter Two establish that demographic, economic, and industry trends have affected youth unemployment over the past three decades. Federal policy responses such as the Manpower Development and Training Act, The Economic Opportunity Act, and the Comprehensive Employment and Training Act are then reviewed. In Chapter Three, data from 1976 are examined and employment, unemployment, and work experience trends are shown for different demographic subgroups of the population. This chapter concludes with a recommendation to target policies to those youths most affected by unemployment including inner city, black and out-of-school youth, and young Vietnam War veterans.

Chapter Four explores the changes anticipated for the economy in the 1980s and looks at its effects on youth unemployment. Growth of occupations are projected and the consequences for youth are discussed. Continued problems for black youth are anticipated and the importance of youth moving into new growth sectors highlighted. Using data from the National Longitudinal Surveys, Chapter Five looks at youth transition from school to work. The chapter first shows that youth tend to enter the labor force gradually, combining school and work for some time period before the transition is completed. Next the nature of entry level jobs is examined concluding that most of these are "secondary" with little opportunity for advancement or permanence. A model is then developed and tested to assess the factors that influence early labor market experiences (employment, unemployment, and income). The explanation and development of the model is not very theoretical and the discussion would have been strengthened had the model been graphically presented. Again, the findings show that the early labor market experiences of blacks, women, and youth from the South are most problematic.

Chapter Six looks at the effect of early labor market experiences on future employability. A number of findings reported in this chapter are very important in terms of policy directions. First, the disadvantages of being out of school and out of work as teenagers or young adults carry over into the early adult years. That is, those youth who had difficult labor market experiences continue to have them later on in their lives. Second, the returns of additional education for blacks are similar to those of whites, suggesting that the returns of schooling increased for blacks during the 1970s. Finally, for out-of-school youth, training used on the job resulted in gains in earnings. This chapter concludes by suggesting that future policies should take these findings into account by providing jobs for out-of-school youth and training for youth during their early work lives.

The final chapter of the book provides a summary of the major findings and recommends a number of youth employment policy options. Recognizing that a single policy cannot respond to the needs of the diverse youth population, the options proposed include policies for job creation, education and training, career information, job placement, and market interventions.

Under job creation policies is the recommendation that youth jobs be created and delivered to those youth most in need (out-of-school youth). The advantages of public sector job creation are recognized as is the need for a combined public-private approach to this problem. Specifically, public sector efforts should be directed where private sector initiatives fail to reach. The need for linking any job creation program to school retention is also discussed. The authors conclude that the jobs created under such programs "should provide useful work experiences, access to training, and openings to new career ladders" (p. 135).

The education and training recommendations emphasize the importance of education and training as they affect labor market experiences of young men and women. Specific policies are aimed at increasing training options outside of the formal education system. In addition, improved career counseling, career information, and job placement programs are called for. Finally, a set of market interventions are suggested. Included here are equal employment opportunity and affirmative action policies which are argued to have positive effects on youth employment and the minimum wage which has been the subject of much debate vis-à-vis its effect on youth employment.

We are left at the end of *The Lingering Crisis* with a set of broad policy recommendations. I feel that more attention could have been given to these recommendations with the specific policy options or program alternatives explored in greater detail. Certainly there are pros and cons with any policy proposal but these are examined in only a cursory manner. In addition, despite the recognition that multiple approaches are best, the policies outlined are neither integrated nor discussed in terms of weighing the benefits and costs of one, or a set, against the others.

This leads me to one of my major concerns with the book. It is not clear who the audience is for *The Lingering Crisis*. Is it the policy maker, policy analyst, basic researcher, average citizen or all of the above? From reading the book, one is left with the impression that the answer is all of the above. While this may be ideal, it is very difficult to accomplish, especially when data analyses are heavily relied on. The book would have benefited from a clearer determination of the primary audience. For policy makers, a greater emphasis on policy options and program alternatives would seem appropriate. For analysts and researchers, more detailed analyses, perhaps in the form of a technical appendix, especially in Chapters Five and Six, seem needed. These should go beyond the percentage tables and provide the information from the more sophisticated regression and multiple classification analyses. Finally, for a "lay" audience, simplification of tables and discussion of data as well as more specific program recommendations would have been beneficial. Despite these criticisms, I feel that all of the audiences listed above can benefit from a careful reading of this book. My concern is that each will want more information to answer questions that may emerge as a function of their unique perspectives.

A final comment of this book is warranted. Perhaps the biggest and most comforting information to come out of this study concerns the positive effect of education and training on reducing youth unemployment, both in the short and long term. I would have liked to see this finding examined in greater detail through further analyses, and its consequences for policies explored more fully.

Adams, Mangum, and their colleagues have provided a most interesting reassessment of the youth unemployment problem. They have opened the door for analysts to further examine these issues and for decision makers to develop policies and programs that may ease the lingering crisis of youth unemployment.

Ivan Charner
National Institute for Work and Learning

Evaluating Federal Social Programs: An Uncertain Art
By Sar A. Levitan and Gregory K. Wurzburg
Kalamazoo, Michigan: The W.E. Upjohn Institute for Employment
  Research, 1979, 148 pp. (with index)

This monograph sharply highlights the confusion that exists in the
minds of some social scientists, government administrators and legislators and the public at large, concerning the role, methods and
limitations of the evaluation of social programs.*

    Evaluating Federal Social Programs, by Sar Levitan and Gregory
Wurzburg, contains five chapters. The first two and the last deal
with a critique of social science methods per se. Chapters 3 and 4
deal with the actual practice of evaluation in government. Taken
together, Chapters 1, 2 and 5 comprise an evaluation of the practical
relevance of social science as an aid to social planning and decision
making in the public sector. These three chapters will be briefly
described first. In them, the prognosis as to the utility of such science is generally not positive. The first chapter, "The Aspirations
and Limitations of Evaluators," argues forcefully that the evaluation
of social programs is flawed and distorted by a slavish devotion to
methodological rigor and narrowness of approach. Instead, the authors assert, "a holistic and judgmental approach" should guide the
evaluation of social programs. A new balance should be struck in
social science evaluation between subjective judgment and empirical
observation on the one hand and modeling on the other such that
more emphasis is placed on the former.

    Chapter 2, "The Tools of the Trade" is the conceptual core of
the book. It discusses the relationship between the analysis of a program's operational structure and its delivery of services to clients
(process analysis) and the analysis of the ultimate effects of the services on the clients (impact analysis). The necessity for properly
identifying program objectives is also discussed as well as the need to
devise accurate indicators to measure these objectives, and the need
for proper control groups. It ends with a general criticism of classical experimentation, drawing upon the New Jersey Income Maintenance Experiment, among others, to demonstrate the difficulties of
operating and evaluating a social experiment in a real world context.
The tone of this chapter is cautionary and critical. Chapter 5, "Can
Evaluation Make a Difference?", focuses on the need for program
evaluation but again restates its potential dangers and limitations.
The limited effects of evaluation in influencing program design and

*This review has benefited from the criticism and suggestions of several of my col-
leagues both at the Department of Labor and elsewhere. However, all opinions and
any errors of fact or judgment are the sole responsibility of the author.

revision are noted, as well as the perverse way in which different policy conclusions can be drawn from a given set of data by persons of divergent polical focus.

Chapter 3 deals with "Evaluation in the Legislative Branch." It discusses the rationale and focus of evaluation in the legislative branch through the general institution of congressional oversight and notes the strengths and weaknesses of this institutional approach. Then the Congressional Budget Office, the General Accounting Office and Congressional Research Service are discussed in terms of their legislative origins and mandate, administrative structure, the nature of evaluation and research performed and its relative strengths and weaknesses. As such, this chapter is relatively complete in its broad outline of evaluation as done by the legislative branch. The criticisms and discussion are generally well taken. Chapter 4, "Evaluation in the Administrative Branch," is much less complete since it effectively deals with evaluation only in the Department of Labor and the Department of Health, Education, and Welfare. Other social agencies, such as the Department of Housing and Urban Development are not considered though major evaluations have been performed there, such as the Housing Allowance Demand Experiment. Indeed, the authors mainly concentrate on two major agencies in the two departments studied—the Office of the Assistant Secretary for Policy Evaluation, and Research (ASPER) in the Department of Labor and the Office of the Assistant Secretary for Planning and Evaluation (ASPE) in the Department of Health, Education, and Welfare. Special sections in the chapter discuss the problems of competitive bidding and the issue of the intellectual and scientific independence of evaluations and evaluators due to the nature of the political and institutional environment surrounding social program evaluation.

General Critique

This study is useful in that it gives interested students a particular view of the problem and issues surrounding the use of social science in analyzing and informing social policy. However, the book has several limitations.

The first limitation is partly a matter of style. The authors have a penchant for polemics and hyperbole. For instance, academics and technicians "search for the Holy Grail;" program planning and budgeting systems were "foisted" on federal agencies; some methodological tools border on "witchcraft;" choosing key variables for analysis is like "shooting in the dark;" and, scholarly criticism of the authors' work is characterized as "attacks." Such expression detracts from scholarly purpose.

More important is the apprehension one gets that the authors do not understand or appreciate the shortcomings to which social science methods are generally subject. They confuse appearance with substance. They castigate "meddling model manipulators" but fail to understand that models and assumptions, whether implicit or explicit, underlie all social science including the "holistic and judgmental" approach they prefer. Throughout the book the authors reserve considerable criticism for "modeling." Models are asserted to provide only partial and often disconnected views of complex, multidimensional programs. Of course, in any given situation, such criticisms can be true. But they are not generally true of the method of modeling—that is, abstracting and theorizing—which characterizes all analysis and is part of the basis of the scientific method. As presented, the authors' criticisms are mainly pertinent to the relative skills of the scientist. Poor analysts do poor science, mathematical, judgmental or otherwise.

A model is simply a way of organizing the salient facts about some important aspect of human behavior. It is best that the model (or models) be made explicit. Modeling is an intellectual method. The fact that mathematics can be used to express the structure of a model is incidental. Done correctly, modeling the operation and the mutual influences of a program on human behavior is a very effective way to arrive at relevant, usable, and verifiable knowledge. It is this aspect of independent verification which distinguishes objective scientific knowledge. However useful and necessary at times, direct judgments about social program outcomes are particularly prone to leaving crucial underlying assumptions implicit or unspecified. Of course, mathematical models which are poorly specified can suffer from the same flaw.

Regardless of the quality and apparent relevance of social science research, one still needs to make distinctions between the political limitations and the methodological limitations on social science research. The following quote suggests an impreciseness on the part of the authors in making such distinctions:

The conditions under which evaluators operate make even the semblance of a scientific methodology impractical. Evaluators are rarely in the position to design programs in such a way as to provide adequate tests for important elements. Claims about the ability to observe results—directly or through proxy measures—are frequently pretentious. The notion of achieving experimental conditions, so central to scientific inquiry, is a virtually unattainable ideal. An enormous number of variables influencing any program are beyond the control of even the most imaginative and powerful policymaker, to say nothing of a lowly evaluator. Yet, in spite of the difficulties of even crude scientific inquiry, policymakers demand assessments of social programs, and evaluators respond, cranking them out with a vengeance.

Hoping to bring to their professions a degree of credibility that the substance of their work sometimes fails to provide, evaluators have collected an impressive array of tools for their trade. Although the collection may seem to border on witchcraft, it is intended to impart a sense of rigorous and systematic inquiry. (pp. 9–10)

Furthermore, the authors do not clearly explain the nature of important tools of social science methods. There is one major and one minor example of this that bear discussion. The major problem surrounds their discussion of experimental design, partially suggested by the above quote. The authors first acknowledge that experiments, presumably with random assignment of program clients to a treatment and a control group, allow one to identify cause and effect between program treatments and program outcomes. In fact, in the absence of strong prior evidence this is the only way to identify cause and effect. However, in subsequent discussion, they allude to the "simplistic notions about cause and effect that underlie experimentation strategies (which) fail to capture either the full effect of program intervention or to satisfactorily document the influence of non-experimental variables" (p. 26). The authors do not clarify why experimentation fails to capture the full effect of a program. They may be referring to measures of outcome, any one of which is only a partial index of program outcomes, but this issue is divorced from the method of classical experimental design and the issue of identifying cause and effect. The latter half of their statement can be construed as correct, though, if random assignment is made on one variable or set of variables and subsequent analysis is performed on another. For instance, a sample can be randomly assigned to a program treatment on the basis of ethnic origin. The effects of ethnic origin on program outcomes is then random and the expected value of its net effect on program outcomes is unbiased. However, the resulting assignment of the same sample by sex may be non-random so that sex interacts with program outcomes and biases those estimates. Even then, analysis of variance, regression analysis or related techniques can eliminate much of this confounding of non-randomness. So, the problem is not severe and is amenable to standard statistical technique.

A less serious problem concerns the dichotomy the authors assert between process and impact evaluation. They argue that a process evaluation assesses whether a program is a workable tool for change while an impact analysis assesses the effects of a program in achieving the desired change. The distinction between the two definitions seems clear until one considers the execution of each type of analysis. For instance, the authors pose as an example of a process question the following: "Will unemployed veterans enroll in training courses for auto mechanics?"

This is, of course, a process question in the sense that the program administrator and Congress wish to know who demands a given program's services. But it is also an impact question in that the composition of clients and their number relative to the intended composition and number is a program outcome. If Congress "throws a party and no one attends" or the wrong people crash it, this is an outcome, an impact.

In short, it is best to view program analysis as a continuum in which process and impact are logically linked. Artificial separation of the two program aspects is sometimes a convenient approach to evaluate a program, however, it risks a misunderstanding or misspecification of how a program is designed, operates and affects outcomes. Of course, a careful modeling of a program should immediately reveal the process-impact link. Much of what is wrong with analysis of social programs can be traced to the artificial separation of process from impact. In this reviewer's judgment millions of dollars of research funds have been wasted thereby, or what is worse, have been used to provide misleading information.

Finally, there are a number of instances of obscure or incorrect reasoning. Two examples are illustrative, though others exist. For instance:

> To determine if education finance programs had equalized per pupil expenditures, educators might look for increases in academic achievement among students in poorer schools. (p. 13)
> Even if indicators (of program performance) are valid, accurate, and reliable proxies for the variables that need to be examined, correlations do not necessarily imply causation because indicators also must have a finite number of components if they are to remain consistent and useful over time. (p. 21)

As for the two descriptive chapters, they are generally informative to the layman who is first introduced to the issues. Their tone is generally factual and while one can disagree with their judgments—for instance, their statement that GAO has a persistent tendency to confine its (evaluation) "recommendations to minor issues involving incremental changes"—the intellectual confusion that the methodology chapters exhibit is relatively absent. The chapter on evaluation in the executive branch, however, exhibits some political naiveté and historical misinterpretation. For instance the authors' understanding

of the relationship between ASPER and the operating agencies, such
as the Occupational Safety and Health Administration (OSHA), is
faulty (p. 96 ff). The authors discuss at some length the interaction
between ASPER and OSHA, especially as OSHA attempted to exe-
cute research which would measure the economic impact of desired
health and safety standards. ASPER is pictured as obstructionist and
opposing the spirit of the law by withholding approval of inflationary
impact statements (IIS's) and otherwise specifying incorrect standards
of program impact. Among other things, the authors ignore the fact
that the IIS's and ASPER's role in the approval process were the
direct result, and had the full knowledge, of the Ford Administration
at the time. They were not generic to the role of ASPER. We should
note, though, that cost assessments of social regulation have received
support from virtually every part of the political spectrum. Although
the Secretary of Labor, by rescinding the secretarial order which
created the IIS review process, could have stopped the process of
"obstruction", it is incorrect to sugest that ASPER, or the Secretary of
Labor, past or present, had great autonomy of action in this matter.
But, given the responsibility to review and pass on the technical quality of the IISs, ASPER executed that responsibility as directed.

This institutional practice of overview of one agency by another
leads us to one final consideration: What is the correct structure for
evaluation and what is its proper locus? While the authors are correct that the effect of the ASPER evaluation of the IISs impeded the
OSHA program in the short run, yet would it be socially useful to
have OSHA, in effect, evaluate itself? This procedure has generally
been rejected in our society. On the other hand, is it socially useful
for an agency such as the GAO, which generally uses a case study
monitoring method of evaluation, sometimes of "worst" cases, to
perform evaluations from which, by definition, insufficient evidence
is presented to generalize to the program as a whole? This approach,
too, is misleading and risks committing serious errors of commission.
There are no immediate solutions to these types of conflicts. The
authors do discuss these matters, but the topic is a difficult one and
additional attention could have been devoted to it in their study.

In conclusion, this monograph is perplexing to one who wishes
to draw an overall judgment of its utility. It provides some valuable
insights concerning problems which surround the institutional and
political context of social program evaluation. But it is exaggerated
in places and exhibits a misperceived role for social science methods.

Ernst W. Stromsdorfer
Abt Associates, Inc.

Education and Jobs: The Imbalancing of the Social Machinery
By Gregory D. Squires
New Brunswick, New Jersey: Transaction Books, 1979, 235 pp.
$19.95

The high unemployment rates of young people, particularly among minorities, has been one of the chief casualties of the recession years. Lack of employment has so engaged public attention in recent years that it has produced one of the federal governments chief social initiatives of the 1970s, the massive Comprehensive Employment and Training Act (CETA) program. The pitfalls of trying to develop a separate and isolated employment policy have been illustrated by the initial efforts of CETA. The CETA mandates to train for and/or provide immediate employment for those most deprived of employment have led to an endless debate over its social and educational implications. This mandate contradicts other social trends (the increase in educational credentialing, for example) by creating a new institutional sector. In this process, the new institution finds itself replicating functions of already existing institutions such as the schools and thus comes into conflict with existing values while still facing the same problems.

Much of the debate and many of the policy questions which currently produce tensions in the educational system and the labor market are actually the result of unrecognized or, at least unresolved, conflicts in values. Gregory D. Squires, in *Education and Jobs: The Imbalancing of the Social Machinery*, while questioning two competing ideologies on the role of education in American society attempts to destroy one with substantial statistical data and makes his own value perspective quite clear: "The major attractions of schooling have been the greater social and economic rewards which are available to the better educated members of society primarily because of the kinds of jobs for which that education qualifies them." William James once said that where there is a contradiction, it is usually the result of the fact that the parties to the dispute have failed to make relevant distinctions. Educators might reasonably complain that Squires has failed to make a distinction between education and training. If we accept his definition then the persuasiveness of his argument is dependent on the assumption that the logical aim of education is to train better for some end.

Squires does an excellent job of developing and describing the two ideologies of education. The conventional interpretation of American education as a democratizing force counteracting the inequalities of the larger society has "provided the nation with skilled manpower required in a modern, industrialized society." The alternative ideology is a class analysis that posits a society in which "education has served primarily as an agency of social control to reconcile the class conflicts in a capitalistic economic system in such a way that the dominant classes could maintain that system and their positions within it." Thus, according to this analysis, the development and expansion of mass public education was "motivated by the concern, on the part of the economic elites, to indoctrinate the masses to accept their positions in society and the legitimacy of the mode of distribution in that society."

I must confess to a predilection against any analysis which proceeds from an ideological position to martial statistical documentation as proof for the viability of the ideology. Certainly in my own field-work experience in both education and work settings, I have found that ideologies do more than shape our ways of thinking, they orient us towards which "truths" we seek and where we go to look for them. Squires proceeds throughout most of the chapters in his book to provide evidence for answers to the following questions:

(1) Can the expansion of formal education in the United States be explained in terms of technological advances or in terms of changes in the technical skill requirements of jobs?
(2) While education has long been associated with income and occupational prestige, is it the noncognitive characteristics or the technical skills inculcated by schools which are rewarded in the occupational structure?
(3) Has formal education performed the democratizing function with which it has been credited? More specifically, has the expansion of formal education led to a greater economic equality?
(4) In light of the answers to the first three questions, to what extent can educational reform contribute to the creation of greater economic equality in the future?

The statistical evidence presented to explore and explain questions 1, 2, and 3 is interesting, very clearly presented, and quite compelling. Yes, the reality in American education in the 1970s is that more people (including minorities such as women and Blacks) are in school for a longer number of years and more money is being spent on schooling both publicly and privately. From these data, Squires then proceeds to an examination of issues in the job market (but, unfortunately, not in the schools) and examines the connection or, rather, lack of connection among technological needs, job training and educational achievement. He points out very clearly that at the operational level, the issue is quite clear: Do people get a better job because of the sheepskin or do they do a better job because of the sheepskin? Following in the tradition of James Coleman and Christopher Jencks he finds little or no relationship but extends their argument by pointing out that since employers demand a higher level of education in entry jobs than is actually necessary to do the job, education does help to get a job. Thus, constantly arguing from his statistical reality to a social reality, Squires pictures the relationship of education to employment as one in which increased education has not led to more equality of income distribution or increased social and occupational mobility, but rather one in which educational credentialing has served to insure the perpetuation of the values enshrined in the personnel director's office. So, the author argues, you don't learn job skills in school but you do learn a set of values, behaviors and motives which the labor market demands. Thus, the educational system serves to socialize youth to the work ethic. He cites the following Mobil Oil Company advertisement aimed at future marketing representatives as empirical evidence of this point:

You need a bachelor's degree to apply. We really don't care what it's in. Because the most important requirements are sales ability and motivation. And those are things you can't major in.

One could also argue, of course, that the ad writer could have benefited from a few more courses in English grammar.

There are some fascinating and unexpected bits of information which Squires explores conscientiously and which enliven the book. He finds, for example, that absenteeism and high job turnover rates are inversely related to education, so he argues, while overeducation for many jobs might seem to be in the service of education and a luxury for the employer since he has a more educated labor supply from which to choose, it can actually be dysfunctional and cause more problems for the employer than undereducation. Here field experience provides some supportive evidence. In a recent study of a police precinct it was quite obvious that the federally funded Law Enforcement Educational Program (LEEP) for police enabling them to obtain higher education free of costs under the assumption that better education makes better cops, seems to provide no evidence of improving job performance. There is considerable evidence, however, that the higher educational opportunities provided for policemen allow many of them to seek alternative careers.

Squires does an excellent job of providing statistical documentation in support of the Marxist class ideology as an indictment of our educational system and the book is must reading for educators as well as those interested in questions of the labor marketplace. What he does less well, and it is because he chooses not to explore it, is to look at the schooling side of the equation. Educators will tell you that there is one belief about American education which is even more pervasive than that which sees it as the great equalizer in American society. That belief is that education can teach solutions to any major social problem. Using education as the means of correcting social inequalities or doing away with unemployment or equalizing opportunities, is little different than producing new curricula to deal with the drug problem or providing courses in ethics in the aftermath of Watergate. To assume that if there is an employment problem, the cure must be in the schools and in designing new curricula around issues of career awareness, career exploration and job skills training may be perpetuating a longstanding myth. The real issue may be a different value question, not whether or not schools can set up career training curricula for students, but whether or not they should. Most of the national commissions which have examined secondary education in the last decade recommend removing job preparation and occupational skill training from the high school and placing it in industrial and business settings.

Throughout his discussions of jobs, equality, educational achievement and efficacy, the author did not explore the other critical role for education in American society, that of transmitting the culture, developing skills of judgement, encouraging creative abilities and providing cognitive growth for youngsters. Is the only cost-benefit of education to be found in the labor market? Can educational attainment only be measured in terms of financial success? Is education really just for marketability? Certainly, it is more difficult to measure and document education's contributions in these areas. Yet, their importance is always visible when social crises for individuals and society threaten the quality of life.

What is most important in Squire's work is that it should present the necessary data to question the role of governmental policy in creating as well as attempting to solve not only the problems of unemployment but the problems of school dropouts as well. The recent youth employment legislation is a policy response to high levels of youth unemployment, high school dropout rates and declining academic achievement among high school students. Certainly legislators would do well to attend to Squires' statistical data of the paucity of any real evidence about the relationship between jobs and education before designing the next round of legislation and expending large sums of money for a reconnection of educational achievement and the realities of the job market. The web of social institutions which develop the sometimes confusing network of remediation programs for youth demand the kind of searching examination Squires' presents. During a recent evaluation of a joint labor and education program in which CETA funds were being used to attract teenage drop-outs back to school by establishing a work-study program, we found an anecdotal example of how the interplay of institutional domains within the same community confounds the social and "problem-solving" context. In this small city, the school representatives were meeting with project staff to decide on admissions requirements to the program. A number of the dropouts from the school system had police records with arrests for crime ranging from prostitution and drug sellling to armed robbery and rape. The job representative was arguing for full-employment, but the principal argued that he didn't want to readmit the drug sellers because they would cause a resurgence of drug selling in the school. The final outcome was a screening process that readmitted everyone except convicted murderers and rapists.

Elizabeth Reuss-Ianni
Institute for Social Analysis

Youth Unemployment, Volume I and Volume II
By the Organization for Economic Co-operation and Development
Paris, 1978, Vol. I, 176 pp., $8.50; Vol. II, 183 pp., $8.50

Most studies of youth unemployment can be understood as variations on two themes. The first theme is, "Will the problem fade away as the economy waxes or the number of youth wanes?" Analysts usually conclude that better conditions won't cure youth unemployment, at least for some important sectors of youth, and that happy days aren't likely to be here again soon for oil-importing nations. The second, and main, theme then sounds: "Which measure is most promising—more jobs, better transitions, or increased employability?" The first measure assumes that more youth are employable and could find their way to jobs if more jobs were available. The second requires belief that jobs and qualified youth both are available if there were better ways to get them together. The third measure assumes the availability of jobs and bridges to them, if youth were better prepared for work.

Analyses vary in the cogency and extensiveness of evidence applied to these themes; in how easily or painstakingly the authors persuade themselves of their case; and the elegance of the means by which they propose to create more job opportunities, improve transitions or increase employability. Few analysts rule out totally any one of the three main strategies; the studies rather differ in the balance of enthusiasm for one or the other. This is, at least in the United States, no small matter. Job creation strategies usually bring power and funds to the systems served by the Department of Labor; employability, to education-related systems; and transitions, to third party groups charged with bringing the first two sectors closer together.

The OECD conclusions are of the genus, youth unemployment will not disappear to any substantial degree until 1985–1990 when demographic shifts and better economic conditions may be expected to have their day; and of the species, increase work opportunities. Despite what we may see as some limitations in the data, the path to these conclusions is well constructed, and the journey worth the trip.

I estimate these volumes cost about $500,000, including OECD secretariat staff work, conference attendance expenses, and work by member agencies in providing information and critiquing drafts. What can be learned by reading these?

Methodology. Secretariat staff have been ingenious in aggregating and disaggregating. Among the indicators presented are the ratio of adult to youth employment (interpreted as good if close to 1.0, unfavorable to youth relative to adults if greater than 1.0, and unfavorable to adults relative to youth if the ratio is more than 1.0, a situation reported by Germany for 1960 through 1975), and youth unemployment rates by age and gender at maximum recession and boom years (interpreted as helping distinguish the position of youth in the labor market from the context of general economic conditions). Staff have been equally ingenious in identifying alternative explanations and in scrounging data to rule out at least some of these. One example is the question of the extent to which unemployment insurance availability may contribute to youth unemployment—apparently it does not, at least not with 1976 or earlier conditions of eligibility and returns. This also is a book in which a product moment correlation of 0.9 between youth unemployment and proportion of youth in the population carefully is dismantled as a causation: in the view of the analysts, economic conditions are a more powerful determinant of youth unemployment than the numbers of youth available for work.

The OECD analysts usefully have cumulated a considerable analytic and empirical literature across many countries, and equally usefully identified alternative hypotheses, a significant accomplishment, considering the care with which the data from 24 countries have been examined and footnoted. There are, however, some methodological differences between the OECD analysis and at least one recent U.S. policy study on youth unemployment (the October 1979 analyses of youth employment policies prepared by Sawhill and her colleagues at the National Commission for Employment Policy for the President) that may seem to us lacunae in the OECD analysis. As one example, quantitative data from large scale reports are the alpha and omega of OECD's cited surveys. Attitudes, skills, opportunities and almost all other process variables are inferred from these or dealt with fairly superficially. On the important question of youth attachment to the labor force, we are told that when job opportunities are plentiful, youth are attracted to the labor market and when aggregate demand contracts, youth are easily discouraged (p. 39). In contrast Sawhill and her colleagues cite, in discussing willingness to accept a job, the quantitative work of Andresani, Berryman, Miller and Simon and also the qualitative studies of Elijah Anderson in a pithy analysis of probable influences on willingness to work. Another methodological difference is that to OECD "youth"—with one exception, that of gender—is treated as homogeneous. In the U.S. analyses, efforts are made to consider youth employment and employability in the context of language backgrounds, parental economic status, ethnicity, cultural group, and other factors which might influence the impact of different measures for understanding and dealing with youth employment. Not for OECD: a youth is a youth is a youth, and how within country differences among youth have shaped various measures is unexamined.

Findings. The OECD diagnosis is that the basic problem is lack of work opportunities in employment, not youth unemployability or too few bridges between adequate education and available work. The emphasis, accordingly, is on strategies developed by different nations to stimulate job creation and work opportunities for youth.

Job subsidies are most widely reported by member nations and receive greatest attention. In the form of direct payments to employers or direct exemptions for usual taxes in employee wages, countries from Austria to Yugoslavia—with the exception of the United States—are pursuing various forms of job subsidies, and the forms make interesting reading. Direct job creation in the public sector is widespread only in the United States, with smaller programs reported by Australia, Canada, Denmark, New Zealand, Norway and Sweden. Community development services, such as the Canadian Works Program which involves youth carrying out community improvement projects proposed at the local level, are viewed favorably as a way of combining swift job creation, community development, and improved employment experiences. Considered with equal approbation are measures to reduce the size of the labor force, such as extended education, paid educational leave, and promoting flexible retirement. Other approaches aim at improving distribution of opportunities through wage and income supports for youth able to find only low-paying jobs, and work-sharing, including partial compensation for lost earnings when "employees and workers agree to share available work as an alternative to some workers being laid off."

The National Commission on Employment Policy (September 26, 1979) Study emphasizes measures to increase youth employability. In contrast, the OECD report describes these with restrained enthusiasm, "Few of the school leavers who enter the labor force during the next few years are likely to benefit . . . in the longer run, fundamental reform of the educational system in the direction of recurrent education may play an essential role" (p. 39). The U.S. seems to be moving toward reform of secondary schooling; OECD, to recurrent education, though less as a way of improving employability and more as a way of increasing job access for youth. Incentives to increase training by employers associated with access to specific jobs (e.g., apprenticeships), training in public institutions, counseling and placement are described with caution. Paid and unpaid work experience are regarded as more likely than is training to complement effectively the other, employment creation focused, measures proposed.

It is unclear how much impact on youth unemployment with what short, intermediate or longer term consequences for other groups might be expected from each strategy described. The Secretariat can be least forthcoming on the most interesting points. As an example, Finland and Sweden had very large increases in both the youth population and the adult labor force with very small increases in youth unemployment

This delightful, but anomalous situation "appears to be the result of conscious policies which were implemented rigorously" (p. 43). What these conscious policy decisions were and what was required to implement them rigorously isn't so much as hinted at in the 141 small-type, packed pages. As another example, we are exhorted to learn from approaches tried and found wanting by member nations, but if any member nation was less than thrilled with an approach, what this was and probable reasons for ineffectiveness aren't presented.

Enthusiasm or caution are signalled subtly. The message

comes across in the number of warnings about possible untoward consequences and in uncertainties about the data (measures which seem less favorably viewed founder in the sea of caveats on lack of information).

Volume II may give some clues to this reticence. Few of the measures reported served many youth or were much more than recent, small-scale experimental projects. Judging from U.S. programs as presented in this report and as seen from Washington, the projects in Volume II should be read as more what the country hopes will happen than as extremely accurate and up-to-date reports on what has occurred. This doesn't detract from the convenience of having such an array of ideas that countries thought well enough of to try out—no small matter as those who have tried to influence policy know.

The OECD reports belong on the desks of all those who are seriously concerned with youth: the information is among the most recent and complete on labor market experiences for youth in other industrialized countries, and is a splendid source of ideas about which one might wish to learn more as well as people (the participants are listed) to contact for further information. One shouldn't expect a very critical analysis from OECD, which strives toward acceptance of national diversity and consensus on broad policies, but rather a sampler of ideas and concerns. The volumes provide this well. They shouldn't, however, be the only books on the desk. Reuben's analysis (*Bridges to Work: International Comparison of Transitional Services*, 1977) has greater depth and scholarship. The *National Commission on Employment Policy 1979* papers are sounding new notes (an emphasis on finding jobs for *prepared* youth, on improving employability, and on incentives for youth to acquire demanded work habits, attitudes and skills through education as well as through training) which were not heard in the OECD reports or heralded there. Perhaps our view of sensible policies has changed from the early 70s when many of the approaches reported in the OECD volumes were planned and as experience has been gained with measures about which, as OECD staff noted, little was known in 1976 when the analyses were prepared. For those who may be responsible for improving employability, the OECD reports offer relatively few ideas. For those who may be responsible, as opinion shifts again, for assuring employment opportunities, the OECD volumes bring together a harvest of a decade of such efforts.

Lois-ellin Datta
Department of Education
National Institute of Education

Creating Jobs: Public Employment Programs and Wage Subsidies
Edited by John L. Palmer
Washington, D.C.: The Brookings Institution, 1978, 379 pp. $14.95

With regard to human resource policy, one of the most important developments of the decade of the 1970s was the revival and expansion of job creation programs. As an instrument of policy intervention, public service employment (PSE) embraces three objectives that are potentially of vital importance to local labor markets. These are the ability of such endeavors to increase the number of available job opportunities; to enhance the income levels of program participants; and to produce useful output which benefits the general community.

The present volume is a collection of essays that were prepared for a conference that was jointly sponsored by the Brookings Institution and the Institute for Research on Poverty at the University of Wisconsin in April, 1977. It also contains a comprehensive overview by John Palmer and Irwin Garfinkel which links the papers together and highlights their major findings. The perspective of the collection is purely from the vantage point of an economist, which all of the authors are. The importance of the papers stems from the fact that much of their work was anticipatory of what was to happen in the future.

PSE was incorporated in the Comprehensive Employment and Training Act of 1973 (CETA) under two titles. Title I simply listed PSE as one of a variety of activities that a local prime sponsor could fund. Title II provided funds for PSE if the local unemployment rate exceeded a specified level. But in 1974 and 1976, significant amendments were made to CETA with the addition of Title VI. This new section of the Act increased both the scope and the scale of PSE. It became a countercyclical weapon of fiscal policy which was greatly enlarged again during the early days of the Carter Administration. It is this expanded role of PSE that is the primary subject of the various essays. The book also contains the remarks of knowledgeable discussants to each of the articles.

One chapter by Jonathan Kesselman is a reflective look backwards to the work programs of the New Deal era. It is quite informative and it should give contemporary policy makers a sense of *déjà vu*. For the policy problems of the past are identical to those bedeviling policy makers in the present. These pertain to the nuts and bolts questions as to the appropriate wage rates; quality of supervision; availability of materials and tools; quality of output; eligibility criteria; degree of training to be provided; the length of time that one could be enrolled; access by minority groups; and possible displacment effects upon the efforts by local and state governments. On balance, Kesselman finds the efforts of the 1930s to be merely camouflaged forms of direct relief. It does seem that he is unduly critical of the pioneering efforts that were made with absolutely no precedents for guidance and given the magnitude of the mass unemployment of that era. Economic efficiency is not necessarily an end in itself.

Most of the remainder of the articles deal with the experience of the mid-1970s and the prospects for future expansion. The general theme of the articles is that, while there is a role for PSE as a countercyclical weapon, its real policy significance lies in its potential as a counterstructural weapon. In this latter role—where wage rates are kept low and the focus is upon providing jobs at the entry level for the long term unemployed or for economically disadvantaged groups, PSE can be a constructive addition to fiscal policy. If PSE is targeted to these subgroups, the prospects for substitution of federal funds for local funds appears to the authors to be minimal. Most of the authors feel that as a countercyclical weapon, the prospects for substitution are too high—especially as time passes. They also feel that, given the political processes involved, it will be very difficult to time a PSE program to have impact when it is needed. They also fear that once local governments have become addicted to PSE that they will lobby to have the programs continued even when aggregate unemployment declines. Hence, it is as a counterstructural device that PSE offers the best promise. Martin Bailey and James Tobin, for instance, show how PSE can "cheat the Phillips Curve" by allowing public expenditures to increase to employ those subgroups of the labor force who, collectively, have inordinately high unemployment rates. In this manner, unemployment can be reduced without triggering unemployment rates since these groups are in surplus.

There is also a very informative article by Robert Haveman on public employment programs in the Netherlands. It deals with an issue that haunts PSE program planning in the United States but which has yet to be carefully researched. Namely, in the Netherlands income transfer programs have increased rapidly in the 1960s and 1970s. Many persons with marginal attachment to the labor force have withdrawn from work. PSE endeavors have been introduced in an attempt to provide jobs for some who are recipients of transfers but who could work. The problem is how to design an effective counterstructural PSE program for low skilled and low wage workers in a context of the availability of liberal income transfer programs. It is a provocative and perplexing subject.

In 1978, PSE under CETA was drastically altered by Congress.

It was virtually converted into a counterstructural policy. It would almost seem that this book was the blueprint for the changes that occurred. For anyone interested in the theoretical as well as practical rationale for this change in policy thrust, this book is a useful primer.

Vernon M. Briggs, Jr.
Cornell University